Women of the English nobilit
1066–1500

While there is increasing interest in the lives of medieval women, the documentary evidence for their activities remains little known. This book provides a collection of sources for an important and influential group of women in medieval England, and examines changes in their role and activities between 1066 and 1500.

For most noble and gentry-women, early marriage led to responsibilities for family and household, and in the absence of their husbands, for the family estates and retainers. Widowhood enabled them to take control of their affairs and to play an independent part in the local community and sometimes further afield. Although many women's lives followed a conventional pattern, great variety existed within family relationships, and individuality can also be seen in religious practices and patronage. Piety could take a number of different forms, whether a woman became a nun, a vowesss, or a noted philanthropist and benefactor to religious institutions.

This volume provides a broad-ranging and accessible coverage of the role of noble women in medieval society. It highlights the significant role played by these women within their families, households, estates and communities.

Jennifer Ward is Senior Lecturer in History at Goldsmiths College, University of London

Manchester Medieval Sources Series

series adviser Janet L. Nelson

This series aims to meet a growing need amongst students and teachers of medieval history for translations of key sources that are directly usable in students' own work. The series will provide texts central to medieval studies courses and will focus upon the diverse cultural, social as well as political conditions that affected the functioning of all levels of medieval society. The basic premise of the new series is that translations must be accompanied by sufficient introductory and explanatory material and each volume will therefore include a comprehensive guide to the sources' interpretation, including discussion of critical linguistic problems and an assessment of the most recent research on the topics being covered.

already published in the series

Janet L. Nelson *The Annals of St-Bertin: ninth-century histories, volume I*

Timothy Reuter *The Annals of Fulda: ninth-century histories, volume II*

Chris Given-Wilson *Chronicles of the Revolution, 1397–1400: the reign of Richard II*

R. N. Swanson *Catholic England: faith, religion and observance before the Reformation*

Rosemary Horrox *The Black Death*

John Edwards *The Jews in Western Europe*

forthcoming titles in the series will include

Simon Lloyd *The impact of the crusades: the experience of England, 1095–1274*

Richard Smith *Sources for the population history of England, 1000–1540*

Alison McHardy *The early reign of Richard II*

Ian Robinson *The pontificate of Gregory VII*

Edward Powell *Crime, law and society in late medieval England*

Jeremy Goldberg *Women in England, c. 1275–1525*

Ross Balzaretti *North Italian histories, AD 800–1100*

WOMEN OF THE ENGLISH NOBILITY AND GENTRY

1066–1500

translated and edited by Jennifer Ward

Manchester University Press

Manchester and New York

distributed exclusively in the USA and Canada by St. Martin's Press

Published by Manchester University Press
Oxford Road, Manchester M13 9NR, UK
and Room 400, 175 Fifth Avenue, New York, NY 10010, USA

Distributed exclusively in the USA and Canada
by St. Martin's Press, Inc., 175 Fifth Avenue, New York, NY 10010, USA

British Library Cataloguing-in-Publication Data
A catalogue record for this book is available from the British Library

Library of Congress Cataloging-in-Publication Data
Women of the English nobility and gentry, 1066-1500 / translated and
    edited by Jennifer Ward.
            p. cm.
        Includes bibliographica references (p.).
        ISBN 0-7190-4114-7. — ISBN 0-7190-4115-5 (pbk.)
        1. Great Britain—History—Medieval period, 1066-1485—Sources.
    2. Women—England—History—Middle Ages, 500-1500—Sources.
    3. Nobility—England—History—Sources. 4. Gentry—England—
    History—Sources.
    I. Ward, Jennifer C.
    DA170.W66   1995
    942—dc20   95-908
                                                                    CIP

ISBN 0 7190 4114 7 *hardback*
ISBN 0 7190 4115 5 *paperback*

First published 1995

99 98 97 95 95   10 9 8 7 6 5 4 3 2 1

Typeset in Monotype Bell
by Koinonia Ltd, Manchester
Printed in Great Britain
by Bell & Bain Ltd, Glasgow

Contents

II: Family   46

V: Household   156

Foreword

Jennifer Ward's recent book on later medieval English noblewomen argued convincingly the importance of those women's roles in shaping and structuring their world. In the present volume, she adds new dimensions to her work. She goes back further in time, situating changes as well as continuities in noblewomen's lives against the nobility's social and political evolution over the centuries from the eleventh to the fifteenth; and, in line with the aims of the series, she opens up the evidence, some of it hitherto unpublished, and presents it accessibly to what will surely be a wide audience. The family and household aptly frame material ranging from marriage-contracts to account-books. But Jennifer Ward succeeds in bringing flesh-and-blood noblewomen to life, not only as resource-managers but as political figures in their own rights, as sometimes ardent practitioners of Christian piety, and lastly and centrally as gendered beings with distinctive experiences as daughters, wives, mothers and widows. Generally lacking formal political roles, noblewomen wielded influence and often power, especially at regional and local levels. How they did so, what were the limits to their activities, what were the costs they paid, can be gleaned from the dossier assembled here. These are not peripheral matters: Jennifer Ward offers a broad highway into and through central areas of medieval English life.

Janet L. Nelson, King's College London

Preface and acknowledgements

The increase in research in women's history in recent years has revealed the importance of women's role in society. Women of the nobility and gentry often found themselves thrust into positions of influence and power as a result of marriage, widowhood, or the accidents of inheritance. The purpose of the present collection of documents is to show the range of interests and activities among this group of women, and by taking the period 1066–1500 it is possible to trace both continuity and change in their responsibilities and relationships within and outside their families. Some of the sources for medieval women's history have long been known, such as the Paston and Stonor Letters. Many of the documents, however, concerning family, household and estates, and religious and cultural attitudes, remain in manuscript, and deserve to be more widely known. Only by careful assessment of such evidence can a full picture of the women of the nobility and gentry be built up.

In working on this book I have incurred a number of debts. I especially want to thank Janet Nelson, who invited me to contribute to the Manchester Medieval Sources series, and the staff of Manchester University Press for their advice and help. Paul Brand, Nancy Edwards, Paul Fouracre, Jeremy Goldberg, Ray Powell and Martin Stuchfield have drawn my attention to particular sources, and discussed various aspects of the lives of medieval noblewomen. Any remaining mistakes are mine. I would also like to thank the staff of the Borthwick Institute, University of York, the British Library, Lambeth Palace Library, the Norfolk Record Office, and the Public Record Office for their help and for permission to publish documents and translations of documents in their care. Material held by the Public Record Office is Crown copyright and is reproduced with the permission of the Controller of Her Majesty's Stationery Office. The investigation of sources is a fascinating process; it is hoped that the collection will provide an insight into the riches of documentation which can be much further explored.

Goldsmiths College, London
October, 1994

Introduction

Throughout the Middle Ages the men and women of the nobility and gentry occupied a position at the top of the social hierarchy. Although there were considerable gradations, depending on size of estates, amount of wealth, and social connections, there were no legal demarcations within the nobility to mark off one social group from another, and there was a great similarity in expectations and attitudes in spite of the differences of degree. The bonds of chivalry, a love of luxury and ostentation, and the desire to enhance the standing of one's family and increase one's estates are found from the highest nobility down to the local gentry from the eleventh to the fifteenth century. These ambitions and concerns give a unity to the period, and affected men and women alike.

At the same time, the way in which the nobility and gentry were envisaged underwent change, and this inevitably had an effect on women who derived their status from their fathers and husbands. The Anglo-Norman baronage of the late eleventh and twelfth centuries comprised the tenants-in-chief of the Crown, men who had been granted their honours, which in some cases consisted of extensive estates, by the Norman kings in return for knight service in the royal host; with good fortune these men were able to pass these lands on to their descendants. The baronage consisted of about 180 tenants-in-chief, and there were wide differences in wealth and landholding.[1] Great changes took place within the group in the 250 years after the Norman Conquest as a result of forfeiture of estates because of rebellion, and the failure of heirs within families; moreover, many new families arose as a result of service and reward, especially from the Crown, and through marriage to heiresses.[2] Only about thirty-six out of 210 English baronies between 1066 and 1327 descended in a single

---

1 D. C. Douglas, *William the Conqueror*, London, 1964, p. 269, comments that there were slightly fewer than 180 tenants-in-chief recorded in Domesday Book holding English estates with a yearly value of over £100.

2 E.g. the Clare family; J. C. Ward, 'Royal service and reward: the Clare family and the Crown, 1066–1154', in *Anglo-Norman Studies: Proceedings of the Battle Conference*, XI, 1988, ed. R. A. Brown, pp. 261–78.

male line for over 200 years.[3] However, in the late thirteenth century the barons of England still comprised a large and varied group. The situation changed in the fourteenth century as the nobles came to be defined as those who received an individual summons to parliament; the English peerage thus came to be a group of between sixty and seventy, becoming both smaller and more distinct. The range of wealth within the peerage was however still very great; the figure of £250 may be regarded as a minimum for a peer in the late fourteenth century, but John of Gaunt's estates brought in revenues of about £12,000. This gulf between the top nobility and the rest was largely the result of marriage and the accumulation of great inheritances in a few hands.[4]

Between 1066 and 1500 the knight had an important role both in war and society. In the Norman period, the knights were not a homogeneous group, and a few of them held as much land as a lesser baron. On many late eleventh- and twelfth-century honours, a distinction can be drawn between the vassals who were responsible for a considerable amount of military service, and the professional soldiers who were responsible for the service of one knight or less.[5] Knights held their fees in return for military service in their lord's contingent in the royal host, and castleguard, the service depending on the agreement made with the lord, not on the amount of land held. Although the knight is seen primarily as a military figure in the twelfth century, the wealthier knight enjoyed high social status, and served his lord as steward or constable, or as counsellor in the honour court.[6] Such responsibilities were to increase from the later twelfth century as the knight became increasingly involved in the operation of royal justice.

For a wide variety of reasons, the number of knights declined in the thirteenth century, and their status grew; partly this was due to inflation, especially severe c. 1200, and consequent economic change,

---

3 E. Miller and J. Hatcher, *Medieval England – Rural Society and Economic Change 1086–1348*, London, 1978, p. 169.

4 The development of the peerage in the fourteenth century is discussed by C. Given-Wilson, *The English Nobility in the Late Middle Ages: the Fourteenth-Century Political Community*, London, 1987, pp. 55–66.

5 S. Harvey, 'The knight and the knight's fee in England', *Past and Present*, no. 49, 1970, pp. 10–13. Fractional fees were normally discharged through a money payment.

6 J. C. Ward, 'The place of the honour in twelfth-century society: the honour of Clare, 1066–1217', *Proceedings of the Suffolk Institute of Archaeology and History*, XXXV, 1983, pp. 195–8.

partly to changing military demands and more expensive equipment, and partly to aspirations for a more luxurious lifestyle.[7] Some men wishing to evade military and the growing judicial and administrative responsibilities of knighthood simply did not become knights at all. As a result of the changes, knights for the rest of the Middle Ages were a select and elite group, prominent in their own localities, often active at court and in parliament, still noted for their military prowess, as well as being engaged in extensive work for the Crown and local lords, ecclesiastical and lay. It has been calculated that c. 1300 the knights in England comprised between 2,500 and 3,000 men, about half of whom had actually been dubbed knight.[8] Whether they were dubbed knights or not, there was never any doubt that they counted as part of the nobility.

During the fourteenth and fifteenth centuries increasing differentiation of rank took place among those below the rank of knight. A distinction came to be drawn in the fourteenth century between knights and esquires, and many esquires came to play a leading part in local society and county government.[9] By the late fourteenth century, the concept of the rank of gentleman had emerged, and was used widely in the fifteenth century.[10] Thus there could be said to be a hierarchy of knights, esquires and gentry, but it has to be emphasised that these were by no means rigidly exclusive groups. Moreover, a distinction has to be drawn between the county gentry, who were men of wealth and standing, and the gentry whose outlook was confined to the parish or their immediate locality. Numbers varied from county to county, as did their estates and income.[11] In his analysis of the income tax of 1436, H. L. Gray suggested that there were eighty-three greater knights in England as a whole, with an income of between £101 and £399, and 750 lesser knights with an income of between

---

7 Changes in the knightly class are discussed by P. R. Coss, 'Sir Geoffrey de Langley and the crisis of the knightly class in thirteenth-century England', *Past and Present*, no. 68, 1975, pp. 3–37, and in *Lordship, Knighthood and Locality: A Study in English Society, c. 1180–c. 1280*, Past and Present publications, Cambridge, 1991, chapters 7 and 8; and by D. A. Carpenter, 'Was there a crisis of the knightly class in the thirteenth century? The Oxfordshire evidence', *English Historical Review*, XCV, 1980, pp. 721–52.

8 Given-Wilson, *English Nobility*, p. 14.

9 The terminology of this evolution is discussed by N. Saul, *Knights and Esquires: the Gloucestershire Gentry in the Fourteenth Century*, Oxford, 1981, chapter 1.

10 D. A. L. Morgan, 'The individual style of the English gentleman', in *Gentry and Nobility in Late Medieval Europe*, ed. M. Jones, Gloucester, 1986, pp. 15–35.

11 Given-Wilson, *English Nobility*, pp. 70–1.

£40 and £100. Below these he ranked 1,200 taxpayers who had an income of between £20 and £39 as esquires; 5,000 men were returned as having an income of between £5 and £19 and many of these were envisaged as gentry.[12] This provides a useful general view of the hierarchy, but few knights would have had an income of over £200, and in practice there was no economic dividing-line between knights and esquires. Similarly the poorer gentry merged into the yeomen. Status was not only dependent on wealth; local reputation and family ambitions and aspirations all played their part.

Although the use of the term gentleman to denote rank is only found in the late Middle Ages, the gentry as a social group below the level of the knights certainly existed much earlier. Gentry whose interests were focused on their home farm and parish church can be traced back at least to the thirteenth century and in some cases to the minor vassals of the twelfth. These local lords of manors were still part of the elite by virtue of the land they held by knight service and the rights which they exercised over it. Furthermore they shared the outlook of the rest of the nobility.[13]

The nature of their tenure can be seen as binding all these noble groups together and it reinforced the attitudes, lifestyle and interests which were common to all. Tenure by knight service was universal among the nobility in the late eleventh and twelfth centuries, and continued to be widespread until its abolition in 1660, even though its original significance had long since disappeared. Social and military changes gradually rendered knight service in the feudal host obsolete,[14] but the vassal remained bound to his lord by homage and fealty, paid relief on his succession to a fee, and was liable to come into the lord's wardship if the heir was a minor. From at least the thirteenth century the operation of these feudal incidents meant that the relationship between vassal and lord was financial rather than personal. In view of this, the ties provided by bastard feudalism often had greater importance for both lord and retainer, as well as contributing to holding noble society together. The service of the retainer to his lord might be military or administrative; the retainer might be an

---

12 H. L. Gray, 'Incomes from land in England in 1436', *English Historical Review*, XLIX, 1934, pp. 620–30.

13 Coss, *Lordship, Knighthood and Locality*, chapter 9, discusses the origins of the gentry.

14 It was summoned for the last time in 1385, but was becoming obsolete well before that date.

official, kinsman, friend or ally, and the relationship could be long-
or short-term. Whatever the nature of the service, the retainer
received his fee and livery from the lord, and the lord's affinity was a
strong influence in noble society from the thirteenth to the fifteenth
century.[15]

The women of the nobility and gentry have to be seen in this
hierarchical setting in order to understand the similarities and
differences between them. On the economic side the differences could
be huge; Elizabeth de Burgh in the first half of the fourteenth century
enjoyed an income of about £2,500 a year, more than 250 times as
much as the revenues of some of the gentry. On the other hand, there
were similarities over concern for family, interest in land, and in
religious beliefs and practices and social conventions. The similarities
make it possible to take these women as a group, always bearing in
mind that they were never an exclusive caste.

A distinction has to be drawn between the subordination of women
found in ecclesiastical and legal writing and what was often the
situation in practice. The didactic treatises stressed the virtues of
meekness, humility and obedience, and emphasised women's religious
duties, while many women found that in practice they needed to be
active, forceful and energetic. Presumably a compromise could be
effected, and it is significant that the knight of La Tour Landry in his
advice to his daughters considered that the wife should be submissive
and obedient but pointed out that there were ways in which she could
influence her husband. The idea that women were inferior and
subordinate was deeply rooted in the Middle Ages. Misogyny was
widespread in the classical world and among the Fathers of the
Church. Women were thought to be disobedient and deceitful; their
beauty was a sexual snare; they were lustful and lacked reason, and
altogether they distracted men and prevented them from reaching
mental and spiritual heights.[16] For churchmen, marriage was considered second-best to a life of virginity. Yet in practice it was essential

15 For a discussion of the early development of bastard feudalism, see S. L. Waugh,
'Tenure to contract: lordship and clientage in thirteenth century England', *English
Historical Review*, CI, 1986, pp. 811–39; P. R. Coss, 'Bastard feudalism revised', *Past
and Present*, no. 125, 1989, pp. 27–64; D. Crouch, *William Marshal*, London, 1990,
pp. 157–68.

16 Translations from these texts are included in E. Amt, ed., *Women's Lives in Medieval
Europe: A Sourcebook*, London, 1993; and in A. Blamires, ed., *Woman Defamed and
Woman Defended*, Oxford, 1992. The latter book includes a number of texts in
defence of women.

to regard women more positively. From the twelfth century, the Church insisted that women as well as men gave their personal consent to marriage, and in the occasional pleadings over marital breakdown both women and men had their say. Women were an integral part of noble society, and occasions arose when it was taken for granted that they would take over duties normally performed by men. This is most obvious in the law of the land where a clear distinction was drawn between the wife and the widow. In the former case the husband was regarded as responsible for his wife, just like a father for his unmarried daughter, but, when a woman was widowed, she counted as a *femme sole*, able to plead in the courts and make her own decisions. The way in which a widow was often expected to take over immediately after her husband's death indicates an acceptance in society of her practical abilities.

In order to understand the position of noble and gentry women, it is essential to see them in the context of their families and of the law of the land; changes in feudal lordship, and, more particularly, the growing authority of the Crown certainly had an effect on their lives. The Norman Conquest brought changes over the inheritance of land; in the late Anglo-Saxon period the will had been used to bequeath land among a wide kindred group, a practice which was ended by the Norman stress on primogeniture. This could be detrimental to both men and women in the kindred group, but what becomes apparent from the charters of the late eleventh and twelfth centuries is the extent to which women had an interest in the land of the family. In the Norman period and later family concerns were usually paramount, normally within the immediate family rather than in a wider kinship structure. Arranged marriages were the norm, and great importance was attached to the birth of children, especially a son and heir. The furtherance of the children's interests, and of family interests in general, was a constant concern throughout life. These interests were normally linked with the husband's family, but there are instances where the wife showed a continuing interest in her own natal family and transmitted this to her descendants.

Change occurred over rights to land and inheritance, and many noblewomen became better off and more secure in their landholding as the Middle Ages progressed. As records from the Domesday Survey onwards indicate, women always had the right to hold land, although during marriage the husband was responsible for it. Down to the fourteenth century, a grant of land, the *maritagium*, was made on marriage, and women were entitled to dower after the death of their husbands. Of considerable significance for many women from the thirteenth century was the development of jointure, land held jointly by husband and wife, which was initially laid down in the marriage settlement, and which the widow held for life in the event of her husband's death. Dower and jointure gave the widow independence, and there was no question that she was in charge of the lands if she chose not to remarry. Levels of wealth varied widely, but the dowager was a common phenomenon in noble society from the late eleventh to the fifteenth century.[17]

Changes in the law of inheritance had an impact on the position of women, and have again to be put in the context of the family and of the authority of the Crown. Where no sons had been born to a family, it was accepted that estates could pass through the marriage of a daughter to a new family. The rule that coheiresses should divide an estate equally between them probably dates from the last years of the reign of Henry I,[18] and from that time it was usually enforced. However, the Crown had the last say over inheritance, especially in the case of major honours, and coheiresses could not automatically assume that they would obtain a share of the inheritance.[19] Moreover, the development of the entail in the fourteenth and fifteenth centuries to ensure that the succession went to a male relation in the event of there being no sons meant that some daughters lost the chance of succeeding to the family inheritance. Daughters and their husbands are known

---

17 There is evidence in the Beauchamp cartulary of some widows disposing of their dower in return for a cash income; E. E. Mason, ed., *The Beauchamp Cartulary: Charters 1100–1268*, Pipe Roll Society, new series, XLIII, 1980, nos. 17, 22, 130–1. For dowagers, see D. Crouch, *The Image of Aristocracy in Britain, 1000–1300*, London, 1992, pp. 79–80; and R. E. Archer, 'Rich old ladies: the problem of late medieval dowagers', in A. Pollard, ed., *Property and Politics: Essays in Later Medieval English History*, Gloucester, 1984, pp. 15–35.

18 J. C. Holt, 'Feudal society and the family in early medieval England: I. The revolution of 1066', *Transactions of the Royal Historical Society*, fifth series, XXXII, 1982, p. 199; J. C. Holt, 'Feudal society and the family in early medieval England: IV. The heiress and the alien', *Transactions of the Royal Historical Society*, fifth series, XXXV, 1985, pp. 9–10; S. F. C. Milsom, 'Inheritance by women in the twelfth and early thirteenth centuries', in M. S. Arnold, T. A. Green, S. A. Scully and S. D. White, eds, *On the Laws and Customs of England: Essays in Honor of Samuel E. Thorne*, Chapel Hill, 1981, pp. 60–89.

19 For examples of Crown intervention, see K. B. McFarlane, 'Had Edward I a "policy" towards the earls?' *History*, L, 1965, pp. 145–59, and reprinted in *The Nobility of Later Medieval England*, Oxford, 1973, pp. 248–67.

to have been angered by this, but usually the only people to gain from a protest were the lawyers.[20]

Treatises like that of the knight of La Tour Landry did not envisage women as landholders and land-managers, and did not consider providing a formal training for a task which they frequently had to assume.[21] The knight stressed the importance of education for women but interpreted this as an ability to read and understand the Scriptures; Humbert de Romans considered that they should be able to say the psalter, the Hours, the Office of the dead and other prayers, and women's possession of books of hours indicates that many could do this.[22] From the point of view of the Crown and the lord, however, women in charge of an estate were expected to know how to meet its obligations. In the Norman and Angevin period, this could well entail the production of knights to serve in the feudal host and to guard royal and baronial castles; later, contributions were demanded for the defence of the realm. Ladies, like lords, held their honour courts, and enforced feudal incidents such as relief and wardship, and women who were their vassals had to carry out their obligations. During the Middle Ages, a growing number of families became tenants-in-chief of the Crown, and were affected by the Crown's right of prerogative wardship;[23] it can be assumed that a large number of noble and gentry women would come up against the demands of the Crown at some point in their lives. A minority found themselves dealing with the Crown as rebels in time of political disturbance.

From the point of view of the family, the woman took over the management of the estates when needed. Certainly this would be the case with her dower if she was widowed, but it was widely expected that

20 E.g. the entail of the Berkeley estates which meant that Elizabeth Berkeley and her husband Richard Beauchamp earl of Warwick were not entitled to succeed to the inheritance; the Berkeley lawsuit lasted from 1417 to 1609. Its early stages are discussed by C. D. Ross, 'The household accounts of Elizabeth Berkeley, countess of Warwick, 1420–1', *Transactions of the Bristol and Gloucestershire Archaeological Society*, LXX, 1951, pp. 81–3.

21 A. S. Haskell, 'The Paston women on marriage in fifteenth-century England', *Viator*, IV, 1973, pp. 463–4. John of Wales, writing his sermons in the later thirteenth century, recommended that children should be taught how to handle their inheritances, but he may well have been thinking of boys rather than girls; J. Swanson, 'Childhood and childrearing in *ad status* sermons by later thirteenth-century friars', *Journal of Medieval History*, XVI, 1990, p. 318.

22 Swanson, 'Childhood and childrearing', p. 324.

23 Under prerogative wardship, the Crown gained custody of all the lands of the tenant-in-chief held by knight service, not just the estates which were held of the Crown.

she would take her husband's place in his absence, relinquishing control on his return. Noble and gentry women needed both practical ability and adaptability. Such activity is described most vividly by Christine de Pisan, who in her *Treasure of the City of Ladies* shows the wise princess presiding over the council and taking decisions in the absence of her husband.[24] Christine, writing *c.* 1400 and familiar with the French court and nobility, probably wrote from personal knowledge, and certainly many noblewomen were called on to do this in the medieval world.

These activities with regard to land and lordship were regarded as very much in the male domain; the woman was virtually taking on a male identity. Other activities were regarded by the treatises as more acceptable for women, such as religion, charity and peace-making. Christine de Pisan's wise princess, like the knight of La Tour Landry's daughters, was enjoined to love and fear God, and to devote herself to the cultivation of virtue and good works. Only a few women, however, were called to the contemplative religious life where they cut themselves off completely from self, family and the world.[25] Most women, even those living as nuns, still have to be seen against the background of family and community.

The noblewoman was therefore expected to be obedient, submissive and virtuous, but to be able to carry out men's duties as needed within the family and on the estates. Her world centred on the family and its interests, and her life and prospects were affected by both the law of the Church and the law of the land, as well as by fortune and accident. The question remains as to how full and vivid a picture of her life and world can be built up from the sources. The dichotomy between subordination and activity comes out in different types of evidence. Treatises like that of the knight of La Tour Landry show what was expected of women by way of character and disposition; the romances like *Sir Gawain and the Green Knight* and Malory's *Morte D'Arthur*, with their emphasis on courtly love, portray wives and maidens in a noble setting, and stress love and temptation, the inspiration women gave to their knights, and the ceremonial life of tournaments and jousts.[26]

---

24 Christine de Pisan, translated by S. Lawson, *The Treasure of the City of Ladies or The Book of the Three Virtues*, Harmondsworth, 1985, pp. 60–1.

25 Christine de Pisan, *Treasure*, pp. 41–55.

26 Both these romances are available in translation in Penguin Classics: *Sir Gawain and the Green Knight*, translated by B. Stone, second edition, Harmondsworth, 1974; Sir Thomas Malory, *Le Morte D'Arthur*, ed. J. Cowen, 2 vols, Harmondsworth, 1986. See also R. Barber and J. Barker, *Tournaments: Jousts, Chivalry and Pageants in the Middle Ages*, Woodbridge, 1989, pp. 206–7.

Although noblewomen attended tournaments and feasts, these were only occasional celebrations, and the didactic treatises warned them to beware of the dangers of courtly love. It is likely that many women enjoyed the romances as make-believe fantasy. The women in the romances epitomised particular traits, good and bad, but they rarely come over as fully developed characters. Chaucer's portrayal of women in *The Canterbury Tales* is much more vivid, and shows the diversity of character and personality which must have existed but which rarely comes over in the historical records.

Chronicles sometimes provide a lively insight into the activities of a particular woman, and they were often interested in family genealogy. Yet their emphasis on events, especially concerning the king, wars, battles, and political affairs generally, meant that they had little interest in social life and economic fortunes. It is therefore essential to turn to more formal records. For the late eleventh and twelfth centuries, charters and documents emanating from royal government reveal more than might be expected about noblewomen. The monastic practice of compiling cartularies, collections of the charters granting lands and possessions, ensured the survival of material which otherwise would probably have been lost. These charters were usually undated, and can present problems of authenticity, but they often throw light on family relationships, household and estate organisation, *maritagium* and dower, as well as religious attitudes. Charters continue to be useful in the later Middle Ages, but by then they can be supplemented by a wide range of other evidence.

The record-keeping practices of the Crown are invaluable for women's history, although it has to be borne in mind that the king was primarily interested in his rights and dues; the records therefore provide details of land, service, feudal incidents and payments made to the Crown. The Domesday Survey of 1086 and royal charters throw much light on women's landholding, whether by way of inheritance, *maritagium* or dower.

The Pipe Rolls of the exchequer of 1130 and after 1155 supplement this material, and are particularly informative over women's involvement in the working of feudal incidents, whether these concerned wardship, relief or the remarriage of widows. Of especial value are the Rolls of Ladies, Boys and Girls, drawn up for Henry II in 1185.[27]

---

27 J. H. Round, ed., *Rotuli de Dominabus et Pueris et Puellis de XII Comitatibus (1185)*, Pipe Roll Society, XXXV, 1913.

These only survive for certain counties, but throw much light on the wardship of the lands and persons of the boys and girls who were minors and in the king's custody, and on the widows who were in the king's gift for remarriage. The descriptions of lands show the resources available to many of these women.

With the growth in documentation in the royal government and elsewhere c.1200, far more material on women becomes available.[28] This is especially important in view of the increasing number of noble and gentry families who were becoming tenants-in-chief of the Crown. Their lands and tenures came to be recorded in dated royal letters, copies of which were kept by chancery, as well as in exchequer records, and their manors were surveyed in the inquisitions *post mortem* taken at the death of a tenant-in-chief. As royal government became more bureaucratic, so greater control was exercised over the localities and more information recorded on the nobility and gentry.

The availability and increasing elaboration of royal writs encouraged men and women to bring property cases before the royal justices; with the emergence of plea rolls in the late twelfth century, additional information becomes available on inheritance, dower and property-holding in general. The need for families to maintain their rights frequently involved resort to litigation in which women were likely to be included at some point. Women brought cases to secure their dower from the late twelfth century, and, as widows, energetically defended their interests. Although they had no right to plead during their married lives, they were often associated with their husbands in cases of alienation of family land. In addition to the plea rolls, a considerable amount of information on landholding and the land market from 1195 onwards is derived from final concords, agreements drawn up in the king's court of which copies were held by each of the parties, while the third copy, the foot of the fine, was kept in the treasury. The development of new legal devices and remedies had a considerable impact on noblewomen, notably the emergence of conditional fees and the entail in the later thirteenth century. Women who held their own franchisal courts were answerable to the Crown for their working, and most of the information on the judicial franchises which they held is derived from the *quo warranto* pleas initiated by Edward I. At that time women had to be ready to defend their liberties as well as their lands.

28 M. T. Clanchy, *From Memory to Written Record: England 1066–1307*, London, 1979, chapter 2.

Royal government influenced record-keeping in other areas, as did the growing use of professional administrators, and this had its effect on the Church and on the noble families themselves. The Church had long been conscious of the importance of documentation, but the range and quantity of its records multiplied from the early thirteenth century. Papal and bishops' registers contain a considerable amount of material on women, ranging from dispensations for marriage to divorce, and from indulgences to visitations of religious houses. Of particular importance are the wills which from the thirteenth century were entered in bishops' registers, and were later to be found in the records of ecclesiastical courts as well.

Many of the records of noble families comprised legal agreements and business documents. They include marriage settlements and an increasing number of estate and household records which throw light on management methods and changing methods of organisation. Such records sometimes enable an assessment to be made of the lady's wealth, and they give information on her lifestyle and standard of living. Letters are found throughout the Middle Ages, but there are no major family collections before the fifteenth century, when the Stonor, Paston and Plumpton correspondence provides material not available earlier, especially concerning family and social relationships and attitudes.

All these records provide a mine of information on issues affecting the women of the nobility and gentry, but they have to be questioned and interpreted. The historian needs to be aware of inherent problems in the records before using them to assess the importance and role of women. Much of the material is factual and formal. Agreements over marriage, wardship and care in old age were couched in legal terms and were clearly business arrangements. What is not recorded is what went on behind the scenes and the feelings and points of view of the parties involved. Without this information, it would be a mistake to conclude that the parties to an agreement saw everything in cold business terms. As far as estates were concerned, there is plenty of information on where they were situated, and what they produced, but the records do not throw light on the discussion which must have gone on before decisions were taken, the relationships between officials and lady, and the pressures on the lady herself. It is sometimes possible to get such information from legal proceedings and more particularly from letters, but often social relationships have to be judged on the basis of factual information, whether this describes actions taken, gifts made, or mutual support offered; there is rarely any knowledge of the emotions involved. There are comparatively few records in which the voice of the woman herself can be heard. Letters and wills are informative up to a point, but it must be borne in mind that they were usually dictated, and in the case of wills most only survive as copies; moreover, it was rare to express emotion. For some women material survives of sufficient variety to enable the historian to get some insight into what they were really like; this is true of Elizabeth de Burgh in the fourteenth century and Margaret Paston in the fifteenth. Elizabeth ranked among the higher nobility. She was widowed three times before she reached the age of twenty-seven, and was caught up in the machinations of the younger Despenser in the 1320s. She was deeply attached to her family and friends, proved to be an energetic manager, loved splendour and display, and had strong religious commitments. Margaret Paston backed her husband in the pursuit of family rights, was busy and forceful, and conventionally religious; some of her children caused her problems. With many other women it is possible to obtain plenty of factual information as to their role and importance but not to produce a fully rounded character.

The language and terminology of the records also has to be considered. By the thirteenth century, many of the gentry were speaking English as well as French.[29] Yet most of the records concerning them were written in Latin down to 1300, and royal government documents and many of the Church records continued to be written in Latin to at least 1500. During the fourteenth century, French came to be used increasingly for letters, wills and household and estate records; Elizabeth de Burgh's clerks used both French and Latin for her household accounts, and Elizabeth used French for her protest about the Despensers in 1326 and for her will. It was not until the fifteenth century that there was extensive use of English. This use of language poses two problems of interpretation, one for the twentieth-century historian in understanding the terminology of the Middle Ages, and one for the clerks themselves who could find themselves writing what to them was not their mother tongue.

In the following chapters, the main areas of activity for noble and gentry women have been examined. For the majority marriage conditioned their future life and responsibilities, and family relationships were often crucial to their well-being. In a society where wealth and status depended on land, it is important to see the types of land that a woman held and the problems she faced in securing her rights.

29 Clanchy, *From Memory to Written Record*, pp. 151–4.

Land had to be managed and exploited in order to secure wealth, and it was important for the lady to secure her income and to exercise lordship over her tenants. It was also important for her to manage her household, since this was the hub of her activities and the place where she exercised patronage and influence. It is also in the context of the household that it is possible to reconstruct her lifestyle. Finally her religious concerns formed an important part of her life and paved her way to the next world. Taking all her activities together, these women had an integral and often an important part to play in noble society.

Many of these activities overlapped, and cross-references have been made as necessary. In making the translations, place-names have been modernised, but surnames have been left in their original form unless there is a common form which is now widely used. Places have been assigned to the counties they belonged to before the local government reorganisation of 1974. Sums of money and measures have been given as in the original document; the modern equivalent for measures will be given in the appropriate chapter. As far as money was concerned, £1 was made up of twenty shillings; each shilling comprised twelve pence, and each penny was divided into two halfpennies or four farthings. The mark was often used as a unit of account, and was worth 13s 4d. Totals have been checked and, where necessary, a corrected total has been put in square brackets.

I: Marriage

Marriage for noble and gentry children was arranged by their families, with the participation on occasion of their lords and of the king, and it was relatively rare for the children themselves to take matters into their own hands. Marriage has to be set in the framework of the rules and conventions of feudal lordship, and was inextricably linked to property and wealth; personal considerations were rarely mentioned, and even then were probably regarded as subordinate. The desirability of securing an heiress and of making advantageous alliances, whether at court or in the locality, strongly influenced families in their choice of marriage partners, and the concern over money and land was underlined in the marriage contract.[1] In many respects marriage was regarded as a source of profit. As a result of marriage to an heiress, new property accrued to the family. Children who were still minors at the time of the death of their fathers came into the custody of their lord or of the king, and their wardship and marriage could be sold or used as the subject of patronage. Although from about 1200 the widow had the freedom to choose whether or not to remarry, pressure could still be applied. All these material considerations applied throughout the period and beyond. At the same time, the Church's doctrine of marriage, developed during the twelfth century, insisted that consent to the marriage had to be expressed by the partners themselves, and the Church's jurisdiction over marriage had some influence over the nobility and gentry in their family arrangements.

Marriage was the end result of complex negotiations, and the family was on the look-out early on for potential marriage alliances.[2] The

---

1 The factors influencing families in making marriage agreements are discussed by, among others, E. Acheson, *A Gentry Community: Leicestershire in the Fifteenth Century, c. 1422–c. 1485*, Cambridge, 1992, chapter 6; C. Carpenter, *Locality and Polity: A Study of Warwickshire Landed Society, 1401–1499*, Cambridge, 1992, pp. 97–107; J. C. Ward, *English Noblewomen in the Later Middle Ages*, London, 1992, chapter 1; S. M. Wright, *The Derbyshire Gentry of the Fifteenth Century*, Derbyshire Record Society, VIII, 1983, chapter 3.

2 Examples of ages at marriage are given by J. R. Lander, 'Marriage and politics in the fifteenth century: the Nevilles and the Wydevilles', *Bulletin of the Institute of Historical Research*, XXXVI, 1963, pp. 119–52. In the Neville family, eleven marriages between 1412 and 1436 involved thirteen children under the age of sixteen, a young man not more than seventeen years old, two girls of eighteen or under, and five men between the ages of twenty and twenty–three.

Paston Letters point to the complications of arranging marriages, and Froissart indicates how the family could defeat a designing son-in-law. However, although the family was of primary importance, the role of the king and the lord must not be discounted. Marriage was inevitably affected by the conditions of feudal military tenure in England after 1066. According to Henry I's coronation charter of 1100, any baron contemplating the marriage of one of his female relations had to consult the king, and a baron's daughter who survived him as his heir was to be given in marriage by the king on the advice of his barons.[3] No king in the Norman period wanted to find an enemy among his vassals. By the thirteenth century, the incidents of feudal tenure were seen increasingly in fiscal terms, but the king's rights and his ultimate control over inheritance continued. The marriages of the higher nobility were especially the subject of political consultation, but co-operation between king and family was frequently found.[4] Royal profit and patronage are clear in the cases of Baldwin fitz Gilbert, Robert Foliot, and Isabella de Bolebec. The importance of consultation with the family was brought out in Magna Carta, where it was laid down that the heir was to be married without disparagement, and a relative of the heir was to be informed before the marriage took place.[5] Because of the custom of prerogative wardship, giving the king custody of all the lands held by a tenant-in-chief, the king's rights of custody and of the marriage of heirs were more extensive than those of lords, but the same considerations apply to lords on a smaller scale. Custody lasted until the male heir came of age at twenty-one; for a female ward marriage with the lord's consent put an end to the wardship at the age of fourteen.[6]

The marriage contract itself specified the property arrangements, which became more complex as the Middle Ages progressed. The contract was normally drawn up by the fathers or male relations of the bride and bridegroom. The bride's father provided a dowry for his

---

3 D. C. Douglas and G. W. Greenaway, eds, *English Historical Documents 1042–1189*, London, 1953, p. 401.

4 E.g. The marriage of Richard de Clare, earl of Gloucester, is discussed by F. M. Powicke, *King Henry III and the Lord Edward*, Oxford, 1947, II, pp. 760–8, where some of the sources are given in translation.

5 Magna Carta, 1215, cap. 6; H. Rothwell, ed., *English Historical Documents 1189–1327*, London, 1975, p. 318. J. C. Holt, *Magna Carta*, second edition, Cambridge, 1992, p. 53, points out that the Crown was accepting so many proffers for the marriage of heiresses and remarriage of widows that Magna Carta did little more than confirm an existing trend.

6 S. S. Walker, 'Proof of age of feudal heirs in medieval England', *Medieval Studies*, XXXV, 1973, p. 307.

daughter, originally in the form of the *maritagium* or a gift of land, and subsequently (from *c.* 1300) in the form of money. The *maritagium* was designed to provide the couple with the means of livelihood for themselves and their children, and, according to Glanvill, if there were no children, the land reverted to the donor.[7] According to the Statute of Westminster II of 1285, the *maritagium* descended to the issue of the marriage, apparently to the fourth generation, and only after that could it be alienated; until that time the donor remained responsible for any feudal services, so that the donor's daughter and her husband, and her son and grandson held freely.[8] The provision of a money dowry necessitated careful planning, as seen in the case of William Berland.

The wife's dower was provided by the husband and his family. To start with, the wife was dowered by a specific gift at the church door when the marriage took place, but in the later thirteenth century it came to amount to one-third of the land that the husband had held in his lifetime. In the thirteenth century it became usual for the bridegroom's father to endow husband and wife jointly with land, and this jointure was then held by the wife for life if she survived her husband, subsequently passing to the children of the marriage. Jointures specified in the marriage contract could be added to during the marriage. In the late Middle Ages family settlements became much more complex as a result of the enfeoffment to use which was used increasingly from the later fourteenth century. By this means, the lands were conveyed to a group of people known as feoffees to uses who held the lands to the use of a particular beneficiary, such as the married couple.[9] Finally some agreements specify a morning-gift,[10] and it was expected that the bride would contribute household stuff. These provisions in the marriage contract were found at all levels of noble society. The change over dower and the practice of jointure often made women more secure and more wealthy from the thirteenth century, to the detriment and sometimes the displeasure of their children.

7 T. F. T. Plucknett, *A Concise History of the Common Law*, fourth edition, London, 1948, pp. 516–17.

8 Statute of Westminster II, cap. 1, *De donis conditionalibus*; Rothwell, *English Historical Documents 1189–1327*, pp. 428–9; A. Harding, *England in the Thirteenth Century*, Cambridge, 1993, p. 201; T. F. T. Plucknett, *Legislation of Edward I*, Oxford, 1949, pp. 131–5; A. W. B. Simpson, *An Introduction to the History of the Land Law*, Oxford, 1961, pp. 77–81.

9 Simpson, *Land Law*, pp. 163–6.

10 F. M. Stenton, ed., *Facsimiles of Early Charters from Northamptonshire Collections*, Northamptonshire Record Society, IV, 1927, no. XXXII.

Jurisdiction over marriage was exercised by the Church, and during the twelfth century marriage law became formalised and widely accepted by the lay world. The Church set the age of marriage at puberty, specifying that boys should be fourteen years old and girls twelve. Betrothal could take place at the age of seven, but marriage before puberty had to be freely confirmed by the parties when they reached maturity, and divorce was permissible if they refused to give their consent.[11] If the children were married young, provision was usually made for them to reside with one set of parents. For the Church, the essence of marriage lay in consent, expressed by the parties in the present tense,[12] and, although the Church stressed that marriages should take place in public, it accepted clandestine marriages as valid when the words of consent *de praesenti* had been exchanged, as in the case of Margery Paston and Richard Calle.[13]

The Church's rule forbidding marriage within four degrees of consanguinity meant that many of the nobility and gentry, who were highly interrelated, had to secure a papal dispensation before contracting marriage. The Church's prohibition of marriage within seven degrees of consanguinity, as found in the late eleventh century, was found to be unworkable, and four degrees was specified at the Fourth Lateran Council in 1215. This meant that, without a dispensation, a marriage was not allowed if the parties had a common great-great-grandparent, as seen in the dispensation for the marriage of John de Hastings earl of Pembroke and Anne Mauny; this not only applied to relations by blood, but to relationships by marriage and spiritual relationships (i.e. godparents) as well.[14] The dispensation was essential in order to secure the legitimacy of the offspring. Only the legitimate heir could inherit.

Ideally, affection and a good property settlement went hand in hand. How often this was the case is unknown, largely because so much of

---

11 C. N. L. Brooke, *The Medieval Idea of Marriage*, Oxford, 1989, pp. 137–40; J. D. Mansi, ed., *Sacrorum Conciliorum Nova et Amplissima Collectio*, XXII, Graz, 1961, cols 251–2.

12 M. M. Sheehan, 'Choice of marriage partner in the Middle Ages: development and mode of application of a theory of marriage', *Studies in Medieval and Renaissance History*, new series, I, 1978, pp. 1–33.

13 A similar case among the higher nobility is discussed in K. P. Wentersdorf, 'The clandestine marriages of the Fair Maid of Kent', *Journal of Medieval History*, V, 1979, pp. 203–31.

14 Brooke, *Medieval Marriage*, pp. 134–6; M. M. Sheehan, 'Marriage theory and practice in the conciliar legislation and diocesan statutes of medieval England', *Mediaeval Studies*, XL, 1978, pp. 417–20; Mansi, ed., *Sacrorum Conciliorum Collectio*, XXII, cols. 1035–8.

the documentation on marriages is legal and formal. However, the letter collections of the fifteenth century show how the two elements could be intertwined; Margery Brews was aware that unless her father reached a satisfactory settlement her marriage to John Paston III was doomed. Letters also show how personal qualities could be taken into consideration. On occasion, parental and royal plans were overthrown by an abduction or elopement, something particularly serious where an heiress was concerned.

Elopement and abduction affected widows as well as girls. Many of the secular and ecclesiastical considerations governing first marriages applied also to remarriage. However, there was one vital difference; the widow was a *femme sole*, entitled to take her own independent decisions and actions, and no longer under the control of father or husband. According to canon and common law, she was entitled to choose whether to remarry or remain a widow. According to Henry I's coronation charter, the widow of a tenant-in-chief of the Crown was entitled to her dower and *maritagium*, and was not to be remarried against her will.[15] Widows, like wards, could be a source of profit and patronage, and the *Rotuli de Dominabus* shows how carefully they and their property were assessed by Henry II. However, by the late twelfth century, many widows were making proffers to the Crown not to remarry, a situation which was regularised by Magna Carta which specified that no widow should be forced to remarry but should give security that she would not marry without the consent of the king or of her lord, whichever was appropriate.[16] With the more bureaucratic administration of the thirteenth century and later, it was usual for the widow to promise not to remarry without consent; widows who broke this promise were punished. However, there still remained occasions when pressure was brought to bear on the widow, often for political reasons.

Marriage negotiations, the securing of the dispensation, and the drawing up of the settlement were all lengthy proceedings. The wedding, when and if it came, was a time for festivity. The bride's father, if a feudal lord, was entitled to levy an aid for the first marriage of his eldest daughter; the rate was laid down in the Statute of Westminster I of 1275 as £1 from a knight's fee.[17] However, feudal

15 M. M. Sheehan, 'The influence of canon law on the property rights of married women in England', *Mediaeval Studies*, XXV, 1963, pp. 111–12; Douglas and Greenaway, *English Historical Documents 1042–1189*, p. 401.

16 Magna Carta 1215 cap. 8; 1216 cap. 8; 1217 cap. 8; 1225 cap. 7; Rothwell, *English Historical Documents 1189–1327*, pp. 318, 328, 333, 342.

17 *Ibid.*, p. 406.

aids became increasingly difficult to collect in the later Middle Ages, and many fathers must have had to meet the expense out of their own pockets. Stress was put on a public ceremony, often at the church door, which might be followed by a nuptial mass. The Fourth Lateran Council with its stress on the publication of banns underlined the importance attached to publicising the occasion when the parties pledged their consent.[18] Afterwards, celebration was the order of the day.

1. Letter from Margaret Paston to John Paston I, probably in 1463, commenting on possibilities for their daughter's marriage [From J. Gairdner, ed., *The Paston Letters, 1422–1509*, 4 vols, reprint of edition of 1872–75, Edinburgh, 1910, II, no. 479; in English]

To my most worshipful husband John Paston, this letter is to be delivered in haste.

Most worshipful husband,[19] I recommend myself to you. May you be pleased to know that I was at Norwich this week to obtain what I needed for the winter. I was at my mother's, and while I was there a man called Wrothe came in, a relative of Elizabeth Clere's, and he saw your daughter and praised her to my mother and said that she was a good-looking young woman. And my mother asked him to get her a good marriage if he knew of any. And he said he knew of one that would amount to 300 marks a year, that is Sir John Cley's son; Sir John is chamberlain to my lady of York, and the son is eighteen years old. If you consider that the matter should be looked into further, my mother thinks that it could be obtained for less money now than later on, and that applies to this or to any other good marriage…

I pray to Almighty God to have you in his keeping. Written at Caister, Sunday after the feast of St. Martin.

From your M. Paston.[20]

18 Banns are discussed by Sheehan, 'Marriage theory and practice', pp. 432–40.

19 The term worshipful was frequently used as a means of address, meaning honourable and respected.

20 The letter refers to Margery, daughter of John Paston I and Margaret Paston, who subsequently married Richard Calle. Margaret referred to her mother-in-law, Agnes Barry, as her mother.

2. The marriage of Mary, daughter of Humphrey de Bohun, earl of Hereford and Essex, and his wife, Joan, 1380–1 [From *Chronicles of England, France and Spain by Sir John Froissart,* translated by T. Johnes, London, 1857, I, pp. 623–4]

From this earl of Hereford there remained only two daughters as his heiresses; Blanche the eldest, and Isabella her sister.[21] The eldest was married to Thomas of Woodstock, earl of Buckingham. The youngest was unmarried, and the earl of Buckingham would willingly have had her remain so, for then he would have enjoyed the whole of the earl of Hereford's fortune. Upon his marriage with Eleanor, he went to reside at his handsome castle of Pleshey, in the county of Essex, thirty miles from London, which he possessed in right of his wife. He took on himself the tutelage of his sister-in-law, and had her instructed in doctrine; for it was his intention she should be professed a nun of the order of St. Clare, which had a very rich and large convent in England.[22] In this manner was she educated during the time the earl remained in England, before his expedition into France. She was also constantly attended by nuns from this convent who tutored her in matters of religion, continually blaming the married state. The young lady seemed to incline to their doctrine, and thought not of marriage.

Duke John of Lancaster, being a prudent and wise man, foresaw the advantage of marrying his only son Henry, by his first wife Blanche, to the Lady Mary: he was heir to all the possessions of the house of Lancaster in England, which were very considerable. The duke had for some time considered he could not choose a more desirable wife for his son than the lady who was intended for a nun, as her estates were very large, and her birth suitable to any rank; but he did not take any steps in the matter until his brother of Buckingham had set out on his expedition to France. When he had crossed the sea, the duke of Lancaster had the young lady conducted to Arundel castle; for the aunt of the two ladies was the sister of Richard, earl of Arundel, one of the most powerful barons of England.[23] This Lady Arundel, out of complaisance to the duke of Lancaster, and for the advancement of the

21 The sisters were in fact named Eleanor and Mary. Humphrey de Bohun died in 1373. Thomas of Woodstock was the youngest son of Edward III and was created duke of Gloucester in 1385. He led an expedition to France in 1380. The marriage took place between July 1380 and February 1381, when Mary was not more than eleven years old; she proved her age in 1384 and died ten years later.

22 This is probably a reference to the convent of the Minoresses outside Aldgate in London where Isabella, daughter of Thomas and Eleanor, later became a nun.

23 Joan de Bohun, Mary's mother, was the sister of Richard FitzAlan, earl of Arundel.

young lady, went to Pleshey, where she remained with the countess of Buckingham and her sister for fifteen days. On her departure from Pleshey, she managed so well that she carried with her the Lady Mary to Arundel, where the marriage was instantly consummated between her and Henry of Lancaster. During their union of twelve years, he had by her four handsome sons, Henry, Thomas, John and Humphrey, and two daughters, Blanche and Philippa.

The earl of Buckingham, as I said, had not any inclination to laugh when he heard these tidings; for it would now be necessary to divide an inheritance which he considered wholly as his own, excepting the constableship which was continued to him. When he learnt that his brothers had all been concerned in this matter, he became melancholy, and never after loved the duke of Lancaster as he had hitherto done.

3. Payment to Joan de Bohun by John of Gaunt duke of Lancaster for the maintenance of her daughter Mary after her marriage until she came of age, 1383–84 [From Public Record Office, London, DL29/ 262/4070, m. 3; in Latin]

£26 13s 4d paid to Joan countess of Hereford for Easter and Michaelmas terms this year, by two acquittances from Joan, in part payment of a certain yearly rent of 100 marks granted to her by the lord [John of Gaunt], namely forty marks to be received yearly from the issues of the manors of Glatton and Holme, and £40 from the manor of Higham Ferrers, to be delivered by the then receivers of the aforesaid manors at the terms of Easter and Michaelmas in equal portions, from 5 February in the fifth year of the reign of King Richard [1382], until Lady Mary countess of Derby, Lady Joan's daughter, reaches the age of fourteen years, or for the time that Countess Mary shall live with Lady Joan at her costs and expenses, by the lord's letter of warranty remaining with the warrants for the sixth year of King Richard.[24]

4. Baldwin fitz Gilbert's acquisition of the honour of Bourne, Lincolnshire, 1130 [From *Magnus Rotulus Scaccarii de anno 31 Henrici I*, ed. J. Hunter, Record Commission, 1833, p. 110; in Latin]

Baldwin fitz Gilbert renders account of £300 36s 4d for the land of William de Rullos together with the daughter of Richard his brother. Paid, £35. And he owes £266 16s 4d.

24 Mary's husband Henry at this time had the title of earl of Derby. The acquittance given by Joan was a receipt.

5. **Grant by Henry II of the lands of Guy de Raimecurt to Robert Foliot together with Margery, the daughter and heir of Richard de Raimecurt, 1154–61** [From British Library, London, Sloane MS. 986, The Chartulary of the Braybroke Family, fo. 21; in Latin]

Henry, king of England, duke of Normandy and Aquitaine, and count of Anjou, greets his archbishops, bishops, abbots, earls, barons, justices, sheriffs, officials, and all his faithful men of the whole of England and Normandy. Know that I have granted to Robert Foliot all the land and honour that was held by Guy de Raimecurt, together with Margery, daughter of Richard de Raimecurt, who is the heir. Wherefore I wish and command that he and his heirs should hold that land and honour of me and my heirs in fee and inheritance as freely, peacefully and honourably as Guy de Raimecurt held them, and Richard his son after him, with soc and sac, toll and team, and infangenetheof, and with all the liberties and free customs that belong to the said honour, in wood and plain, meadows and pastures, waters and mills, inside and outside cities, and in all places.[25] Witnessed by Thomas the chancellor and others.

6. **The marriages of the daughters of William earl of Gloucester, d. 1183** [From W. Stubbs, ed., *Gesta Regis Henrici Secundi Benedicti Abbatis*, 2 vols, Rolls Series, London, 1867, I, pp. 124–5; in Latin]

In the same year [1176] the earl of Gloucester at the request of the king made John, the king's youngest son, the heir to his earldom. And the king conceded that the aforesaid John his son should marry the earl's daughter, if it was allowed by the Roman Church, for they were related. And if the Roman pontiff did not permit a marriage to be contracted between them, the king promised the earl that he would marry off the earl's daughter with the greatest honour, and that in return for this concession the king himself would give £100 worth of rents in England to the wife of Amaury count of Evreux, and another £100 worth of rents to the wife of the earl of Clare; for both were daughters of the earl of Gloucester. And if the earl of Gloucester had a son legitimately born of his wife, that son and the aforesaid John, son

---

25 Further information is given by F. M. Stenton, *First Century of English Feudalism*, second edition, Oxford, 1961, p. 264; and by I. J. Sanders, *English Baronies*, Oxford, 1960, p. 33. In 1086, Guy de Reinbuedcurt's honour lay in Northamptonshire, Leicestershire, Lincolnshire, Oxfordshire and Cambridgeshire, with the centre at Chipping Warden, Northamptonshire. Margery was Guy's granddaughter. Thomas the chancellor was Thomas Becket, subsequently archbishop of Canterbury.

of the king, would divide the earldom of Gloucester between them.[26]

7. The wardship of Isabella, daughter of Walter de Bolebec, 1185
[From Public Record Office, London, E198/1/2, *Rotuli de Dominabus et Pueris et Puellis*, Rolls 4, 5, 11; in Latin]

Buckinghamshire. The daughter of Walter de Bolebec, who was nine years old at Michaelmas [29 September], has been in the custody of Earl Aubrey since the beginning of Lent. Her land at Whitchurch, which belongs to the fee of Walter de Bolebec, has been in the custody of Reginald de Curteni since the feast of St. John nine years ago,[27] and it is worth £20 a year, not counting aids, and the profits from demesne land and the garden. It is stocked as follows: three ploughs, one boar, five sows, and twenty-one piglets.

Buckinghamshire. Chesham was held by Walter de Bolebec, and for ten years has been in the custody of Reginald de Curteni, together with Walter's daughter, and it is worth £30 a year.

Cambridgeshire. The daughter of Walter de Bolebec is in the gift of the lord king and is ten years old. The vill of Swaffham Bulbeck is part of the barony of Walter de Bolebec, and his daughter is the heir, and Swaffham has been given in dower to the wife of Gilbert Basset.[28]

8. Grant of the marriage of Belesent, daughter and heiress of Roger son of Odo, by her lord, Richard de Clare, earl of Hertford, 1173–90
[From British Library, London, Harley Charter 111 E45; in Latin]

Richard de Clare earl of Hertford greets all his men and friends, both present and future. Know that I have given and granted and by this my

---

26 The passage shows the king's ability to override the customary division of an estate between the heiresses, Henry II doing this in the interests of providing for John. John married the youngest daughter Isabella whom he divorced in 1199. The eldest daughter Mabel married Amaury count of Evreux, and the second daughter Amicia married Richard de Clare earl of Hertford, d. 1217. In 1217 after the death of Isabella the Clare family succeeded to the earldom.

27 It is likely that the feast referred to was the Nativity of St. John the Baptist on 24 June which was a usual term for the payment of rent.

28 Presumably Walter's widow had been married to Gilbert Basset. It was usual for the custody of the heir and of the lands to be in different hands. These entries did not comprise the whole of Walter's barony. In 1190, Aubrey de Vere earl of Oxford paid 500 marks for permission to marry Isabella to his son Aubrey; *Rotuli de Dominabus et Pueris et Puellis de XII Comitatibus*, ed. J. H. Round, Pipe Roll Society, XXXV, 1913, pp. xxxix–xli; D. M. Stenton, ed., *The Great Roll of the Pipe for 2 Richard I, 1190*, Pipe Roll Society, new series, I, p. 110.

present charter have confirmed to Hugh, brother of Master Robert de Kent, in return for his service Belesent, daughter and heiress of Roger son of Odo, together with all the land which Roger and his father Odo held of me and my father within and outside the borough of Tonbridge, namely the land at Sandhurst and 'Helham', with all appurtenances, in wood and plain, in meadows, pastures and fisheries, to have and to hold to him and his heirs of me and my heirs wholly and fully and freely and peacefully in all things by the service of half a knight for all service. And in return for this my gift Hugh has done homage and fealty to me. And in order that this my gift may be firm and permanent I have confirmed it with the present writing and with the testimony of my seal. Witnessed by Richard de Clare, John the steward, William de Watevile, Master William de Tunebrege, Master Robert de Kent, Guy son of Odo, Ralph Canutus, Ralph de Penecestre, Gilbert de Cortune, John de Clare, Richard de Marem, Hugh de Cestre, William Scurleg, John son of Godfrey, Richard of the chamber.

9. **Extracts from the proof of age of Joan, daughter and heiress of William de Welles, held at Great Sampford, Essex, 23 June, 1351**[29]
[From Public Record Office, London, C135/113/16; in Latin]

John Walram, knight, aged sixty, was examined on oath concerning Joan's age, and says that she was fifteen years old on the feast of the Nativity of the Blessed Mary last past [8 September]. He knows this because he was present as her godfather at her baptism in Great Sampford church on the feast of the Nativity of the Blessed Mary, in the ninth year of the reign of Edward III [1335], and her name was written in the church's missal. This is his memory of Joan's birth and age.

Richard de Welle, aged forty, was examined on oath about Joan's age, and says that she was fifteen years old on the feast of the Nativity of the Blessed Mary last past. Asked how he knows this, he says that William de Welles, Joan's father, was at Sampford on the day of Joan's birth, and gave Richard a tenement in Sampford by a charter dated the feast of the Nativity of the Blessed Mary in the ninth year of the present king, and he then heard how the news of Joan's birth came to

---

29 Statements were taken from twelve jurors altogether. Joan became a ward of the Crown on the death of her father, and her wardship was granted to Guy de Brian; his attorney was summoned to the proof of age (as was the usual practice with guardians) but did not appear. John de Coggeshale paid £400 to Guy for Joan's marriage to his son Henry; J. C. Ward, 'Sir John de Coggeshale: an Essex knight of the fourteenth century', *Essex Archaeology and History*, XXII, 1991, p. 65.

William, and this is his memory of the birth and age of Joan.

Simon Maynard, aged sixty, was examined on oath about Joan's age, and says that she was fifteen years old on the feast of the Nativity of the Blessed Mary last. Asked how he knows this, he says that he met Margery Kellehog, the midwife of Agnes, Joan's mother, coming from the church and the baptism with Joan on the feast of the Nativity of the Blessed Mary in the ninth year of the present king. On that day his son Reginald died. And this is his memory of Joan's age.

Nicholas Stonespol, aged fifty, was examined on oath concerning Joan's age, and says that Joan was fifteen years old on the feast of the Nativity of the Blessed Mary last past. Asked how he knows this, he says that he was present when Margaret atte Hyde, Joan's wet-nurse,[30] swore on the Book[31] that Joan was aged fifteen on the feast of the Nativity of the Blessed Mary, and this is his memory of Joan's birth and age.

The jurors say that Henry de Coggeshale, son of John de Coggeshale, married Joan, and they have legitimate offspring.

10. **Grant by Henry I to Miles of Gloucester of Sibyl, daughter of Bernard de Neufmarche, and of her inheritance, and giving details of her *maritagium*, 1121**[32] [From Public Record Office, London, DL10/ 6; in Latin]

Henry king of England greets the archbishops, bishops, abbots, earls, sheriffs, and all his barons French and English, and his faithful men of the whole of England and Wales. Know that I have given and firmly granted to Miles of Gloucester Sibyl, daughter of Bernard de Neufmarche, together with all the land of Bernard her father and of her mother after their deaths, or earlier during their lifetime if they so wish, and with this *maritagium* comprising Talgarth, the forest of Ystradyw, the castle of Hay, and the whole land of Brecknock up to the boundaries of the land of Richard fitz Pons, namely up to Brecon and Much Cowarne, a vill in England; and also the fee and service of Roger de Baskerville, the fee and service of William Revel, the fee and service

---

30 The Latin word *nutrix* can simply mean nurse, but in this context wet-nurse is the more likely meaning.

31 Presumably the Bible or a Gospel-book is meant.

32 The grant illustrates co-operation between the family and the king. It is further discussed by J. E. Lloyd, *A History of Wales from the Earliest Times to the Edwardian Conquest*, 2 vols, third edition, London, 1939, pp. 436–9, and by D. Walker, 'Miles of Gloucester, earl of Hereford', *Transactions of the Bristol and Gloucestershire Archaeological Society*, LXXVII, 1958, pp. 66–84.

of Robert de Turberville, and the fee and service of Picard. And I wish
and command that all the tenants of the *maritagium* do him liege
homage, saving fealty to me as their lord. And all the tenants of the
whole land of Bernard should similarly do him liege homage as their
lord, saving fealty to me and to Bernard for as long as he wishes to
hold the land. And I give and grant this to him as Bernard's purchase
which he has rendered to me, and at the request of Bernard himself and
his wife and his barons. And I wish and firmly order that Miles should
hold as well, honourably, peacefully and freely as Bernard ever held.
Witnessed by Roger bishop of Salisbury, Robert bishop of Lincoln,
Ranulf the chancellor, Robert son of the king, William de Tankerville,
Nigel de Albini, Pain fitz John, Geoffrey fitz Pain, Geoffrey de Clinton,
Ralph Basset, and William de Albini Brito, at Winchester, between
Easter and Pentecost in the same year that the king married the
daughter of the duke of Louvain.[33]

11. Arrangements for the marriage of Hugh de Vere and Hawise de
Quency, 1223, giving details of Hawise's *maritagium* and the fine paid
to the king for her marriage. [From British Library, London, Harley
Charter 55, B5 (first document); and C. Roberts, ed., *Excerpta e Rotulis
Finium in Turri Londinensi Asservatis Henrico Tertio Rege, 1216–72*, 2 vols.,
Record Commission, London, 1835–36, I, p. 101 (second document); in
Latin]

Know men present and future that I Margaret de Quency countess of
Winchester have given, granted and by this my charter confirmed to
Hugh de Ver in free marriage with Hawise my daughter £4 8s worth
of rent, namely 20s rent which Roger de Belegrave owed me with the
homage and service which was due to me, and 17s 6d rent in Laughton
which Geoffrey de Cranford owed me with the homage and service
which was due to me, and 50s 6d rent in Thurmaston which Alexander
de Witeby owed me with the homage and service which was due to me.
To have and to hold of me and my heirs to them and their heirs who
will be born of Hawise, well, peacefully, freely and quietly in free
marriage.[34] And if it should happen, which God forbid, that Hawise
should die without an heir begotten by Hugh, all the said rent will

33 Henry I's second wife was Adeliza, daughter of Godfrey of Louvain, duke of Lower
Lorraine.

34 Stipulations concerning succession are more precise in the thirteenth century and
later than in the twelfth. The warranty clause guaranteed the tenure of Hugh and
Hawise. Margaret was the widow of Saer de Quency earl of Winchester who died

revert peacefully together with the homage and service into my hands
or the hands of my heirs. And be it known that if I Margaret or my
heirs can acquire and deliver to Hugh those six virgates of land with
appurtenances which the prior of Brackley and Henry de Faffinton
hold in the vill of Wigston Magna or if we have made an exchange to
the value of the said six virgates in the same county before he takes
Hawise his wife to his home, then the aforenamed £4 8s rent will
revert peacefully to me and my heirs. And I Margaret and my heirs
will warrant to Hugh and Hawise his wife and their heirs who will be
born of Hawise all the said rent, as is aforesaid, against all people. In
order that this should be valid I have affixed my seal to the present
writing. Witnessed by John de Beauchamp, Ernald de Boys, William
de Cnapwell, Everard de Trumpithon, John de Hulecotes, Fulk de
Vaux, Geoffrey de Capell, Peter de Beche, and many others.

Margaret countess of Winchester made fine with the lord king for 400
marks in order that her daughter Hawise might be married to Hugh
son and heir of R[obert] de Vere, late earl of Oxford. She will render
100 marks to the lord king at Easter in the seventh year of his reign
[1223], 100 marks at Michaelmas [29 September] in the same year,
100 marks at Easter in year 8 [1224], and 100 marks at the following
Michaelmas in the same year.[35]

12. The grant of a *maritagium* by Warin de Bassingburn to Sir
Laurence de St Maur who married Warin's niece Emma, 1265–66
[From British Library, London, Cotton Charter XII 27; in Latin]

Know men present and future that I Warin de Bassingburn have given,
granted, and by this my present charter have confirmed to Sir Laurence
de St Maur, knight, in marriage with Emma my niece, and to his heirs
born to him and Emma, the manor of Claycoton next to Lilbourne in
Northamptonshire with the advowson of the church and all other
appurtenances belonging to the said manor both within the vill and
outside it, together with £4 16s rent of assize in the vill of Lilbourne,
namely 19s 7d from the tenement of John le Mercer; 8s 9d from Richard
son of Isaac; 12d from William son of Henry; 12s 4d from John Samson;
6s 8d from William son of Hugh; 8s 4d from Gilbert son of Geoffrey;

in 1219. Hugh de Vere's wardship had been bought by his mother from the king in
1221; *Patent Rolls 1216–25*, pp. 319, 341. Hugh did homage to the king for his
inheritance in 1231.

35 A fine denoted an agreement with the king or a lord for which a sum of money was
paid, often in instalments.

3s 10¹/₂d from Roger the clerk; 10s 2d from John Scot; 12d from
Alexander the Carpenter; 3¹/₂d from Nicholas the Miller; 8s from William
son of Geoffrey; 8s from William de Rowell. To have and to hold of me
and my heirs to the aforesaid Laurence and Emma and their heirs born of
Emma freely, peacefully and wholly, without claim from me or my heirs,
saving forinsec service if any is due. However if it should happen that
Sir Laurence and Emma should die without an heir being born to them,
the aforesaid manor with the advowson of the church and all other
appurtenances, together with the £4 16s rent of assize shall revert fully
to me or to my heirs without any objection. And I Warin de Bassingburn
and my heirs will warrant and defend the manor of Claycoton with the
advowson of the church and all its other appurtenances together with
£4 16s rent of assize in the vill of Lilbourne to the aforesaid Laurence
and his heirs born of Emma against all men and women. And in order
that this my gift and the confirmation of my charter may remain in
force for ever, I have affixed my seal to this charter. Witnessed by
Sir Pain de Chaworth, Sir John de Musegros, Sir Robert de Tybetot,
Sir Patrick de Chaworth, Sir John Russel, Sir Baldwin de Bassingburn,
Sir Hugh de Plogenet, and Sir Alexander de la Dune, and many
others.[36]

13. Agreement for the marriage of Hugh de Courtenay and Margaret
de Bohun, 28 February 1315, giving details of jointure and dowry
[From Public Record Office, London, DL27/13; in French]

On Friday after the feast of St Mathias the apostle in the eighth year
of the reign of our lord King Edward son of King Edward, the
agreement was made between the very noble lady, Lady Margaret
queen of England, and Sir Humphrey de Bohun earl of Hereford and
Essex and Lady Elizabeth his wife on one side, and Sir Hugh de
Courtenay on the other. It was agreed that Hugh, son of Sir Hugh,
should take as his wife Margaret, daughter of the earl and countess. Sir
Hugh grants that, at the time when he and the earl and countess can
agree that the marriage will take place, he will enfeoff Hugh his son

---

36 The version of the charter in L. C. Loyd and D. M. Stenton, eds, *Sir Christopher
Hatton's Book of Seals*, Oxford, 1950, no. 121, adds after the reversion clause
'rendering yearly 1d at Easter for all service save forinsec service'. Forinsec or
foreign service denoted service outside the manor or estate. Warin acquired this
property from the land of the Disinherited on 25 October 1265; Andrew de Astley
redeemed his lands from Warin by 10 July 1266, but did not regain Claycoton
which by then had been granted to Sir Laurence de St Maur; *Calendar of Patent Rolls,
1258–66*, p. 615.

and Margaret his wife jointly with 400 marks worth of land assessed at its true value and in a suitable place. To hold to Hugh and Margaret and to the heirs begotten by Hugh and entailed according to the will of Sir Hugh the father, rendering each year to Sir Hugh for the whole of his life, and while his son Hugh is alive, 400 marks at the four terms of the year. And if it should happen that Hugh the son should die during the lifetime of his father, Margaret should have and hold the above 400 marks worth of land, charged with the yearly sum of 400 marks, for the whole of her life, rendering each year a rose at the feast of the Nativity of St John the Baptist [24 June] to Sir Hugh and his heirs. And Sir Hugh wishes and concedes that, if it should happen that Margaret should survive him and Hugh his son, she should have dower both of all the lands and tenements that Sir Hugh the father holds, and of the lands and tenements of his inheritance that are held in dower as they revert to him, so that Margaret cannot demand dower nor bring an action to recover dower in the lifetime of Sir Hugh the father. And the earl agrees to be bound to pay on the day of the marriage to Sir Hugh 1,000 marks sterling for the above marriage. And Sir Hugh grants that as soon as the marriage shall take place he will charge himself with the maintenance of Hugh his son and Margaret his wife. And for greater security Sir Hugh concedes that Hugh his son will inherit all his inheritance to hold to him and the heirs begotten by him and entailed according to his will, so that all the aforesaid lands remain entirely in Sir Hugh's hands for the whole of his life except the 400 marks worth of land with which he will enfeoff Hugh his son and Margaret his wife as has been said above at the time that the earl obtains leave from the king to do this. And the earl and countess and Sir Hugh have promised in good faith to abide by all the above agreements and faithfully to carry them out. In witness of this the parties have alternately put their seals on this indenture.[37] Given at Westminster, on the above day and year.

14. Arrangements for the marriage of Hugh Courtenay and Elizabeth Audley involving feoffees to uses, 1387 [From Public Record Office, London, E210/494; in Latin]

Know men present and future that Edward Courtenay earl of Devon and Hugh Courtenay his brother have given, granted and by this their

---

37 Each family held a copy of the indenture, sealed with the other family's seal. Hugh the father became earl of Devon in 1335; his son succeeded him in 1341 and died in 1377; Margaret died in 1391.

present indented charter have confirmed to Hamo de Breirton clerk, Roger Spey, John Wadham and Thomas Kerdyngton clerk their manors of Goadrington, Stancombe and 'Klyngton' with appurtenances in Devon, and also the earl has given, granted and by this his present charter confirmed to the said Hamo, Roger, John and Thomas his manors of Hinton and Mudford with appurtenances in Somerset to have and to hold to the same Hamo, Roger, John and Thomas, their heirs and assigns for ever according to the following conditions: namely, that the said Hamo, Roger, John and Thomas should have seisin of the said manors, and that, after Hugh takes Elizabeth Audley as his wife, and Hamo, Roger, John and Thomas are required by Hugh and Elizabeth, or by the earl or his heirs, within three months of the request being made at Okeford Fitzpaine in Dorset they will give and grant the said manors with appurtenances to Hugh and Elizabeth to have and to hold to Hugh and Elizabeth and to the male heirs begotten by Hugh; if there is no such issue the said manors and appurtenances are to remain to the earl and his heirs for ever. And if, after the marriage between Hugh and Elizabeth has been celebrated, Hugh dies before the re-enfeoffment has been carried out, the said Hamo, Roger, John and Thomas are to give and grant the said manors and appurtenances to Elizabeth to have and to hold for the whole of her life, and to remain after Elizabeth's death to the male heirs begotten by Hugh and for lack of such issue to remain to the earl and his heirs for ever. Provided always that, if Hugh dies before the marriage between him and Elizabeth is celebrated, the said Hamo, Roger, John and Thomas are to give and grant the said manors with appurtenances to the earl and his heirs for ever without making any estate to Elizabeth, or the earl and his heirs should be allowed to re-enter the aforesaid manors with appurtenances and to retain them in their former good state. And the earl and Hugh and their heirs will warrant the aforesaid manors of Goadrington, Stancombe and 'Klyngton', and the earl and his heirs will warrant the said manors of Hinton and Mudford with appurtenances to the said Hamo, Roger, John and Thomas in the above form. In witness of this, both the earl and Hugh and the said Hamo, Roger, John and Thomas affix their seals alternately to this indented charter. Witnessed by William Bonevyll, John Beauchamp of 'Lyllesdon', John Streith, James de Chuddelegh, John Prydeaux, knights, Nicholas Kyrkham, William Carent, Thomas Knoyel and others. Given on Thursday after the feast of St Gregory the pope [14 March] in the tenth year of the reign of King Richard II.

15. Agreement for the marriage of Thomas Danyell and Grace Ogle, 1 December, 1458 [From Public Record Office, London, E40/12478; in English]

This indenture made between John Danyell of Dersbury esquire on the one side, and John Ogle esquire on the other bears witness that the two parties have reached an agreement as follows. John Danyell grants to John Ogle the wardship and marriage of Thomas Danyell, son and heir apparent of the said John Danyell of Dersbury, to be married and wedded to Grace, daughter of the said John Ogle, between the present time and the Purification of our blessed Lady next.[38] John Danyell grants to John Ogle that he will make or cause to be made for the said Thomas Danyell and Grace a sufficient and lawful estate in fee simple of his lands to the yearly value of six marks, over and above all charges and outgoings discharged of all manner of actions and encumbrance, within the county of Lancaster before the feast of the Purification, to have and to hold to Thomas and Grace and to the heirs of the body of Thomas lawfully begotten, the remainder ever being at the will of the said John Danyell; with the proviso in the deed that, if it should happen that Grace dies without issue born to her and Thomas living at the time of her death, the said grant, estate and seisin that was delivered and made to Thomas and Grace is to be void and of no value, and then it is to be lawful to the said John Danyell of Dersbury and his heirs to re-enter and hold and grant the said six marks worth of land yearly, notwithstanding the estate made previously. Also John Danyell grants to John Ogle that all the residue of his manors, messuages, lands, tenements, reversions, rents and service, with the appurtenances, which he has or at any time had in demesne, or through reversion of inheritance, or that any other person or persons has to his use within the county of Lancaster or within the county of Chester over and above the said six marks worth of land shall immediately after the death of John Danyell descend, remain and fall to Thomas Danyell and to his heirs, without any alienation, rent charge, statute merchant, recognisance, or any other encumbrance made in any way by him or by any other person or persons enfeoffed to his use upon the said manors, messuages, lands, tenements, reversions, rents and service, with their appurtenances, or any part of them; excepting always all those lands and tenements which Alice, mother of Thomas, now holds in jointure for her life, and except also all such lands and tenements as any wife of John Danyell shall after his death have and hold by right

38 The feast of the Purification of the Virgin Mary falls on 2 February.

and title of dower, which land and tenements so held in jointure or in dower shall immediately after the death of the said Alice and after the death of any such wife so holding them in dower shall each descend, remain and fall to the said Thomas and to the heirs of his body lawfully begotten, the remainder ever being at the will of the said John Danyell. Provided always that it be lawful for John Danyell to be bound for himself or his friends in any of the bonds for surety of the peace or for any other reasonable cause, so that the bonds be not made by fraud or collusion with the purpose or intention to charge or encumber the said manors, messuages, lands, tenements, reversions, rents and service, or any part of them. For this grant of marriage and estate John Ogle and three sufficient persons with him shall be bound by their individual obligations to pay John Danyell or his assigns 100 marks, that is to say, on the day of making these indentures twenty marks, and at the following feast of the Nativity of St John the Baptist [24 June] ten marks, and at the following Christmas ten marks, and so paying ten marks at each of these feasts until the sum of 100 marks is fully paid to John Danyell or his assigns. Also John Danyell grants to John Ogle that, if it happens that Grace dies within eight years of the date of the indenture without issue born to her and Thomas alive at the time of her death, he will repay or cause to be repaid to John Ogle half of any payment made by John Ogle to him or to his assigns at any time before Grace's death, except for the first payment, and all payments not paid at the time of her death should cease, and he should then deliver to John Ogle or to his assigns all sureties and bonds in which John Ogle and his friends are bound to John Danyell. John Ogle grants to John Danyell that, if it should happen that he should die without a male heir, Grace shall keep and have her lawful share of his lands and tenements which he has or may have in the future, if any other of his daughters have any share of his land. In order to ensure that the covenant will truly be observed, John Ogle and three sufficient persons with him are bound to John Danyell in the sum of £15; and John Danyell and three sufficient persons with him are bound to John Ogle by an obligation of £100, for the performance by John Danyell of the covenants above specified, and also so that no divorce shall be obtained between Thomas and Grace, the cause arising on Thomas's part or by his suit. John Danyell of Dersbury grants to John Ogle that he shall have the keeping and governance of Thomas and Grace during the said eight years, and also have and take all the sales and profits of the said six marks worth of land yearly during the eight years to maintain Thomas and Grace in all things needed by them. Provided always that, if

Thomas will not abide nor be governed by John Ogle at any time within the eight years, then it be lawful for Thomas to have half of the said six marks worth of land to support himself. In witness of this the parties have alternately set their seals to each part of the indenture, on 1 December in the thirty-seventh year of the reign of King Harry the sixth.

16. Will of Sir William Berland making provision for the marriage of his daughters in the event of his death, 1383 [From Public Record Office, London, C54/224, m. 34d; in French]

The will of Sir William Berland knight made by him on the day of the feoffment of his lands in the seventh year of King Richard II, all done to strengthen the said will or to amend or relinquish it during his lifetime.[39] First my will is that those who are feoffees in my lands are enfeoffed on the following condition, namely that, if it pleases the said Sir William to be re-enfeoffed in the future, the said feoffees are bound to re-enfeoff him without warranty. After my death and during the lifetime of Christian my wife I wish that all the lands, tenements, rents and services with their appurtenances which I have in the vill of Goldhanger, and all the lands, tenements, rents and services with appurtenances called 'le Vanne' in the vills of Hockley and Rawreth, which used to belong to John Viel, and also all the lands and tenements with appurtenances that I have in the vill of Prittlewell, except the lands with appurtenances called 'Serles', should be sold to aid the marriages of my daughters Joan and Elizabeth, or of one of them if the other die or be married by other means. They should be married before the age of fifteen if they want to be married, or, if one or the other or both desires or desire to be a nun or nuns, by their free will and without compulsion, I wish that she or they should have aid from the aforesaid lands after they are sold. If Christian my wife dies before they are married, I wish that the said feoffees should keep the aforesaid lands in their hands without waste or destruction and without any sale together with all the other manors, lands, tenements, rents, fees and services with all appurtenances which they have of my feoffment until my debts are fully paid as quickly as possible, in case I or my wife are then in debt, and so as to maintain my children, and also until the sum of £200 be levied from the said lands, tenements, rents, fees and services with appurtenances for the marriage of my aforesaid daugh-

39 The feoffment was made on 13 September 1383, and was enrolled immediately before the will on the Close Roll; *Calendar of Close Rolls, 1381–5*, pp. 394–5.

ters well and honourably according to my estate, and another £200 be
levied for alms for my soul and the souls of Christian my wife, my
father, mother, sons, daughters, brothers, sisters and all Christians,
and to aid the poor of my family, and to repair public bridges and
highways where there is most need in the vills and lands aforemen-
tioned, and principally in the hundred of Rochford, and also to aid my
tenants who are poor or distressed, by the good discretion of the
aforesaid feoffees. When the said sum is levied in the aforesaid manner
and form, I wish the feoffees to make enfeoffment in fee simple to the
heirs begotten of my body in the form and manner that the common
law of England demands, and, in case all the heirs begotten of my body
are dead before the said enfeoffment is made, I wish the feoffees to
make enfeoffment in fee simple in tail to my next heirs of blood of all
the lands, tenements, rents, fees and services with appurtenances
which are in the vills of Prittlewell, Milton, Southchurch, Leigh,
Ashingdon, Goldhanger and Fambridge, with remainder to the heirs
of Sir John de Brennsoun. I wish that all the other lands that they have
of my feoffment shall be sold without long delay, having no regard for
too great a price, but they should not be sold to purchase lordship of
lords, nor otherwise to my damage. The sum taken from the sale of the
aforesaid lands I wish to be spent in the above way for the aforesaid
souls, and in other ways by the good discretion of the feoffees for the
greater profit of my soul and the aforesaid souls, and especially in the
region where the aforesaid lands are.

17. Dispensation for the marriage between John de Hastings earl of
Pembroke and Anne daughter of Lord Mauny and Margaret de
Brotherton, 1368 [From Lambeth Palace Library, London, Register
of Simon Langham, fo. 68; in Latin]

Simon [archbishop of Canterbury] to the noble lord John de Hastings
earl of Pembroke and the noble lady Anne, daughter of the noble lord
Walter Mauny knight of our and of Cambrai dioceses, greetings, grace
and blessing. We have recently received the letters of the most holy
father in Christ and our lord, Lord Urban V, by divine providence
pope, sealed with his genuine lead seal, with the cord of hemp in the
manner of the Roman Curia, complete and undamaged, absolutely free
of all flaw and sinister suspicion.[40] They read as follows: Urban, bishop,

---

40 Simon Langham was bishop of Ely between 1362 and 1366, and was translated to
   Canterbury where he was archbishop between 1366 and 1368. Urban V was pope
   between 1362 and 1370, and was in Italy for the last three years of his pontificate.

servant of the servants of God, to his venerable brother...[41] the archbishop of Canterbury, greetings and apostolic blessing. The contents of the petition presented to us recently on the part of our beloved son the noble man John de Hastings earl of Pembroke and our beloved daughter in Christ the noble woman Anne, damsel, daughter of our beloved son the noble man Walter Mauny knight of your diocese of Canterbury and the diocese of Cambrai contained the information that with the consent of their parents they were once betrothed to one another by words *de futuro*, but because the said Anne and the late Margaret, damsel, daughter of our most dear son in Christ Edward, illustrious king of England, with whom in her lifetime the said earl contracted marriage by words *de presenti*, were related in one case in the third degree of consanguinity and in two cases in the fourth degree, they cannot contract marriage without obtaining an apostolic dispensation.[42] Wherefore on the part of the said earl and Anne we have been humbly petitioned that, since much good may be hoped to come from this marriage if it takes place, we may think it worthy to provide them with the grace of a fitting dispensation. Therefore for the aforesaid reasons and also in consideration of the said king's supplication to us on behalf of the earl and Anne, being favourably disposed to the petitions of the king and of the earl and Anne, we commit the matter by apostolic letter to your brotherly love, concerning which on this and other things we have special trust in the Lord. We order that, if the said Anne has not been abducted and if the parents and the majority of the relatives around the third degree of consanguinity of the said earl and Anne give their consent, you may grant a dispensation with our authority, so that, notwithstanding the impediments which proceed from consanguinity of this kind, the earl and Anne may freely contract marriage with each other and remain in it lawfully after it has been contracted, pronouncing the offspring to be born of this marriage legitimate. We urge the said earl and Anne diligently, if this dispensation is granted to them by you, to bestow in alms 1,000 gold

Cambrai is now in northern France, but in the fourteenth century was part of the Holy Roman Empire; the lead seal was the papal *bulla*. All papal bulls had to be carefully checked by the recipient to ensure that they were not forgeries.

41 A small portion of text is missing.

42 A promise to marry at some time in the future constituted betrothal, not marriage. True marriage was contracted when the parties expressed their consent to marry in the present tense. Margaret and Anne were related in the third degree because they were both great-granddaughters of Edward I, and in the fourth degree because their great-great-grandfather was Philip III of France twice over through their descent from his sons Philip IV and Charles of Valois.

florins towards the repair of the church of the monastery of St Paul in
Rome of the order of St Benedict. Given at Montefiascone on 1 July in
the sixth year of our pontificate.

These apostolic letters were received by us with the reverence which
was fitting, were read thoroughly, and their whole contents considered, and because we found that you Anne had not been abducted, but
that your parents and the majority of your relatives around the third
degree consent to the marriage, we grant you a dispensation by
apostolic authority, notwithstanding the impediments which come
from this consanguinity, to contract marriage freely with each other
and to remain in it lawfully after it has been contracted, and by the
same authority we decree that the children to be born of this marriage
will be legitimate. We wish however that in return for this dispensation there shall be a bestowal of alms in the form expressed above in
the said apostolic letters. In testimony of this we have issued these
letters. Given at Mayfield on 31 August AD 1368 and in the second
year of our translation.

18. The marriage of William de Roos and Margaret de Neville, 1342 [From Public Record Office, London, C66/206, m. 1; in Latin]

The king greets all those to whom the present letters come. You
should know that when William de Roos, son of our beloved and
faithful William de Roos of Helmsley, marries Margaret, daughter of
our beloved and faithful Ralph de Neville, William the son is of so
young an age that he cannot consent to the marriage. Therefore a
divorce between him and Margaret could possibly by chance occur in
the future, and William's marriage could belong to us if his father, who
holds of us in chief, died during his minority. Wishing to exercise
special grace towards Ralph because of his good service up to now and
in the future, we have granted him of our gift whatever belongs or
could belong to us in the aforesaid marriage. In testimony of this we
have had these our letters patent drawn up. Witnessed by the king at
Westminster on 15 May.

19. Excerpt from the matrimonial case concerning John de Carnaby esquire and Joan Mounceaux, lady of Barmston in Holderness, 1390– 91, showing the importance attached to the words of consent in the present tense [From Borthwick Institute of Historical Research, York, CP E.179, document 10; in Latin]

John Dawson of Newburgh in Tyndale, thirty years old and more, of free condition, related by marriage to John Carnaby but unknown in what degree, was sworn and examined. He says that the first article contains truth. Asked about what he knows, he says that he was present in the hall of the house of Joan Mounceaux in Barmston. He does not remember the day, but it was the first, second or third day after the Purification of the blessed Mary last. He heard John and Joan make a sworn contract between themselves in this form, with first John saying, 'I take you Joan as my wife, and on this I give you my troth.' Immediately Joan replied, 'I take you John as my husband, and on this I give you my troth.' Asked who were present there and heard this, he says that Robert and Richard, his co-witnesses, heard this sworn contract, and no others whom he remembers. He says on the second article that on divers occasions after the contract was made, whose dates he does not remember, he heard Joan acknowledge this contract in the presence of the said John and others whose names he does not remember. He says on the last article that this matter was notorious and manifest in the aforesaid vills and places according to news and rumour. Asked whether they were standing or sitting when they made the contract, he says they were standing by a cupboard in the aforesaid hall.

20. The examination of Margery Paston and Richard Calle by Walter Lyhert bishop of Norwich to see whether their marriage was valid, 10 or 11 September 1469[43] [From J. Gairdner, ed., *Paston Letters*, II, no. 617, extract from a letter from Margaret Paston, Margery's mother to John Paston II, Margery's brother; in English]

On Friday the bishop sent Asschefeld and others for her [Margery], and they are very sorry about her behaviour. And the bishop spoke to her very plainly, and reminded her of her birth, and of her relations and friends, pointing out that she would have more if she accepted their rule and guidance, and why they would abandon her and not offer any good or help or comfort. He said that he had heard that she loved her status, and that her friends were not pleased with what she wanted to do, and therefore he told her to take very good advice as to how she acted. He said that he wanted to know the words that she had spoken to Calle, as to whether they constituted marriage or not. And she went

43 This should be compared with no. 1. The marriage is discussed by C. Richmond, 'The Pastons revisited: marriage and the family in fifteenth-century England', *Bulletin of the Institute of Historical Research*, LVIII, 1985, pp. 31–4.

over what she had said, and said boldly that if those words did not
ensure marriage she would make it surer before she left, because, she
said, she thought that she was bound in conscience whatsoever the
words were. This wicked speech grieves me and her grandmother as
much as all the rest. And then the bishop and the chancellor both said
that neither I nor any of her friends would receive her. And then Calle
was examined on his own, as to whether her words and his agreed, and
when and where it had been done. And then the bishop said that he
supposed that there might be found other things against him that
might prevent the marriage, and therefore he said that he would not
be too hasty in giving sentence. He said that he would wait until the
Wednesday or Thursday after Michaelmas, and so it has been delayed.
They wanted to be married quickly according to her wish, but the
bishop stated that he would do as he said. I was with my mother at her
place when she was examined, and, when I heard about her behaviour,
I ordered my servants that she should not be received in my house.

21. Extract from a letter from Richard Calle to Margery Paston, 1469
[From J. Gairdner, ed., *Paston Letters*, II, no. 609; in English]

My own lady and mistress, and in the eyes of God very true wife, I
with a very sad heart recommend myself to you as one who cannot and
will not be happy until it be otherwise with us than it is at the moment;
for the life that we lead now gives no pleasure to God or the world,
considering the great bond of matrimony uniting us.

**22. Extract from a letter from John Paston II to his mother Margaret
Paston, discussing the marriage of his brother John III to Margery
Brews, 28 March 1477** [From J. Gairdner, ed., *Paston Letters*, III, no.
797; in English]

May you be pleased to know that I have received your letter in which
you wrote of the great injury likely to affect my brother John if the
matter between him and Sir Thomas Brews's daughter does not come
about. I would be as sorry as he would be, and as glad as any man over
the wealth and suitability of the marriage if it should take place. I am
happier now that he should have her than I was over any previously
contemplated marriage, considering her person, her youth, her family,
the love on both sides, the tenderness of her father and mother
towards her, her father's and mother's kindness to her in parting with
her, the favour and high opinion that they have of my brother, the

honourable and virtuous disposition of her father and mother which indicates that the girl should probably be virtuous and good...

Item, there is another drawback. I understand that the manor [Sparham, Norfolk] is given to my brother and his wife and to the issue born to them. If it should happen that they have one or more daughters and his wife dies and then he marries again and has a son, that son would have no land although he was his father's heir.[44]

23. Extract from a Valentine letter from Margery Brews to John Paston III, February 1477 [From J. Gairdner, ed., *Paston Letters*, III, no. 784; in English]

Most worshipful and well-beloved Valentine...

And as for me, I have understood and done what I can in the matter, as God knows. And I give you clearly to understand that my father will only part with £100 and fifty marks for that purpose which is much less than what you want. So if you could be happy with that and with my poor person I would be the happiest girl on earth. And if you are not satisfied or if you might have much more, as I have previously understood from you, do not take it upon yourself to come again on the matter, good, true and loving Valentine, but let it go and do not speak of it any more, as I may be your true lover and humble servant during my life.

No more to you at this time, but may Almighty Jesus preserve you both body and soul etc.

From your Valentine Margery Brews.

24. Extract from a letter from Thomas Mull to Thomas Stonor, 1472 [From Public Record Office, London, SC1/46/62; in English]

Most worshipful brother, I recommend myself to you. Please you to know that my cousin William has been with a very good-looking gentlewoman, and talked to her in love's way, and I certainly know that they are very well pleased with each other. She was formerly the wife of Lord Mountjoy's son. As for what my cousin will have with her, if God provides that they marry, it is sure that she has of her father's inheritance 100 marks worth of land, and after her father's death she

---

44 Margaret Paston gave the couple her manor of Sparham in order to bring about the marriage, and although John Paston came to accept his mother's decision he was critical on some points.

will have in addition all the rest of her father's land, and out of Lord Mountjoy's land she has an annuity of eighty marks by indenture; she has exchanged land worth 100 marks for this fee of eighty marks. I have these details from my bedfellow Thomas Powtrell who is a member of Lord Mountjoy's council and belonged to the council at the time she married his son; and as I understand from my bedfellow, the whole value of Sir Thomas Etchingham's land, as shown in writing at the time of the marriage, was between 300 and 400 marks, not fully 400 but better than 300, but by how much my bedfellow cannot remember.[45]

25. The abduction of Margaret de Multon, 1314–15 [From *Chronicon de Lanercost*, ed. J. Stevenson, Bannatyne Club LXV, Edinburgh, 1839, p. 223; in Latin]

In the same year [1313] Sir Thomas de Multon, lord of Gilsland, died on 26 November, and left an only daughter as heir, named Margaret, whom Robert, son of Robert de Clifford, was betrothed to at Hoffe in the seventh year of her age, lying in the same bed. And during Robert's lifetime, Ranulf, son of Sir William de Dacre, married the same Margaret because he had the right to her on account of an agreement made before the above wedding between Thomas de Multon, Margaret's father, and William de Dacre.[46]

26. The abduction of the widow Elizabeth de Burgh by Theobald de Verdun, 1316[47] [From *Rotuli Parliamentorum*, 6 vols, London, 1783, I, pp. 352–3; in Latin]

Theobald de Verdun was summoned before the king's council because by force and arms he abducted Elizabeth from Bristol castle. Elizabeth

---

45 The lady was Margery, daughter of Sir Thomas Etchingham, whose husband William, son of Walter Blount, Lord Mountjoy, died in 1471. She subsequently married Sir John Elrington, not William Stonor; C. L. Kingsford, ed., *The Stonor Letters and Papers, 1290–1483*, 2 vols, Camden Society, third series, XXIX, XXX, 1919, I, p. 123.

46 Ranulf abducted Margaret from Warwick castle. He was later pardoned by the king and Margaret's lands were handed over to the couple after she had proved her age in 1317; *Calendar of Patent Rolls, 1313–17*, p. 39; *Calendar of Close Rolls, 1313–18*, p. 504.

47 Elizabeth de Burgh was the daughter of Gilbert de Clare earl of Gloucester and Hertford and Joan of Acre (see no. 28); after the death of her brother at the battle of Bannockburn, she was one of the heiresses to the Clare lands. Her first husband, John de Burgh, died in 1313; Theobald died later in 1316.

was the wife of the late John de Burgh, one of the sisters of Gilbert de Clare late earl of Gloucester, and niece of the king, and on the king's orders she came from Ireland to England on Wednesday after the feast of the Purification of the Blessed Virgin Mary [3 February] in the ninth year of his reign [1316], and was living in Bristol castle by the king's arrangement and at his expense. Theobald married her outside the castle without the king's licence and in contempt of the king of £1,000. Theobald stated that he was betrothed to Elizabeth in Ireland before he married her, and that on that Wednesday she came one league from the said castle on his orders, and there he married her; he added that he did not enter the castle and he did not believe that he had done anything in contempt of the lord king. However if it seemed to the lord king's council that he had done anything wrong he was prepared to make amends according to the will and grace of the lord king. Afterwards Roger Mortimer of Chirk and Bartholomew de Badelesmere undertook to have Theobald before the king at the king's order to do what the lord king with his council should consider ought to be done.

27. **The king's role in the remarriage of widows** [From *The Great Roll of the Pipe 22 Henry II, 1175–6*, Pipe Roll Society XXV, London, 1904, p. 30 (Matilda of St Hilary); *Rotuli de Oblatis et Finibus in Turri Londinensi asservati tempore Regis Johannis*, ed. T. D. Hardy, Record Commission, London, 1835, p. 37 (widow of Ralph de Cornhill, 1199); in Latin]

The sheriff [of Oxfordshire] renders account of £6 12s 9d from the farm of the land of the countess of Clare in his bailiwick before the king gave her to William d'Aubigny [earl of Arundel]. He delivered the money. And he is quit.[48]

Essex. The widow of Ralph de Cornhill gives the lord king 200 marks and three palfreys and two goshawks in order that she should not be married to Godfrey de Louvain, and that she can marry whom she wishes, and for having her lands. An inquiry was ordered which reported that she had married of her own free will.

48 Matilda's first husband, Roger de Clare earl of Hertford, died in 1173.

28. The secret remarriage of Joan of Acre, daughter of Edward I and Eleanor of Castile, and widow of Gilbert de Clare earl of Gloucester, to Ralph de Monthermer, while her father was negotiating her marriage to Amadeus V, count of Savoy, 1297 [From *Johannis de Trokelowe et Henrici de Blaneforde Chronica et Annales*, ed. H. T. Riley, Rolls Series, London, 1866, pp. 26–7; in Latin]

In Acre, Eleanor conceived and bore a daughter whom they called Lady Joan of Acre who in the process of time was handed over to Lord Gilbert earl of Gloucester in lawful matrimony. She bore him two sons. On his death she took for herself a certain knight elegant in appearance but poor in substance. I do not say that all the lords of the land received this news with pleasure; no one in the land attacked it. All for fear or respect kept quiet; for fear because she was the daughter of the king, of royal stock; for respect because she was the principal countess of the realm. However, one of the magnates of the land came and thundered in the king's ear that a marriage of this kind was contrary to his honour, since several nobles, kings, earls and barons selected her for marriage. To him she replied, 'It is not ignominious or shameful for a great and powerful earl to marry a poor and weak woman; in the opposite case it is neither reprehensible nor difficult for a countess to promote a vigorous young man.' Her reply pleased the lord king, and thus his anger and that of the magnates was appeased.[49]

29. Levying an aid for the marriage of an eldest daughter, 1251 and 1235–36 [From H. R. Luard, ed., *Annales de Theokesberia* in *Annales Monastici*, 5 vols, Rolls Series, London, 1864–69, I, p. 146 (Richard de Clare); F. W. Maitland, ed., *Bracton's Notebook*, 3 vols, London, 1887, no. 1146, 1235–36 (extract from the case concerning Henry de Tracy); in Latin]

Richard de Clare earl of Gloucester demanded an aid from his men for marrying his daughter, although he did not yet know to whom.[50]

Henry [de Tracy] came to the Devon county court and acknowledged the seizure of the animals [of Walter de Reygni], and asked for seisin,

---

49 Joan was born in 1272 during her father, Edward I's, crusade. She bore Gilbert one son and three daughters. The chronicler does not comment on Edward I's anger over the marriage, and the details may be apocryphal. The story does however underline the widow's freedom to choose her next husband and the pressures which could be put on her.

50 Isabella de Clare married William marquis of Montferrat in 1258. The aid was levied at the rate of two marks per knight's fee; *Close Rolls, 1254–6*, pp. 192–3.

and said that he took the goods justly, because he had the lord king's writ directed to the sheriff of Devon to levy a reasonable aid from his fees to marry his eldest daughter, and, when all his knights had come to his court as a result of his summons, and especially the steward Richard de Chartray, they granted him twenty shillings from each fee. Because payment was not made from the ten fees that Richard de Chartray held of him, he took Walter's beasts as action against Richard, since Richard had nothing in demesne that was sufficient to pay £10.[51]

30. The importance of a public marriage ceremony, 1225 [From *Bracton's Note Book*, 3 vols, London, 1887, no. 1669; in Latin]

Alice who was the wife of James de Cardunville petitioned against Hugh bishop of Lincoln for one-third of two carucates of land with appurtenances in Chiselhampton as her dower with which the said James dowered her on the day that he married her. And the bishop comes and says that he does not consider that she ought to have dower because she was never married in the face of the church, but he married her in his last illness and in his house. He knows well that while he was in good health she was always his mistress, and he seeks judgment as to whether he ought therefore to give her dower.

And Alice says that indeed she was married to the same James in his illness in that house, and he placed the ring on her finger, and afterwards he got better and went from place to place. She says that the banns were announced at the three neighbouring churches for three Sundays before he married her, and he married her in the aforesaid way in his house on the day after the feast of St George [23 April], and he died on the feast of the Nativity of St John the Baptist [24 June]. Similarly she asks for judgment whether she ought to have dower or not. And because she knows that she was not married at the church door nor dowered there, it was decided that the bishop should be quit, and Alice in mercy,[52] and she should have no dower, because James acted for the salvation of his soul and in peril of death.

---

51 Presumably Walter was a vassal of Richard de Chartray.

52 Alice was liable to pay an amercement because of her false claim for dower.

31. The weddings of the daughters of Roger Mortimer earl of March, 1328 [From *Chronicon Galfridi le Baker de Swynesbroke*, ed. E. M. Thompson, Oxford, 1889, p. 42; in Latin]

However, after the marriage of his sister,[53] the young king of England journeyed to Hereford soon after the feast of Holy Trinity where the marriages were solemnised between the daughters of Roger Mortimer and certain nobles, namely the son of the Earl Marshal and the heir of Sir John de Hastings etc. Item, there were solemn tournaments there at which the queen mother was present.[54]

---

53 Edward III's sister Joan married David Bruce.

54 Beatrice married Edward, the son of Thomas de Brotherton earl of Norfolk, and Agnes married Laurence de Hastings earl of Pembroke.

II: Family

As with marriage, the woman's relationship to her husband and children has to be seen within the framework of canon and common law, the Church being concerned with the marriage itself, and the royal courts with property. Throughout the period, the family and its continuity were regarded as of prime importance, and the birth of the heir, preferably a son, was considered crucial. Far more can be learned about family relationships in the later Middle Ages than earlier because of the existence of a wider range of documentation, notably wills and letters, although legal and administrative documents also throw valuable light on the nature of families. For the late eleventh and twelfth centuries information has to be gleaned largely from chronicles, saints' lives, charters and exchequer material.

Many monastic chroniclers were principally concerned with tracing the family of their patrons and therefore concentrated on births, marriages and deaths, and the exploits of the best known male members of the family, not necessarily giving accurate information. Descriptions of women, where they occur, stress their family, property and offspring. Attention was focused on the eldest line of the family. This gives the impression that on marriage a woman became absorbed by her new family, and her identity was submerged under husband and offspring. Wills and other material however show that women acted as transmitters of their own family tradition, and they and their children might well relate to maternal kin, as is seen with Eleanor de Bohun's bequests to her son.

According to law, women were under the control of their husbands and could not take independent action; Margaret Beaufort, the mother of Henry VII, was exceptional in becoming a *femme sole* during the lifetime of her third husband.[1] Wives were expected to be obedient, and Adam Marsh criticised Eleanor de Montfort, countess of Leicester, for her quick temper. Yet husbands were expected to treat their wives well, as Warin de Montchensy found when his conduct was investigated by Robert Grosseteste, bishop of Lincoln. Letters especially make it clear that great variety existed in the relations between

1 M. K. Jones and M. G. Underwood, *The King's Mother: Lady Margaret Beaufort, Countess of Richmond and Derby*, Cambridge, 1992, pp. 98–9.

husband and wife. Behind the humble forms of address, real affection can be detected, and strong evidence in many cases of a working partnership between husband and wife; on the other hand some marriages were clearly unhappy. The fifteenth-century letters of the Pastons, Stonors and Plumptons are invaluable here. Although some wives, like Cecily duchess of York, accompanied their husbands on business, many were left at home and became responsible for the family and its interests during the absences of their husbands, which could be frequent and lengthy. Where letters do not survive, far less is known of marital relationships and the terminology of wills in particular has to be used with caution; however, the nature of the bequests and more especially the appointment of the wife as supervisor or executor of the husband's will points to trust, partnership and a knowledge of affairs on the part of the wife.[2] Many wives chose to be buried beside their husbands and provided masses for their souls.

Complications certainly arose on occasion in the life of husband and wife, and here legal evidence is of the greatest value. Although the wife lost her rights to dower if she committed adultery, as seen in the extraordinary case of Margaret de Camoys, the decision of a husband to take a mistress, although condemned by the Church, did not incur secular penalty. The mistress however had no legal protection and her children no right to inherit. It is likely that tricky situations resulted, as when John of Gaunt placed his mistress in the household of his daughter-in-law. The widower's decision to marry again could also lead to difficulties especially if it led to favouritism of the second family, as seen in the marriage of Ralph Neville, earl of Westmorland to Joan Beaufort. Relationships between stepchildren and stepparents again show great variety, but close relationships existed, as in the family of Margaret Beaufort.[3]

Divorce, in the sense of the annulment of the marriage, occasionally occurred, if it could be proved that there was an impediment prior to the marriage, such as the failure to secure a dispensation because of consanguinity or a precontract or an earlier marriage; the absence of consent and cruelty were also grounds for annulment.[4] However, other

2 The importance of the wife in the execution of wills is discussed by R. E. Archer and B. E. Ferme, 'Testamentary procedure with special reference to the executrix', *Medieval Women in Southern England*, Reading Medieval Studies, XV, 1989, pp. 3–34.

3 Jones and Underwood, *The King's Mother*, pp. 31–4.

4 Divorce and matrimonial litigation are discussed by R. H. Helmholz, *Marriage Litigation in Medieval England*, Cambridge, 1974; and examples are given in N.

factors played a part, such as incompatibility, lack of children and political considerations.[5] As a lesser step, separation *a mensa et thoro* (from board and bed) could be arranged, but this did not allow the parties to remarry. As in the law of marriage, the Church's role here came to be crucial, but a secular element in the proceedings can often be detected especially where property was involved.

The birth of children, especially of an heir, was an all-important event for the family and an occasion for rejoicing. Much information is found in household accounts and in proofs of age, dating from the thirteenth century on. The midwife was present at the birth, and the baby was then often handed over to a wet-nurse; a doctor is occasionally mentioned, as is the presence of relics. The father was immediately informed of the birth. Baptism took place on the day of the birth or very soon after, the godparents being chosen from local notables, ecclesiastical or lay. The churching of the mother was usually followed by a feast and celebration. In the cases where the child died, the burial and prayers for the soul would be carried out with solemnity.

What is difficult to elucidate from the evidence is the extent of the mother's responsibility for the young child. The nurse was responsible for physical care, and a mistress of the children was appointed in larger households. Preachers however stressed the responsibility of parents in the training of children, and the necessity for discipline. It was widely felt that parents' love for their children should be reciprocated by the love, respect, and, if necessary, support of children for their parents.[6] It is likely that the mother had a supervisory role, as seen in Mary de Bohun's purchases for her young children. Once the children were sent to other households for their education, the mother would only see them occasionally, and instead was often responsible for sons and daughters of other families. In the event of her husband's death, she was often given responsibility for the children, although this guardianship was often shared with other relatives or with the king. According to Henry I's coronation charter, in such an event the keeper of the land and the children should be either the wife or another relation who was more suitable.[7]

Adams and C. Donohue Jr., ed., *Select Cases from the Ecclesiastical Courts of the Province of Canterbury, c. 1200–1301*, Selden Society, CXV, 1978–79.

5 Ward, *English Noblewomen*, pp. 30–2.

6 Swanson, 'Childhood and childrearing', pp. 309–16.

7 Douglas and Greenaway, eds, *English Historical Documents 1042–1189*, p. 401.

Letters, household accounts and to some extent wills, all giving information from the thirteenth century onwards, indicate that there was plenty of variety in the relationships between mothers and children. Teenagers could be difficult, as already seen with Margery Paston. What is clear is that many parents saw it as important to ensure that their children enjoyed a good livelihood, as seen in marriage settlements and in provisions in wills where the father was looking to the future.[8] Mothers might endow younger children with part of their own inheritance.[9] Arrangements over land did cause tension and dispute,[10] but the evidence of visits and bequests points to friendship between the mother and her grown-up children and sometimes their children as well. Putting relationships on a business footing must not be assumed as precluding affection.

The extent to which brothers and sisters kept in touch is again varied. As already seen, John Paston II was concerned over his siblings, especially in connection with money and property arrangements.[11] It is likely that some contact was maintained where wills record bequests to brothers and sisters, and the appointment of brother or sister as executor points to the same conclusion. On the whole, however, the combined evidence of chronicles, letters, household accounts, wills and records of royal government shows that interest was focused on the nuclear family. Nobles and gentry were aware of wider kindred groups, and knew that death and accidents of inheritance might well lead to a distant relation achieving prominence. The evidence that they have left behind shows their interests centred on their immediate family group.

32. An excerpt from the Dunmow chronicle showing the genealogy of the early lords of Little Dunmow priory, Essex[12] [From British Library, London, Cotton MS. Cleopatra CIII, fo. 291r; in Latin]

1111   William Baynard, of whom Lady Juga [Baynard] held the vill of Little Dunmow, lost his barony through ill-fortune and felony.

8 See no. 16, the will of William Berland.

9 See no. 99.

10 See no. 90.

11 See no. 22.

12 The chronicle dates from the late thirteenth century, and shows the priory's interest in the family of its patrons, but its dating is often inaccurate; e.g. William Baynard suffered forfeiture in 1110; Robert fitz Richard died in 1137; Robert earl of Gloucester was captured in 1141.

Henry king of England gave the whole of the barony to Robert fitz Richard fitz Gilbert earl of Clare,[13] and to his heirs, together with the honour of Baynard Castle and its appurtenances in the City of London; Robert was then steward of the lord King Henry.

1112   Robert fitz Richard married Matilda de Senlis who was lady of Bradenham, and she gave two-thirds of the tithes of the same vill to the canons of Dunmow.

1127   Britric, first prior of Dunmow, died, and Augustine succeeded him.

1134   Robert fitz Richard, first patron of the canons of Dunmow, died, and is buried at St Neots, near the tomb of Richard earl of Clare, his father, and others of his family. Walter his son and heir succeeded him, and he gave churches, tithes and other property to his church of Dunmow for the salvation of their souls.

1140   Matilda de Senlis, wife of Robert fitz Richard, died.

1142   Walter fitz Robert married Matilda de Bohun, and Earl Robert was captured, and in return for his release King Stephen was freed.

1146   Matilda de Bohun died.

1148   Walter fitz [Robert] married Matilda de Lucy and begot Robert and others.

33. Excerpt from the Lanthony chronicle[14] [From *Monasticon Anglicanum* VI, p. 135; in Latin]

Humphrey VII de Bohun [*c.* 1249–98] married Matilda de Fiennes, and they had a son, Humphrey VIII de Bohun, earl of Hereford and Essex, constable of England and lord of Brecon. And on the feast of St Leonard [6 November] his mother, the aforesaid Countess Matilda, died, and is buried at Walden.[15] Humphrey VII for a long time survived his wife and is also buried at Walden.

13 Richard fitz Gilbert was not earl of Clare; his great-grandson was created earl of Hertford *c.* 1140.

14 This chronicle was particularly interested in the earls of Hereford. The priory of Lanthony by Gloucester was founded in 1136 by Miles of Gloucester who was created earl of Hereford five years later.

15 The abbey of Walden was founded *c.* 1136 by Geoffrey de Mandeville earl of Essex. The Bohun family succeeded the Mandeville family as earls of Essex in the thirteenth century.

Humphrey VIII de Bohun married Elizabeth, daughter of King
Edward, son of King Henry III [1302]. They had six sons and four
daughters: namely, Margaret who died young; Humphrey IX who also
died young on 10 September 1304; John earl of Hereford and Essex,
constable of England and lord of Brecon; Humphrey X earl of
Hereford and Essex, constable of England and lord of Brecon; Edward
and William born as twins; Eleanor; Margaret II; Eneas; Isabella who
died young. Countess Elizabeth, wife of Humphrey VIII, is buried at
Walden [d. 1316]. Humphrey VIII died at Boroughbridge on 16
March 1322 and is buried at York in the church of the Dominican
friars.

34. Excerpt from the will of Eleanor de Bohun, duchess of Gloucester,
bequeathing personal and family possessions to her son Humphrey,
1399 [From J. Nichols, *A Collection of all the Wills of the Kings and
Queens of England*, London, 1780, pp. 181–2; in French]

Item, a chronicle of France in French with two silver clasps, enamelled
with the arms of the duke of Burgundy. Item, one book of Giles [of
Rome], On the Rule of Princes. Item, a book of vices and virtues, and
another, in rhyme, of the history of the knight of the swan, all in
French.[16] Item, a psalter well and richly illuminated with gold
enamelled clasps, with white swans and the arms of my lord and father
enamelled on the clasps, and with gold mullets on the binding;[17] this
psalter was left to me with remainder to my heirs, and was to pass
from heir to heir.[18] Item, a coat of mail with a latten cross on the
spot over the heart which belonged to my lord his father. Item, a gold
cross hanging by a chain with an image of the crucifix and four pearls
round it, with my blessing, as the possession of mine which I loved
most.

16 The swan was the Bohun badge.

17 The mullet was a term used in heraldry for a star, usually with five, but sometimes
   with six or more points.

18 The Bohun family were great patrons of manuscript illumination in the fourteenth
   century. Works associated with them are described in J. Alexander and P. Binski,
   eds, *Age of Chivalry*, pp. 501–4.

35. A father's advice to his daughters, c. 1372[19] [From T. Wright, ed., *The Book of the Knight of La Tour Landry*, Early English Text Society, original series, XXXIII, 1868, revised edition 1906, chapters 10, 18, 53, 90, 96; in English]

Daughters, you must be meek and courteous, for there is no greater virtue to get the grace of God and the love of all people; for humility and courtesy overcome all proud hearts, just as you may tame a sparrowhawk, be he never so wild, with good and courteous behaviour, and make him come from the tree to your hand... Also I have known many ladies and gentlewomen who have gained much love from great and small by courtesy and humility. Therefore I teach you to be courteous and humble to great and small, to show courtesy and respect, to speak to them kindly, and to be meek in answer to the poor, and they will praise you and give you a better name and reputation than will the great men whom you are courteous to. The great receive the courtesy which is their due, but the courtesy shown to poor gentlemen and others of lower rank comes from a free, gentle, courteous and humble heart.

Therefore the wife ought to allow her husband to be spokesman and master, as that is her duty, and it is shameful to hear strife between them, especially in front of other people. When they are alone, she may talk to him pleasantly, and advise him to mend his ways if he has done wrong. If he can do this he will thank her very much, and say that she is acting as she should. A good woman ought to do this, like Hester the queen of Syria. Her husband the king was fierce and quick-tempered, but when he was angry she would say nothing until he had calmed down. When his anger was over, she might rule him as she pleased. This was very clever of her, and so should all women do.

Fair daughters, hold it in your heart not to put any paint or make-up on your faces which were made in God's image. Keep them as your Creator and nature have ordained. Do not pluck your eyebrows, or your temples or forehead. Do not wash your hair in anything but soap and water.

I shall give you another example of a good woman and a lady who had a daughter named Deborah whom she put to school. By virtue and

19 The Knight compiled his book for the instruction of his daughters; he felt that this was necessary because of his frequent absences from home. He compiled a similar book for his sons, but this has not survived. The book was translated into English in the fifteenth century, and printed by Caxton in 1484.

grace of the Holy Spirit, Deborah showed great patience and wisdom. She loved holy Scripture, lived a holy life, knew the secrets of God, and prophesied the future. Since she had such great wisdom, people took her advice, especially of what was to happen concerning the realm. Her husband was harsh and cruel, but through her great ability and good management she could behave in such a way towards him that she always pleased him more and more, brought him out of his anger, and made him behave peaceably towards her and all other people. With this good example in mind, young women and maidens should be put to school to learn about the virtues from Scripture, so that they may have a better idea and knowledge of their salvation, and avoid everything that is evil in manner, as did the good lady Deborah. In the same way St Katherine through her wit and learning, by the grace of the Holy Spirit, overcame the greatest philosophers of Greece, and by her learning and steadfast faith won the victory of martyrdom. Her body was taken on a twelve-day journey by the angels of Heaven to Mount Sinai where her blessed body yields oil to this day... There are men who consider that they do not want their wives and daughters to know anything of the Scriptures. It is not enough for women only to be able to read the Scriptures; every woman is the better for being able to read and know the law of God, and to have been taught to have virtue and knowledge so as to withstand the perils to the soul, and to carry out the works of salvation. That is something approved and necessary for all women.

A good woman who everywhere bears a good name for honour and goodness must always ensure that she keeps her body clean and undefiled, and refuse the delights of youth and foul pleasures. In this way she wins a good reputation and much honour, and will be numbered with the good ladies and all good women for ever; she also wins the love of God, and of her husband, and of the world, and the salvation of her soul which is the worthiest and best thing of all.

36. Letter from Adam Marsh to Eleanor de Montfort, countess of Leicester, *c.* 1250 [From J. S. Brewer, ed., *Monumenta Franciscana*, 2 vols, Rolls Series, London, 1858–82, I, pp. 294–6; in Latin]

Friar Adam to the illustrious Lady Eleanor, countess of Leicester.

I have written briefly because there is no time to write more. From that sentence of God which says, 'Let us make for him a helper similar to him' [Genesis, chapter 2, verse 18], we are clearly instructed, since the wife is bound very strictly to the husband, that through constant strength, prudence and discretion, and the clemency of kindness, the yoke of help and zeal apply to everything affecting the worship of God, or the just life, or right judgement. On account of this, every conjugal feeling which does not fulfil it in every way is convicted of damnably violating the individual sharing of life which she swore to keep undefiled according to the law of marriage. On this departure from duty, minds are above all proved to incur guilt when through the demonic furies of anger they are not afraid of disturbing the very loving peace of marriage. Therefore there occurs this formidable statement, 'Propensity to anger kills the stupid man, that is in spirit, and envy murders the young.' Truly through anger gentleness is abandoned, the likeness to the divine image is spoiled, wisdom is ruined, life is lost, justice relinquished, companionship destroyed, harmony broken, truth clouded. From anger there come forth quarrels, mental passion, insults, clamour, indignation, feebleness of mind, and blasphemies. Of necessity melancholy follows from which are born malice, rancour, feebleness of mind, despair, sluggishness over precepts, and the mind wandering towards illicit things. In anger the heart beats quickly, it urges excitement, it drives the tongue to evil-speaking, it devastates the mind within, it generates hatred of those most dear, and it dissolves the treaty of friendship. Let it not be that so cursed a scourge drives a spirit exalted with such manifold glory of illustrious titles into the detestable ignominy of the fatal abyss! Let the gentlest grace of the most pious Virgin help, I pray, with the blessed Author of peaceful love, so that the peace of God, which passes all understanding, keep your heart and mind.

Nor is my acuteness of clear reflection to be wondered at, I beseech you, in that I pursued the most serious matter more zealously with the eloquence of the saints. For the rest, why does more lascivious dress lead matronly modesty into sinister suspicion? Surely the harlots were not different from chastity in expression and appearance? Who is there who does not curse this madness which is carried on from day to day at so great a cost, with so many occupations ministering to the insane fondness for superfluous decoration, through which both the Divine Majesty is provoked and worthy countenances offended, except that it is pleasing to the wantonness of the pimps? Is it not a wrong to the Divinity to make up a face which it embellished with the gift of beauty with I do not know what exotic follies? Let us hear the divine Apostles among whom the chief said, 'Women should be subject to their husbands, so that if any men do not believe the Word, they may gain from the conversation of women, reflecting in fear on holy talk. Be not outwardly concerned with hair or wealth or clothes; he who in the depths of his heart has the incorruptibility of a quiet and modest spirit is rich in the sight of God' [First epistle of St Peter, chapter 3, verses 1–4]. The teacher of the Gentiles, who became all things to all men so that all might gain, proclaims to all people, 'Women should dress themselves with modesty and sobriety, not with curled hair, or gold, or pearls, or costly robes, but, as is fitting, showing piety through good works.' Would that the heart should be open! How great is the fear of the terrified heart because it is proper to insist, among so many concerns for salvation, on opposing the follies of such great destruction. Unless it is stopped by this sort of foolishness, such necessary talk on the business of salvation would concentrate on the very splendid diligence of your piety. Not in vain do I beseech you, on account of God's wounds, I shall have launched weapons of heavenly emulation into the holy heart; I trust that, by Divine mercy, the more unrestrained extravagance of dress, protracted by so lasting an ignorance, will henceforth fall inwardly into neglect on account of the eagerness for worthy maturity. May I be pardoned, I entreat, because in anxious solicitude I have not held back the rod of bitter chiding, nay rather of persuasion leading to salvation, since I do not know whether the divine element is allowed to live in the flesh until I, who am eager for your advancement, may enjoy a talk with you. I am unwilling to finish this letter. For the talk should be extended to greater length on as many matters as possible, if opportunity were given.

Farewell to your dearest excellence. Farewell illustrious earl. Farewell also to your excellent offspring. May your worthy house also remain in Christ and the most blessed Virgin.

37. Extract from a letter from Adam Marsh to Robert Grosseteste bishop of Lincoln (1235–53) concerning Warin de Montchensy's treatment of his wife [From J. S. Brewer and R. Howlett, eds, *Monumenta Franciscana*, I, p. 112; in Latin]

I have spoken to Sir Warin de Montchensy concerning the summons by which he was cited to appear before you, and about always treating his wife both properly and with respect, as is fitting, according to the lawful demands of the sacrament of marriage. He promised that, God willing, he would do this from this time on. However, I have received through most deservedly credible testimony from a certain man constrained more strictly by spiritual necessity who on account of special companionship and familiarity with Sir Warin and his private and public conversation swore a multiplicity of oaths (however, an excuse of this kind should not influence a judge) and knew better that the same Sir Warin was completely free of the crime he was accused of.

38. Letter from Elizabeth Stonor to her husband William Stonor, 12 September, 1476[20] [From Public Record Office, London, SC1/46/115; in English]

Most revered and worshipful and entirely best beloved cousin, I recommend myself to you in the humblest possible way. Today, sir, your servant Thomas Mathew brought me a letter from you which tells me that you have somewhat recovered and by the grace of God will get better and better every day. Also, noble cousin, I understand that my brother and yours is very ill with the pox,[21] and I am very sad and sorry that you are there, as the air of the pox is very contagious, especially to those who are closely related. I would therefore ask you, noble cousin, to come here, if you would like to do so. And if you do not want to do this, noble cousin, I ask you to let me have some horses so that I may come to you, for I am truly willing to put myself in danger there just like you, and shall feel like this while my life lasts to the pleasure of God and yourself. For I really thought it a long time since I saw you, as I truly hoped that your horses would have been here tonight; and indeed I thought this and planned to be with you tomorrow night by God's mercy, and this would have been a very great comfort to me. For truly I have not been happy in my heart for the past week over certain matters I have been told of. Therefore I wished very much several times that you had been here, because I know well that you could have dealt with certain matters better than me. Truly I have not had such a busy week since I came here, except for one day, and Sir William and John Mathewe can both tell you about part of it. Concerning my children, I thank you very much, sir, that you are so pleased to look after them. Yet, noble cousin, if you like to send them with such horses as you are pleased to send for me, I would certainly ask you to do this, as the pox has passed out of this region and city as far as I know, blessed be God. Noble cousin, I entreat you eagerly that I may hear from you by Saturday night at the

20 Elizabeth was the daughter of a London alderman, John Croke; William Stonor was her second husband; Thomas Betson was her son-in-law.

21 This name was given to several diseases characterised by pustules on the skin.

latest, for truly I cannot be happy until the time that I know truly what arrangements you want to make for me. No more at present, but may Almighty Jesus preserve you, and keep you long in good bodily health, and long to live virtuously to God's pleasure, and so to your greatest heart's desire, amen. At London, 12 September, year 16.[22]

My son Betson recommends himself to you as heartily as possible, and asked for your prayers etc., and you will receive two letters from him by John Mathewe. He took his barge today at eight o'clock in the morning. I pray God to send him good speed, amen.

From your own Elizabeth Stonor.

This is to be delivered to my most honourable cousin, William Stonor esq.[23]

39. Letter from Katherine Chadyrton to Master George Plumpton at Bolton Abbey, *c.* 1450–55 [From *Plumpton Correspondence*, ed. T. Stapleton, Camden Society, IV, 1839, pp. xxxix–xl; in English]

My best brother, I am truly sorry that I shall not see you, having come as far as York. God knows that my intention was not desire for goods, but I know well now that you thought the opposite. However, it is known, brother, that I am in poor health, and my heart would have been greatly comforted to have talked to you, but I believe, and so does my daughter, that you are displeased, and are taking no notice of my earlier letter, because she wanted a book from you. As I ever hope to be saved, she asked me to write for a psalter or a primer, and my husband said, half jokingly, ask my brother to get something for my new chapel. God knows he did not mean gold or silver, but some other thing for the altar. However, if I had known that you would be displeased, I would not have written, seeing that I have displeased my best brother. My sister Dame Isabel lives as sad a life as any gentlewoman born, and this is why I have never been well since I saw her last month. She has no woman nor maid with her, but is on her own. And her husband comes every day to my husband, and talks in the fairest language that you ever heard, but everything has gone wrong, he is always in trouble, and all the joy she has on earth is when my husband visits her. She swears that there is no one that she loves better. Moreover, brother, I entreat you, if you or anyone on your

22 This is a reference to the regnal year, 16 Edward IV.
23 This was written on the back of the letter.

behalf can find any agreeable young woman, who is strong and able to work for her pay, twenty-four years old or more (and I would prefer one of my kindred if there were any), I beseech you to get her for me as quickly as you can, at Easter if possible. I can write no more because of great haste over my journey, but I pray the blessed Trinity with all the saints in heaven to give me grace to see you before I die, to God's pleasure and your bodily well-being. Furthermore, brother, I went to Lord Scrope to see my lady, and in truth I stood there more than an hour and yet I saw neither lord nor lady. And I had the strangest welcome that I ever had from Mistress Darcy, and yet I was accompanied by five men; there are no such five men in his house, I daresay.

From your sister, Katherine Chadyrton.

40. **Evidence that Cecily duchess of York accompanied her husband to Normandy when he was reappointed king's lieutenant there** [From *Annales Rerum Anglicarum of William of Worcester*, in J. Stevenson, ed., *Letters and Papers Illustrative of the Wars of the English in France during the Reign of Henry VI King of England*, 2 vols, Rolls Series, London, 1861–64, II, part 2, p. 763; in Latin]

1441   Henry, the eldest son of Richard duke of York, was born at Hatfield on Friday, 10 February, at five o'clock in the morning. In this year on 16 May the duke departed for France, and was made regent of France for five years.

1442   Edward, second son and heir of Richard duke of York, king of England and France, was born in Rouen at 2 a.m. on Monday morning, 28 April. He was conceived in the chamber next to the chapel of the palace of Hatfield.

1443   Edmund, third son of Richard duke of York, was born in Rouen at 7 p.m. on Monday, 17 May.

1444   Elizabeth, second daughter of Richard duke of York, was born in Rouen at two o'clock in the morning of Tuesday, 2 April.

41. **Extracts from the wills of Sir Michael de Poynings, knight and his wife Joan, 1368 and 1369** [From Lambeth Palace Library, London, Register of Archbishop William Whittlesey, fos. 99r, 100v; in French]

Will of Sir Michael de Ponynges, knight.

First I leave my soul to God and to Our lady and all his saints, and my body to be buried at Poynings next to my lady my mother towards the south. And I wish that my burial be carried out with the advice of my executors who will be Joan my wife, Master Adam Wykemere, Robert Rotiller, John de Borle parson of the church of Tarring and John atte Hyde. And I bequeath to my executors, that is to say to Joan my wife one pair of new basins with the ewers of silver and two silver pots each containing half a gallon, and one silver almsdish, and twelve dishes and twelve silver salt-cellars, and all the stock and other goods that are in the manor of Westdean...

Will of Lady Joan de Poynings, widow of Sir Michael de Poynings, knight.

First I leave my soul to God and to Our Lady and all his saints, and my body to be buried in the church of Poynings next to my lord towards the north...

42. The testaments and last wills of Sir William Septvans, knight, and his wife Elizabeth, 1448[24] [From Lambeth Palace Library, London, Register of Archbishop John Stafford, fos 161v–162r; in Latin]

Testament of William Septvans, knight.

First I leave my soul to Almighty God, the Blessed Virgin Mary, and all the saints of heaven, and my body to be buried in the church of Christ, next to my father at Canterbury.[25] To each monk of Christ Church to pray for my soul, 20d. To the church of Milton for tithes forgotten, 6s 8d. The rest of all my goods not bequeathed, after the payment of debts, legacies and expenses, I give and bequeath to Elizabeth my wife. I make, ordain and constitute as my executors the aforesaid Elizabeth, together with Thomas Ballard, William Manston, and Roger Manston esquires, Robert Artour clerk, and Richard Hunte of Milton.[26]

Last will of William Septvans, knight.

This is the last will of me William Septvans, knight, concerning all my manors, lands and tenements, farms, woods, rents and services, with

24 The testament dealt with personal property, and the will with real property, i.e. land.

25 This is a reference to Canterbury cathedral.

26 Only the references which relate to his wife and her will and testament have been translated.

all and each of their appurtenances, lying and being situated in the liberty of the Cinque Ports or elsewhere within the counties of Kent and Sussex, as are known in the same, made and recited by me on 4 March in the twenty-sixth year of the reign of King Henry VI [1448] to Sir John Smyth, rector of the parish church of Milton, then my curate, Simon Morle, John Byrcholte, Richard Carpenter, John Pykering, William Smyth, Peter Fygge, Thomas Troyes, William Gros, Henry Barbour, Henry Simon and Robert Carslake, on the instructions and with the full knowledge of my feoffees. First I wish that my feoffees quickly after my death enfeoff Elizabeth my wife of a tenement of mine in the parish of All Saints in the city of Canterbury, to have and to hold the said tenement with all its appurtenances to the same Elizabeth, her heirs and assigns for ever. Moreover I wish that my said feoffees quickly after my death enfeoff the said Elizabeth of my manor of Milton with all its appurtenances together with all my other manors, lands and tenements, farms, woods, rents and services whatsoever in the said counties and liberty, to have and to hold all the aforesaid manors, lands and tenements, farms, woods, rents and services with all their appurtenances to the said Elizabeth for life. So that after Elizabeth's death all the said manors, together with all other lands and tenements, farms, woods, rents and services, should remain to that child, male or female, whom Elizabeth is now bearing, with God's favour. To have and to hold all the aforesaid manors, lands and tenements, farms, woods, rents and services with all their appurtenances to the said male or female child, its heirs and assigns for ever. And if it should happen that the said male or female child should die in the lifetime of Elizabeth, the child's mother, then I wish that the manor of Milton with all its appurtenances should remain after Elizabeth's death to Reginald Wydyhall, his heirs and assigns for ever. And if it should happen that Reginald should die in Elizabeth's lifetime then I wish that the said manor of Milton and all other manors, lands and tenements, farms, woods, rents and services of mine, with each and all of their appurtenances, should be sold after Elizabeth's death by my feoffees, and the money received used by the said feoffees and my executors for the salvation of my soul, and the souls of my father and mother and all the faithful departed, as shall seem to them best and most salutary. Moreover I wish that Richard Hunte, my servant, should have and receive yearly from the said manor of Milton and from all my other lands and tenements in Kent 40s sterling for the whole of his life, with sufficient distraint ordained by my feoffees to obtain security from Richard himself. Given at Canterbury on the above day and year.

Testament of Elizabeth, widow of William Septvans, knight.

First I bequeath my soul to God Almighty, blessed Mary and all the saints of heaven, my body to be buried in the church of Christ at Canterbury next to Sir William Septvans formerly my husband. Item, I bequeath to the convent of the same church to pray for my soul and the souls of all my benefactors five marks to be distributed among them... Item, I bequeath ten marks to a priest to celebrate mass for my soul and the souls of William Septvans, my late husband, and all my benefactors in the church of All Saints Canterbury for one year. Item, I bequeath to Thomas Wydyhall my brother one horse, one saddle and one bridle. Item, I bequeath to the same Thomas one set of bed-hangings embroidered with lions with all the fittings ...

The last will of Elizabeth, widow of William Septvans.

This is the last will of me Elizabeth, formerly wife of William Septvans, knight, made and recited to Richard Carpenter, William Smyth, Thomas Dryvere, Thomas Troye, Thomas Burdon and John Boteler then present. Since the said William Septvans, my late husband, in his last will from among his lands and tenements granted to me Elizabeth one tenement situated in the parish of All Saints next to the Franciscan friars of the city of Canterbury, to hold to me, my heirs and assigns for ever of the capital lords of that fee by the due and rightful customary services, I wish that the feoffees of the said William Septvans, my late husband, quickly after my death enfeoff John Wydyhall my son of the said tenement with its appurtenances to have and to hold to the said John, his heirs and assigns for ever of the capital lords of the fee, by the due and rightful customary services. Moreover I wish that my executors should have custody of Simon Wydyhall and John Wydyhall, my sons. And they are to receive yearly all the profit of all the lands and tenements of the said Simon and John until they come of age. And my executors will put Simon and John to school for all the above term, and find everything necessary for them. Given on the feast of the Annunciation of the blessed Virgin Mary [25 March] in the twenty-sixth year of King Henry VI of England.

43. Extract from the dower case brought by William Paynel and Margaret de Camoys, 1300 [From *Rotuli Parliamentorum*, I, p. 146; in Latin]

William Paynel and Margaret his wife petitioned the lord king at his parliament at Westminster in the twenty-eighth year of his reign, asking that he should render to them one-third of the manor of 'Torpell' with appurtenances as Margaret's dower which belonged to her of the free tenement that used to be held by John de Camoys, her first husband.

And Nicholas de Warwyk who prosecuted for the lord king said that Margaret ought not to have dower, and she ought not to be heard nor admitted to any of the dower petitioned for, because for a long time before the death of the said John, sometime her husband, of her own accord and willingly she left her same husband and lived in adultery with the said William, now her husband, during John's lifetime, and she was not reconciled to John before his death. For this reason, according to the form of the lord king's statute now issued, concerning women estranged from their husbands and living with their adulterers, and not reconciled of their own accord without ecclesiastical coercion before the death of their husbands, Margaret's petition should be totally rejected.[27] And he seeks judgment for the king.

And on this the said William and Margaret proffered a writing made in the name of John de Camoys her first husband in these words:

John de Camoys, son and heir of Sir Ralph de Camoys, greets in the Lord all the faithful men of Christ to whom the present writing shall come. You should know that I have handed over and surrendered of my free will to Sir William Paynel, knight, Margaret de Camoys, my wife, and the daughter and heir of Sir John de Gatesden, and I have given and granted, released and quitclaimed to the same Sir William all the goods and chattels which Margaret has, or from henceforth could have, and also whatever of mine belongs to Margaret in goods or chattels with their appurtenances. So that neither I nor anyone else in my name from henceforth will be able or have a right to demand or claim Margaret's goods or chattels with their appurtenances for ever. I wish, grant and confirm by this present writing that the said Margaret should remain with the said Sir William according to William's will. In testimony of this, I have affixed my seal to this present writing. Witnessed by Thomas de Repeston, John de Ferring, William de Icombe, Henry le Brunz, Stephen Chamberlain, Walter le Blund, Gilbert de Batecombe, Robert Wood and others.

And they say that the same Margaret lived with William in the way set out in the said writing, with the assent and by the will of John, then Margaret's husband, during his lifetime, and by John's grant and

27 This is a reference to the statute of Westminster II of 1285; H. Rothwell, ed., *English Historical Documents 1189-1327*, p. 448.

release, as expressly could be made clear to the lord king and his court
by the words contained in the same writing, and she did not live in
adultery with William. And on this they asked for judgment. And then
William and Margaret were told that they should be at the next
parliament to hear its judgment.[28]

44. The maintenance of Lady Katherine Swynford and her daughter
in the household of Lady Mary de Bohun, countess of Derby, John of
Gaunt's daughter-in-law, 1387 [From Public Record Office, London,
DL28/1/2, fos 21, 24, Lady Mary's chamber and wardrobe account; in
Latin]

Of the lady's livery, delivered to Lady Katherine Swynford and Joan
her daughter at Christmas two lengths of silk brocade, white and blue,
together with furs of pured minever, as entered below.

Delivered to Lady Katherine Swynford for her livery at Christmas 7½
timbers of pured minever, with one length of white and blue brocade,
as above.

Delivered to Joan, daughter of Lady Katherine Swynford for her livery
at Christmas five timbers of pured minever, with one length of white
and blue brocade, as above.[29]

45. Provision made by Adam son of Warin for his second wife and
family, c. 1140–52 [From British Library, London, Harley Charters
76 F35; in Latin]

Gilbert earl of Clare to all his men and friends, French and English,
greeting. Be it known to you all that I have agreed to the gift made by
Adam son of Warin to Hugh his son and Princa his wife, namely the

28 Judgment was given against Margaret and William in 1302 and she lost her claim
   to dower; *Rotuli Parliamentorum*, I, pp. 146–7. John de Camoys' hand-over of land
   for Margaret and her sons, and the two compurgations by which William and
   Margaret cleared themselves of the charge of adultery are entered in *ibid.* p. 147
   (the latter were not believed by parliament). The case is discussed in F. Pollock and
   F. W. Maitland, *The History of English Law before the time of Edward I*, 2 vols, second
   edition, Cambridge, 1898, II, pp. 395–6; and by J. H. Round, 'The Stophams, the
   Zouches and the honour of Petworth', *Sussex Archaeological Collections*, LV, 1912, pp.
   19–34.

29 The furs were used for lining the robe. Pured minever was the white belly skins of
   the Baltic squirrel with the grey trimmed off, and a timber denoted a bundle of forty
   skins; E. M. Veale, *The English Fur Trade in the Later Middle Ages*, Oxford, 1966, pp.
   223, 228. Joan Beaufort married as her second husband Ralph Neville, first earl of
   Westmorland.

land of Martin the chaplain of Poslingford that was held by Bernard and whatever belongs to it. And at Clare the meadow which Martin held and the messuages in which the monks' barns were together with the garden, and from the sokemen of 'Stratesleia' and 'Fernleia' in Stansfield 20s 6d with their homage. I concede this gift to Hugh and Princa his mother in fee and inheritance to hold to them and their heirs of me and my heirs. They are to hold of Adam in his lifetime, and if Hugh dies it is to be held by Hervey his brother, and if Hervey dies it is to be held by the rest of Princa's children, whether male or female. And after Adam's death they are to hold of me and my heirs by the service of one-fifth of a knight, and that one-fifth part of a knight is included in the service of one knight from Pebmarsh. And while Princa remains unmarried after Adam's death, I grant and give all the said holding to her in order to bring up her children. If however she takes a husband, I only give and grant her the aforesaid sokemen rendering 20s 6d, and three burgage tenements in Sudbury on the Essex side, and ten marks which Adam will give to her in dower. Witnessed by Roger my brother, Robert de Creuechor, Simon de Thoni, Roger de Hastinges, Walter son of Humphrey, Ralph Walensis, Alan de Dampmartin, Stephen his brother, Hugh de capello, Thomas de capello, Gilbert son of Humphrey, William de Mundaville, Warin son of Adam, Gerard nephew of Adam, Geoffrey his nephew, Fulk his brother, William son of Ansgod, Matthew de Lundoniis, Roger de Dalham, William the clerk, Baldwin the clerk, Elinal and Alured his brothers.[30]

46. The two wives of Gilbert Pecche, d. 1291 [From J. W. Clark, ed., *Liber Memorandorum Ecclesie de Bernewelle*, Cambridge, 1907, p. 50; in Latin]

Sir Gilbert Pecche had two wives. One was called Matilda de Hastinges, and was renowned for her family, but much more celebrated for her way of life; they had sons and daughters. She died in London. Her body was buried in the church of the canons of the Blessed Virgin Mary over the water, because it could not be brought back here honourably at that time, as she had chosen, on account of the disturbance in England.[31] However, her heart was brought here in a

---

30 This grant and the service specified are discussed by Ward, 'The place of the honour in twelfth-century society', pp. 193–4. Land in Pebmarsh was inherited by Ralph son of Adam, presumably Adam's eldest son by his first marriage, and in the thirteenth century the one–fifth fee was a sub-tenancy of Pebmarsh.

31 This is a reference to the Barons' Wars; Matilda died in 1264 or 1265, and was buried in the church of St Mary Overy, Southwark.

lead shrine, and buried before the high altar next to her children. On
its arrival Sir Gilbert gave our church 10s yearly rent in Cheveley.
After this Sir Gilbert took another wife called Joan, the daughter of Sir
Simon de Creye. He loved and honoured her much, because she was
very beautiful and good. By her he fathered sons and daughters, and
on account of his love for the mother he came to love the children of
his second wife more than those of the first, as appeared later. For
Gilbert gave certain manors to his second wife and her children and
prudently provided security of tenure which was necessary for holding
them in perpetuity. He left John Pecche, his eldest son, and Edmund
his brother, the sons of the first wife, as it were almost destitute, for
I do not know by what spirit or counsel he was influenced when he
made the lord King Edward, son of King Henry, and Queen Eleanor
the heirs of the rest of his barony.

47. The struggle between the children of the first and second marriages
of Ralph Neville, first earl of Westmorland;[32] this royal letter dates
from 1432–40 [From S. Bentley, *Excerpta Historica*, London, 1833, pp.
2–3; in English]

From the king.

Worshipful father in God, most trusted and well beloved, we have
recently heard and fully understand to our great displeasure of certain
misgovernances and quarrels recently stirred up between our cousin
the earl of Westmorland, Sir John Neville and Sir Thomas Neville on
one side, and our cousins the countess of Westmorland, the earl of
Salisbury and Lord Latimer on the other.[33] Both sides have recently
assembled great bands and companies on the field as if to war and
revolt, and have moreover committed other great and horrible offences
including the slaughter and destruction of our people. This is very
much contrary to our estate and the well-being and peace of this our
realm, and also expressly against our laws. The subversion of good
governance and other great dangers and evils are likely to follow,
which God forbid and prevent in our time, unless by our authority

---

32 The settlement for the marriage of Joan Beaufort, daughter of John of Gaunt and
   Katherine Swynford, to Ralph Neville, first earl of Westmorland, was weighted in
   favour of Joan's children, and as a result the earl's grandson and heir, by his first
   marriage, succeeded in 1425 to a diminished inheritance; hostilities broke out which
   were only settled in 1443, after Joan's death in 1440; *Calendar of Close Rolls, 1441–
   47*, pp. 150–1, 195–9.

33 Richard Neville earl of Salisbury was Joan's eldest son.

peace be re-established and the quarrel settled. We therefore wish and command you to have our writs issued to each of the said earls, and to Lord Latimer and the knights, ordering each of them strictly upon his allegiance to appear before us in person on the day after the feast of St Hilary next [14 January] wherever we are in this our realm to answer in the said matters as law and reason will require. Moreover you are to order them strictly to abstain and cease from all the above misconduct from now on, and to see that our peace is kept by them and their servants and adherents, on peril of condemnation. Given under our signet at our castle of Kenilworth, 28 December.

To the honoured father in God, our most trusted and well beloved, the bishop of Bath, our chancellor of England.

48. The projected divorce between John de Warenne earl of Surrey and Joan of Bar, 1314[34] [From *Historical Papers and Letters from the Northern Registers*, ed. J. Raine, Rolls Series, London, 1873, pp. 228–30; in Latin]

William etc. [Greenfield, archbishop of York] to his beloved son the Official of the archdeacon of York, greeting. At our audience, it came to our knowledge from the allegation of the noble man Lord John de Warenne earl of Surrey, our parishioner, that, while he was a minor and in the custody of Lord E [Edward] late king of England of famous memory, he was forced by certain nobles and magnates of the realm to contract matrimony with the noble woman Lady Joan, daughter of the late count of Bar, who is related to him in the third and fourth degree, which is forbidden by law. He was completely ignorant of this impediment, and indeed contracted marriage by force and fear (which could be a matter for agreement), and disowned the contract as soon as he could and dared. When afterwards he learned of the impediment, in order to exonerate his conscience, on account of the evident danger to souls, he demanded with great insistence that we should provide him with a suitable and quick remedy. Wishing therefore to take care of the salvation of the same souls, as we are bound to do, and to show them in all things the fulfilment of justice according to the nature of the business, since we are in duty bound to show justice to all our

34 This letter only gives part of the story and, as far as the issue of consanguinity was concerned, a dispensation had been obtained from Pope Clement V. The earl later alleged a pre-contract with Maud de Nerford who was his mistress at the time, and Joan's childlessness, though never mentioned, may well have been an additional factor. The divorce was in fact never granted. For the whole story, see F. R. Fairbank, 'The last earl of Warenne and Surrey and the distribution of his possessions', *Yorkshire Archaeological Journal*, XIX, 1907, pp. 198–206.

parishioners and subjects, we firmly order you to summon Lady Joan peremptorily in the castles of Conisbrough and Sandal, where she is known to have residences, if she may be found there in person; otherwise summon her procurator if she has left one; if not, proclaim this citation publicly and announce it to her relatives and to notables and friends on any Sunday or feast day while Mass is sung in the parish churches of the said vills and in other noted and important places in the archdeaconry, wherever you think it expedient, so that she has no true reason for ignoring the case. Summon her to appear in person or by her procurator, who should be sufficiently instructed, before us or our commissary for this case in our greater church of York on Wednesday after Michaelmas next, to reply to the earl on these matters to be put forward according to canon law, and to take the case further according to the quality and nature of this business which shall be dealt with according to the canons. You are to announce publicly that, whether she comes or not, the matter will proceed according to law. You are to take care to certify us or our commissaries distinctly and openly at the said time and place by your letters patent which are to contain the sequence of events so as to show you have carried out our order. Farewell. Given at Cawood, 8 September, in the year of grace 1314 and in the ninth year of our pontificate.

49. The importance of the birth of an heir: the reputed pregnancy of the countess of Gloucester, 1316, after the death at the battle of Bannockburn on 24 June 1314 of her husband Earl Gilbert de Clare[35]
[From *Rotuli Parliamentorum*, I, p. 354; in Latin]

At the next parliament of the lord king, namely at Lincoln on the quindene of St Hilary in the ninth year of his reign, Hugh [le Despenser the younger] came and petitioned for his pourparty etc. reciting the reasons stated above. And the said Gilbert [de Tondeby] and Geoffrey [le Scrope] said on behalf of the lord king that no pourparty of the aforesaid lands and tenements should be delivered to the said Hugh, reciting the reasons given above, adding also that the said countess after the death of her late husband the earl at the due time and according to the course of nature felt a living child. This was

35 There were political reasons why Edward II postponed the division of this earldom for three years until 1317, but the extract underlines the importance attached to the birth of the heir. The partition of the Clare estates is discussed by M. Altschul, *A Baronial family in Medieval England: the Clares, 1217–1314*, Baltimore, 1965, pp. 165–74.

well known in the parts where she was living. Although the time of the birth of that child, which nature allows to be put off and hampered for divers reasons, may still be delayed, this should not prejudice the aforesaid pregnancy, at least while nature does not put an end to it but supports it, and the lord king ought to protect it in all things. They said that since these matters were well known, as has been said, the said Hugh, if it seemed to him expedient, could and ought to have obtained a writ from the lord king's chancery, according to the law and custom of the realm and the course of chancery followed in a case of this kind, to have the belly of the countess inspected by discreet knights and matrons to see whether the countess was pregnant or not, and, if she was, then at what time it was thought she would give birth. And since the aforesaid countess had always been ready to allow an examination of this kind, and since Hugh and Eleanor had not abided by the due process, their negligence should not prejudice the said pregnancy but rather redound to the loss and prejudice of Hugh and Eleanor. And the lord king, wishing to proceed in the aforesaid business considerately and prudently, had had certain prelates and other men experienced in civil and canon law nominated by himself and the justices and others knowledgeable in the laws and customs of the realm, ordering them to deal with the said business; and when they had deliberated and discussed this, they could not agree on a final decision, according to their report to the lord king because of the case's difficulty and rarity. Because of this a day was given to the said Hugh and Eleanor in the quindene of Easter in the presence of the king and his council wheresoever they were.

50. **Entries in the household accounts of Elizabeth countess of Hereford relating to the birth of her son Humphrey, 1304**[36] [From Public Record Office, London, E101/365/20 m. 8; in Latin]

To Robert de Bures and Guy de Asshewell, monks of Westminster, coming to Knaresborough and staying there with the girdle of the Blessed Mary and returning to Westminster, for their expenses, of the gift of the countess by her own hands on 15 September, 40s.

To Robert the king's minstrel and his fifteen minstrel-companions making their minstrelsy in the presence of the countess and other magnates on the day the countess was purified, of the gift of the countess by her own hands on 11 October, 6 marks.

36 This extract should be compared with no. 33.

On 11 October, in offerings at Mass on the day of the purification [churching] of the countess, 4s 5d.

51. Entries from the accounts of the journey bringing the body of Humphrey de Bohun to Westminster for burial, starting on Thursday 15 October 1304[37] **[From Public Record Office, London, E101/365/ 17, m. 1, 2; in Latin]**

Thurday 15 October at Aberford. Wages of four grooms carrying the infant, 8d. [This entry is repeated until the company reached Fulham on Tuesday 27 October.]

Friday 30 October at Fulham. To Richard de London, plumber, for making a lead coffin for the body of Humphrey son of the earl of Hereford, 4s 1d.[38]

Saturday 31 October at Fulham. For four candles bought to put round the body of the said Humphrey, each weighing three pounds, twelve pounds in all, 6s.

Sunday 8 November at Westminster. For 120 poles for making the candles for the burial of the said Humphrey, each costing $\frac{1}{2}d$, 5s [sic].[39] For working up 524 pounds of wax, at $\frac{1}{4}d$ a pound, 10s 11d. For transporting the wax and the 'herse' from London to Westminster, 3s. For hiring the 'herse', 6s 8d. For offerings at the mass celebrated for the said Humphrey's soul on the day of his burial, 5s 4d. To the friars preachers of London, by gift, to pray for the soul of the said Humphrey, 5s.[40] To William de Westminster and his companions for ringing the bells for the soul of the said Humphrey, 4s.

52. The birth of a first child to Henry earl of Derby, later Henry IV, and Mary de Bohun, 1382 [From Public Record Office, London, DL28/1/1, fo. 5r; in Latin]

Given by order of my lord Lancaster on 16 April to an esquire of my lord Buckingham called Westcombe who brought my lord the news that his lady was delivered of a child, 66s 8d. And at Rochford on 18 April the lord gave to the mistress of the said child by mandate of my

37 These accounts give details of the provisions consumed each day. Only the entries relating to the burial have been translated.

38 A plumber was a worker in lead.

39 The candles were set on a 'herse' which was a frame over the coffin.

40 This is a reference to the Dominican friars.

lord Lancaster, 40s. And given on the same day to the nurse of the said child, 26s 8d.[41]

53. The birth of Thomas, son of Henry earl of Derby and Mary de Bohun, 1387–88 [From Public Record Office London, DL28/1/2, fo. 17r; in Latin]

To a midwife named Joan who was with the lady at the birth of the young lord Thomas, of the gift of the lord in London, 40s.

54. Extracts from the proof of age of Ralph son and heir of Richard Basset of Weldon, 1322 [From Public Record Office, London, C134/72/1; in Latin]

Martin Love, aged 60, sworn and examined concerning the said age, says that Ralph, son and heir of the said Richard Basset, was aged 21 and more on the feast of St Rufus the martyr last [27 August], because on that feast in the twenty-eighth year of the reign of King Edward formerly king, of famous memory, [father] of the present king [1300], he was born at Huntingfield in Suffolk, and on the second day following he was baptised in Huntingfield church. He knows this because he, Martin, on that feast-day was present at a banquet with Sir Roger de Huntyngfeld, then lord of the manor, and a maid announced to Sir Roger that Lady Joan Basset, Ralph's mother, had given birth to a son, and this son on the second day was baptised and called Ralph. From this he is sufficiently knowledgeable about his age.

Alexander son of John, aged 50, sworn and examined concerning the said age [makes the same statement] and knows this because he came with a certain Joan, his sister, to Huntingfield on the said feast, and she stayed as nurse [presumably wet-nurse] to the same Ralph. From this he is sufficiently knowledgeable about his age.

William le Keu, aged 60, sworn and examined concerning the said age [makes the same statement] and knows this because at that time he was living with Sir Roger de Huntyngfeld and on Sir Roger's orders went to Norwich to find a doctor for Joan, Ralph's mother, and on the day of his birth they arrived in Huntingfield. For this reason he remembers Ralph's age.

41 See above, nos. 2, 3. Thomas of Woodstock earl of Buckingham was Mary's brother-in-law, and Mary was presumably with her sister, Eleanor de Bohun, at the time of the birth. Lancaster was John of Gaunt, Henry's father. The reference to the nurse is presumably to the wet-nurse. This child did not survive.

55. Extract from the proof of age of John, son and heir of John de Grey of Rotherfield Greys, 1321 [From Public Record Office, London C134/72/2; in Latin]

John Bakon, aged 40, Thurstan de Ewelme, aged 50, Robert of St Faith, aged 50, John de Harewell, aged 40 and more, Gilbert Dru, aged 60, and Robert de Padenhale, aged 40 and more, sworn and individually examined about the age of the said heir, say that he is aged 21 and more, and they are in full agreement with those sworn previously on the date of his birth. They know this because of the great banquet which John de Grey, the father of the same heir, gave at Rotherfield on the feast of St Andrew [30 November] after the heir's birth, when Margaret, the heir's mother, purified herself; that banquet is still well remembered in those parts, because abbots, priors, and almost all other good men of that region were present.

56. Extract from the proof of age of Alice, wife of John de Newentone, and daughter and co-heiress of the late Peter de Southcherche, 1329 [From Public Record Office, London, C135/19/2; in Latin]

Adam Sare, aged 44, sworn and examined concerning the heir's age, says that she is 21, because she was born at Southchurch in Essex on 1 November in the thirty-second year of King Edward son of King Henry [1304] and was baptised in the church of the same vill. He knows this because at the time of the heir's birth he was in a garden where he heard the cries and groans of the heir's mother in labour. This is how he remembers the time of the heir's birth.[42]

57. A second miracle performed on James de Clare, son of Roger earl of Hertford and Matilda of St Hilary, 1170–73[43] [From J. C. Robertson, ed., *Materials for the History of Thomas Becket*, 7 vols, Rolls Series, London, 1875–85, II, pp. 255–7; in Latin]

Some weeks after his recovery, namely in the middle of the following Lent, James was seized by another sickness and breathed his last. His mother had set out to church to attend divine service; members of the

---

42 Alice was clearly more than 21 years old; but she shared her father's inheritance with her sister Joan, wife of Thomas de Rocheforde, who was also investigated in this proof of age and was born on 13 March 1308.

43 James had previously been cured of a hernia in the second year of his life by St Thomas Becket who was martyred in 1170. Roger de Clare earl of Hertford died in 1173.

household had remained at home. There was no one found to announce the death of the boy to his mother, lest he should be said to have been the cause of the calamity. At length a little boy, the brother of the dead infant, ran to the church (it is known for a fact that no boy keeps a secret) and exclaimed over and over again to his mother, 'Madam, my brother is dead. Madam my brother is dead.' At once she turned pale and jumped up, and throwing off her clothes ran back to the house. She found the infant taken out of the chamber into the large outer hall, with his mouth open, but inwardly without breath, the tongue and lips retracted, the eyes sunk and with only the white of the eye to be seen, cold and stiff, and, so as to speak briefly, well and truly dead. She seized him in her arms and said, 'St Thomas, restore my son to me. When he had a hernia previously you restored him to health. Now he is dead restore him to life, holy martyr.' Moreover she ran and took the relics of the saint which she had brought from Canterbury out of a chest. She put the blood of the saint on the mouth of the dead infant and thrust a piece of the cloth into his throat, continuously crying and saying, 'Holy martyr Thomas, give me back my son. He will be brought to your tomb if he revives. I will visit you on bare feet. Hear me.' But all the knights who stood by, and also the countess of Warwick and the rest of the women, told her to be quiet. Yet she knelt with bare knees again and again on the ground, and cried much more, 'Holy martyr, have mercy on me.' Then her chaplain Lambert, a respected man of a good age, spoke: 'How are you behaving, my lady? You are acting foolishly. You are being stupid. What you are doing and saying smacks of madness. Surely the Creator should be allowed to do what he wishes with his creature. Stop! Put down the infant, and let him be treated as dead. It is the height of stupidity for you to want to strive for what is impossible to obtain.' Everyone spoke similarly. However, she said, 'I will certainly not stop, nor will I put down the infant, for I trust that he will be given back to me. Martyr, glorious martyr, most pious, beloved martyr, have mercy on me; give me back my son.' After she had cried out in this way for about two hours, the martyr had mercy and restored her infant to life. First there was a sign of red on his face, and after a little while he cried and opened his eyes. They blessed the Lord who gives death and life, and goes down to the depths and back. There was great joy in the house, and rejoicing replaced the extremes of grief: 'for they obtained joy and gladness; sadness and groans fled away'. The countess, mother of the restored boy, took on unaccustomed toil, and setting out to Canterbury on bare feet with the boy performed her promised pilgrimage. There followed the countess of Warwick and many other women, and also the chaplain called Lambert, and many knights who all testified that they had seen the boy both truly dead and truly restored to life.

58. Entries from the accounts of Mary de Bohun countess of Derby, giving details of purchases for her children, 1387–88 [From Public Record Office, London, DL28/1/2, fos. 19r–24v; in Latin]

Hugh Waterton accounts for the delivery of 1³/₄ yards of scarlet for two robes lined with tartarin for the young lords.[44]

Delivered to William Lecham 2 yards of white shortcloth for kirtles and hose for the young lords.

Delivered for two robes and hose for the young lords 1³/₄ yards of blue shortcloth. And also for the same 2 yards of blue shortcloth for two robes and hose and hoods.

Delivered to John Clyf 3 yards of red tartarin and 3 yards of blue tartarin for lining two robes of scarlet and two of blue cloth for the young lords.

Delivered for the bed of the nurse of the young lord Thomas at Kenilworth 5 yards of white shortcloth.

Delivered to cover the cradle of the young lord Thomas two yards of blue shortcloth.

Delivered of the lady's livery to Joan nurse of the young lord Henry, Joan nurse of the young lord Thomas, and to Amy Melborne, Katherine Chamberer and Juliana Rokster for their Christmas livery, namely to each of them 3 yards, in all 15 yards of motley cloth.

Delivered to Joan nurse of the young lord Henry, Amy Melborne, Katherine Chamberer and Juliana Rokster for their livery at Christmas four furs of poppelen.[45]

44 Scarlet was an expensive woollen cloth, dyed in grain with kermes. Tartarin was a type of silk.
45 Poppelen were the early summer skins of the Baltic squirrel; Veale, *English Fur Trade*, p. 226.

59. Evidence of children remaining with their widowed mother, 1185 [From Public Record Office, London, E198/1/2, roll 3, *Rotuli de Dominabus*, in Latin]

Beatrice who was the wife of Robert Mantel, the lord king's serjeant of the honour of Nottingham, is in the lord king's gift and is thirty years old. Her dower land in Roade is worth 30*s* a year, and is stocked with one plough; there are six virgates there. She has three sons and one daughter. The eldest is ten years old, and is in the custody of Robert de Saucei, as the jurors say, by the king's command, and the rest of the children are with their mother.

60. Part of a letter from Adam Marsh to Robert Grosseteste bishop of Lincoln, mentioning the proposal for Simon de Montfort's son Henry to stay with the bishop, *c.* 1252[46] [From J. S. Brewer and R. Howlett, eds, *Monumenta Franciscana*, I, p. 110; in Latin]

After discussing the matter with the lady countess and with me, the lord earl of Leicester proposes to send back his eldest son Henry to your fatherly care, if it should happen that he returns earlier to Gascony, so that while he is young he may make progress for as long as possible under the protection of your holiness, God willing, in the learning of letters and in moral discipline. If however the earl should remain in England he proposes to make different arrangements for the boy according to your salutary advice.

61. John, son of Henry duke of Hereford and Mary de Bohun, in the household of Margaret de Brotherton at Framlingham, 1397[47] [From Public Record Office, London, DL28/1/6, fo. 25v; in Latin]

For one horse hired in London and going from there to Framlingham and back to carry the winter clothing and other necessaries for the young lord John on 10 November, together with the expenses of the same horse and one man for six days outside the household, 7*s* 8*d*.

For one hired horse going from London to Framlingham and back on 20 December taking the equipment of the young lord John at Christmas, with the expenses of one horse and one man outside the household for seven days, 10*s*.

46 Simon de Montfort was Henry III's lieutenant in Gascony between 1248 and 1252.
47 Henry earl of Derby was created duke of Hereford in 1397; Mary de Bohun died in 1394.

62. Extract of a letter from Elizabeth to William Stonor, 1476 [From Public Record Office, London, SC1/46/121; in English]

Sir, my lady Suffolk is half displeased because my sister Barantyne is not better clothed, and also my sister Elizabeth. She says that unless they are arrayed differently she may not keep them, and she says that my mother and yours ought to say that you have enough wealth to provide my sister Elizabeth with all she needs.[48]

63. Extracts from the roll of the receiver of Michael de la Pole earl of Suffolk, referring to the children of the family, 1416–17[49] [From British Library, London, Egerton Roll 8776, m. 4, 5; in Latin]

Money received for the maintenance of the sons and daughters of the late lord earl, the father, and of his son the late earl. He renders account of £16 13s 4d received from Sir Robert Bolton, clerk of accounts, from the goods and chattels and from the receipts of lands in the hands of feoffees of Sir Michael de la Pole, late earl of Suffolk, the father, as appears in Sir Robert's roll of receipts and of the aforesaid goods, for the maintenance of Lady Elizabeth de Burnell (ten marks), Joan her sister (five marks), Alexander (five marks) and Thomas (five marks) their brothers, sons and daughters of the late lord earl the father, namely from Easter in the fourth year of the reign of the present lord king [1416] to the following Michaelmas in the same year; this was not accounted for previously. He renders account of £26 13s 4d received from the same Sir Robert Bolton clerk, as appears in his account, of which £13 6s 8d a year was assigned for the maintenance of Elizabeth Lady Burnell, £6 13s 4d assigned for the maintenance of Lady Philippa daughter of the late earl, and £6 13s 4d for the maintenance this year of Alexander son of the late earl, but nothing was assigned this year for the maintenance of Thomas, son of the same earl, because [he was provided for] by the bishop of London.[50] However he renders account of £6 13s 4d received from the

48 Elizabeth of York was the wife of John de la Pole, second duke of Suffolk. Sister Barantyne was William Stonor's sister Mary whose husband, John Barantyne, was under age; C. L. Kingsford, ed., *Stonor Letters and Papers*, II, p. 13.

49 The roll is dated in the heading to 4–5 Henry IV, whereas it in fact covers the year 4–5 Henry V, 1416–17; as usual the accounting year ran from Michaelmas (29 September) to Michaelmas. The later date is proved by the reference to the funeral of Isabel dowager countess of Suffolk who died on 29 September 1416, and the references to the late earls, father and son, both named Michael de la Pole, who died at Harfleur and Agincourt respectively on 18 September and 25 October 1415.

50 Presumably Richard Clifford, bishop of London, was providing for his education.

same Robert Bolton, as appears in his account, for the maintenance for the year of the daughters of Sir Michael de la Pole, late earl of Suffolk, son of the late earl his father, at the feasts of Easter and Michaelmas, namely to each of them five marks this year.

Sum total: £50

[Extracts from] the wardrobe payments for the sons and daughters of the lady[51]

For Joan de la Pole. £6 13s 4d paid on 17 May this year to the aforesaid Joan, daughter of the lady, as for her maintenance granted to her by the lady for Easter term this year, because she received nothing at Stamford, with 26s 8d paid to her formerly by Clement Liffyn, and with 30s paid to her by William Green her servant as for her fee and clothing up to the aforesaid date paid in arrears. Paid to Joan on 9 February for her expenses in riding from Wingfield to London, 26s 8d. Paid to Joan by the lord earl her brother, as in money granted to her by the lady her mother, for the repair of his armour, 100s.[52]

For Thomas de la Pole. Paid to John Aleyn by Clement Liffyn for items taken by John, as is said, for Thomas son of the lady before 1 November, year 4 [1416], 33s 4d. Given to Thomas son of the lady in September this year while studying at Oxford for play and his small expenses, together with 8d paid for one purse for him to put his money in, 4s. Given at the same time to Master Robert Rowebury, Thomas's master and tutor, as payment made to him by the lady, 20s. Paid by Clement Liffyn for 2½ yards of violet cloth sent to Oxford, price 4s 8d a yard, 11s 8d.

For Alexander de la Pole. For the expenses of Alexander, son of the lady, riding to Ipswich to school there in September in the fourth year of the present king, paid by John Hedon, 4s 6d. Paid to Master William Bury, master of the school there, for Alexander's stay with him from the Sunday before Michaelmas, year 4, to the feast of St Arnulf, namely 18 July, in the fifth year of the present king, that is for forty-two weeks at 20d a week, 70s ... For the expenses of John Hedon and others riding to Ipswich on 13 July to bring Alexander from Ipswich to Wingfield on the following day, 3s 11½d.

For Philippa daughter of the lady. Paid to the prioress of Bungay by John

51 The lady was Katherine Stafford, wife of Earl Michael de la Pole, the father.

52 The next entry for Lady Elizabeth Burnell records payments for shoes and cloth, and does not throw light on her activities over the year. Elizabeth was the widow of Katherine Stafford's grandson, Edward Burnell, who was killed at the battle of Agincourt.

del Hill mason for Philippa's stay with her damsel[53] from the feast of St
Mary Magdalen [22 July], year 4, until Christmas this year, for twenty-
two weeks at 3s a week, 2s being deducted because her damsel had time
off for two weeks, 64s. Paid to the same prioress on 8 May in full payment
for Philippa's stay from Christmas to the eve of Pentecost following,
namely 29 May, for twenty-two weeks, at the same price, two weeks
being deducted in which Philippa and her damsel were at Wingfield
with the lady her mother, 60s ... Paid to the prioress of Bungay for
Philippa's sojourn for twenty weeks from 29 May until the eve of the
feast of St Luke the evangelist [17 October], at the same price, 60s.

For Elizabeth and Isabella, daughters of Sir Michael the son. Paid to
Christian Fastolffe for Elizabeth's stay at Bungay from the feast of St
Anne [26 July] to the feast of St John the Evangelist [27 December]
in the Christmas season, for twenty-two weeks at 8d a week, 14s 8d, in
two instalments. Paid to the same Christian for Elizabeth's stay from
the feast of St John to Sunday 9 May for nineteen weeks at 8d a week,
as above, 12s 8d. Paid to Joan Baker of Fressingfield for Isabella's stay
from the eve of the Assumption of the Blessed Virgin Mary [14
August] in the fourth year of the present king until the feast of
Pentecost in the fifth year, namely 30 May, for forty-one weeks, at 6d
a week, 20s 6d.[54] ... For the expenses of Robert Bolton esquire and
John Hedon at Bungay with seven horses to bring Elizabeth to
Wingfield, 16d. Paid to Joan Baker for Isabella's stay from 30 May
until the Sunday before Michaelmas this year for seventeen weeks at
6d a week as above, 8s 6d ... Paid to the abbess of Bruisyard for
Elizabeth's stay from 10 May this year until the following Michaelmas
for twenty weeks, at 12d a week, 20s. Given by the lady to a friar there
called 'le President' for his labour in teaching Elizabeth while she was
there, 6s 8d. Paid to a woman serving Elizabeth for the same time, 6s 8d.

64. Agreement concerning the upbringing of Isabella, daughter of
Thomas Stonor, 1432[55] [From Public Record Office, London, C146/
1229; in Latin]

---

53 The use of the word *domicella* implies a lady-in-waiting rather than a servant.

54 Joan is described in another entry as Isabella's nurse.

55 In his will Thomas Stonor arranged for his wife to be responsible for his daughters;
   he left lands to his wife for life, the proceeds of which were to be used for his
   daughters' maintenance. His son Thomas was to be in the governance of Thomas
   Chaucer; his marriage was to be sold and the money used for the daughters'
   dowries.

Richard Drayton esquire and Alice his wife, who was the wife of Thomas Stonor esquire, late of Oxfordshire, greet in the Lord all the faithful of Christ to whom the present indenture may come. Know that we, the aforesaid Richard and Alice, have granted to John Hampden of Hampden, Edmund Hampden, Richard Restwold, Peter Feteplace and Thomas Ramsey a yearly rent of eight marks to be received and levied from and in our manors of Penton Mewsey in Hampshire and Bierton near Aylesbury in Buckinghamshire, and in all the lands and tenements which we have in the vill of Westminster and elsewhere in Middlesex. To be received by the aforesaid John, Edmund, Richard Restwold, Peter and Thomas and their assigns from the feast of St Gregory the pope next [12 March] for the term of the next ten years, at the feasts of Easter, the Nativity of St John the Baptist, St Michael the archangel, and Christmas, in equal portions, yearly. And if it should happen that the said rent at any of the said feasts should be partly or wholly in arrears during the aforesaid term, then the aforesaid John, Edmund, Richard Restwold, Peter and Thomas and their assigns shall be allowed to distrain in all the said manors, lands and tenements, on all goods and chattels in the same manors, and to take and carry away and drive off the distraints thus taken, and to keep them until they are fully satisfied of all the arrears of the said rent. Provided always that as long as we, the aforesaid Richard Drayton and Alice, during the said term sufficiently and honestly maintain and cause to be maintained Isabella Stonor, daughter of the said Thomas Stonor and Alice, in food, clothing and teaching suitable for her age and status, then we, the aforesaid Richard and Alice and our assigns shall be exonerated and quit of the said yearly rent and payment, as shall be the said manors, lands and tenements. Provided also that if the said Isabella should be married or die within the said term, or Thomas Stonor and John Stonor, Isabella's brothers, die within the said term, then this present writing shall be void. Provided also that if Alice should die in the lifetime of me, Richard Drayton, then the present indenture would lack all its strength and force, and be void. In testimony of this, the aforesaid parties have affixed their seals alternately on these indented writings. Given at Stonor in Oxfordshire on 1 December in the eleventh year of King Henry VI.

65. Arrangements for the wardship of Hamo Lestrange, 1317 [From Norfolk Record Office, Lestrange of Hunstanton Collection, no. A7; in French]

Isolda who was the wife of Sir John Lestrange of Knockyn greets in God all those who see and hear these letters. Be it known to you all that Margaret who was the wife of Sir Hamo Lestrange, lord of Hunstanton, has been acknowledged in our lord the king's chancery on the quindene of the feast of St Martin [11 November] in the eleventh year of the reign of King Edward II to be bound to me in £510 to have the wardship of the lands of Hamo son and heir of Sir Hamo Lestrange who is a minor.[56] And if the said Hamo dies as a minor in my lifetime without issue of his body, she has of my grant the custody of the said lands until Edmund his brother comes of age, saving to me the custody of the reversion of the tenements that the said Margaret holds in dower if she dies before the aforesaid heirs come of age. And she is to pay at the next feast of the Purification [2 February] after the completion of this writing, £10. At the feast of the Nativity of St John next following [24 June], £10, and at the feast of St Michael next following, £10, and so £30 from year to year, at the same terms, and similarly £30 at the end of seventeen years, for which time we have calculated the minority of the said children will last. And it is for this that the said recognisance has been made. In order to ensure the payment of the said farm, I, Isolda, wish and grant for me, my heirs and assigns that I have reserved for myself the wardship of Hamo's issue if he marries and has children of his body. If after my death the said Hamo dies without issue before he comes of age, so that Margaret cannot retain the wardship of the lands until the end of the aforesaid seventeen years, as I have granted, and Margaret, her heirs and assigns have paid the debt according to the terms in the recognisance before Hamo's death, then Margaret, her heirs and assigns should be quit for ever of all the debt due after Hamo's death, and I, Isolda, my heirs and assigns will forbear to demand any of the debt contained in the said recognisance for the terms to come after Hamo's death. And if it happens that Hamo dies without issue of his body, and she holds the wardship for Edmund's minority, I have granted that she should pay me at the terms laid down in the recognisance. And if it should happen that the said Edmund, Hamo's brother, should die a minor, and she cannot have and hold the wardship of the lands until the end of the

56 The deed was enrolled on the chancery rolls; *Calendar of Close Rolls 1313-18*, pp. 582–3.

seventeen years, she should pay me fully for the terms up to Edmund's death, and she, her heirs and assigns should be quit for ever of the payments due after Edmund's death and of the remainder of the debt contained in the said recognisance, and we will forbear to make any demand. And in witness of these things I, Isolda, have affixed my seal to the part of the indenture remaining in Margaret's hands. And Margaret's seal has been put on the other part to be kept by me. Given in London on the Friday after the feast of St Andrew in the year of the reign of the above-named king.

66. Arrangements for Lady Alice de Plumpton to live with her son, 1428[57] [From *Plumpton Correspondence*, pp. xxvii–ix; in French]

This indenture made between Lady Alice de Plumpton on one side and Robert de Plumpton her son on the other witnesses that Robert has granted and freely given to Lady Alice his mother her board, suffcient and suitable to her status, and board for Elizabeth and Isabel, Lady Alice's daughters, and for Richard her son, and for a nurse for one full year, starting on the feast of St Martin [11 November] in the next winter after the date of this indenture. The said Robert has also freely granted to Lady Alice a chamber, called 'le closetts', with a little chamber made high in the said room, for her own use, and sufficient light and fuel. And if Lady Alice desires or wishes at the end of the year to stay longer with Robert, then Lady Alice will give for her board 12*d* a week, and for Elizabeth her daughter 8*d*, and for Richard her son 6*d*, and for Isabel her daughter 6*d*, and for a companion 8*d*, and for a maid 6*d*. And the said Lady Alice is to have all the easement and everything specified above during the time that she makes her home with the said Robert.[58] And in order to abide by and fully perform each and every condition, both parties have set their seals to the present indentures. Witnessed by John de Mureton, Henry de Mureton, Robert de Skelton chaplain, Roger de Spofforth and Nicholas Thornby chaplains. Given at York, on 9 October, in the seventh year of King Henry VI.

---

57 Alice was the daughter and co-heiress of John Gisburn, mayor of York.

58 The term 'easement' covers Alice's rights of accommodation including free access.

67. Evidence from the household accounts of Elizabeth de Burgh of her close links with her daughters, Isabella de Ferrers and Elizabeth Bardolf, her grandchild, Elizabeth de Burgh countess of Ulster, and her half-brother, Edward de Monthermer; the extracts date from 1339, 1343, and 1351–2 respectively.[59] [From Public Record Office, London, E101/92/12, m. 6, 8; 92/24, m. 4; 93/12, m. 3d; in Latin]

For the expenses of the lady [Elizabeth de Burgh], Sir Edward de Monthermer, and some of the lady's household being at Clare from 23 November to 28 November.

For the expenses of Lady Bardolf at Anglesey on her journey to Bardfield. For the expenses of five destriers from the lady's carriage being there to transport Lady Bardolf from 3 December to 10 December.[60]

Furnished and used for the distribution to the poor for the soul of Sir Edward de Monthermer eight quarters of wheat from Erbury which made 2,497 loaves. Item, expended 4,280 herrings from stock[61]

For the expenses of Lady de Ferrers coming from Groby to Bardfield with the expenses of Robert Mareschal, Lady Joan de Strecheleye and others of the lady's household going from Bardfield to Groby to seek her and to return with her, from 14 October to 26 October.[62]

Item, for 4½ ells of scarlet and 4½ ells of tawny cloth bought for the countess of Ulster on 4 June, £4 12d.

Item given to the masons of the Augustinian friars at Clare working on the tomb of Sir Edward de Monthermer on 23 July, 2s 6d.

59 Further details are given in no. 135.

60 Anglesey, Cambridgeshire, and Great Bardfield, Essex, were both residences of Elizabeth de Burgh. Sir John Bardolf's estates were mainly in Norfolk, and his wife was often picked up at Anglesey on her visits to her mother. The Latin word *dextrarius* means a war-horse or destrier; obviously strong horses were needed for this type of conveyance.

61 Edward de Monthermer was mortally wounded at Vironfosse in October, and died at Clare; Elizabeth de Burgh looked after him and arranged his funeral. Erbury was the name given to the demesne manor at Clare.

62 The funeral of Sir Henry de Ferrers of Groby took place on 20 October.

68. Elizabeth de Burgh's bequests to the Bardolf family; the will is dated 1355, but Elizabeth did not die until 1360 [From Lambeth Palace Library, London, Register of Simon Islip, fos 165v–166r; in French]

Item, I bequeath to my daughter Bardolf my bed of green velvet striped with red with whatever belongs to it, with one coverlet of fine cloth lined with pured minever, a half coverlet to match, and a kerchief of blue samite lined with … and one coverlet of tawny motley lined with gris.[63] Item, I bequeath to my said daughter a great room of worsted-hangings, with blue parrots and cockerels on a tawny field, and whatever belongs to them. Item, I bequeath to my said daughter my great carriage with the horse-cloths, hangings and cushions, and whatever belongs to it.[64] Item, I bequeath to Sir John Bardolf and to my said daughter, his wife, jointly in my manors of Caythorpe and Clopton 26 quarters of wheat for seed for the winter season, and 7 quarters and 4 bushels of maslin and rye.[65] Item, for the Lent season 17 quarters and 4 bushels of peas, 37 quarters and 4 bushels of barley, 9 quarters and 4 bushels of dredge,[66] and 22 quarters and 1 bushel of oats, 4 cart-horses, 12 draught animals, 22 oxen, together with my carts and ploughs which belong to the said manors, and all their apparatus.[67] Item, I bequeath to my young daughter [grand-daughter] Isabel Bardolf to help her to marry one goblet of gold plate, two great cups partly enamelled, and twelve large silver dishes, my bed of pure sendal[68] with a coverlet of grey motley lined with minever. Item, to Agnes her sister to help her to marry one silver cross, two candlesticks, two salt-cellars, one goblet, one great almsdish, one goblet of embossed silver, one incense-boat, one censer, one clasp with the Annunciation depicted on it, and six new silver chargers. Item, to the said Agnes a bed of indigo of which the hangings and coverlet are of woollen cloth, and one blue coverlet lined with gris.

63 Bequests of beds in medieval wills meant bequests of their hangings and furnishings, not of the wooden bed itself. The nature of the kerchief's lining is not clear in the manuscript, but was presumably some sort of fur. Samite was a heavy silk material; gris was the grey back of the winter skins of the Baltic squirrel; Veale, *English Fur Trade*, p. 228.

64 This type of carriage, drawn by five destriers, is depicted in the Luttrell psalter; J. Backhouse, *The Luttrell Psalter*, British Library, London, 1989, pp. 50–1.

65 Maslin was a mixture of wheat and rye.

66 Dredge was a mixture of barley and oats.

67 These manors were to pass to the Bardolfs, but, unless agricultural equipment was specifically bequeathed, it counted as the property of the executors.

68 Sendal was a silk material.

69. Extracts from the will of William de Ferrers of Groby[69] referring to his mother, wives, daughters and siblings [From Lambeth Palace Library, Register of William Whittlesey, fos 124v–125r; in Latin]

I bequeath to divers chapels to sing masses for my soul and the soul of my wife recently departed according to the disposition of my executors, £100.

I bequeath to the abbess and convent of the Minoresses of London outside Aldgate, ten marks. I bequeath to Elizabeth my daughter, a nun in the same house, £20. I bequeath to the abbot and convent of Croxden to sing masses for my soul and the soul of Lady Isabella my mother, ten marks.[70] I bequeath to the Dominican friars of Chelmsford and the Franciscan friars of Leicester ten marks each for two chaplains in each house to sing masses for my soul. I bequeath to the abbot and convent of Tilty to sing masses for my soul and the souls of my ancestors, ten marks. I bequeath to the Dominican and Augustinian friars of Leicester and the Carmelite friars of Maldon five marks to each house for one chaplain to sing masses for my soul in each house.

I wish Margaret my wife to have £100 as in silver vessels of the ornaments of the chapel and wardrobe and in brass vessels not bequeathed, and to have this quantity of whichever type according to the disposition of my executors or in cash at my wife's choice. Item, I wish that the said Margaret my wife should have £100 of silver as in live and dead stock of the manors according to the disposition of my said executors or in cash at my wife's choice, on the condition that, if my executors are vexed, molested or in any other way impeded by Margaret my wife or by any other person in her name, or if she should seek any of my other goods, the legacies of the said £200 or the goods and chattels in place of the above-named sums should be void and have no validity but should be completely annulled.

I bequeath to Henry my son my green bed adorned with my arms, with its hangings and with the hangings belonging to the hall. And if it should happen that Henry should die before he comes of age, then I wish that the aforesaid bed and hall with the hangings belonging to them should remain to my daughter Margaret.

Item, I bequeath to Margaret my daughter one white bed with all its

---

69 He was the son of Henry and Isabella de Ferrers of Groby referred to in no. 67; the will was made in 1368, shortly after his second marriage; he died in 1371.

70 Croxden was a foundation of the Verdun family; Isabella de Ferrers was the daughter of Theobald de Verdun and Elizabeth de Burgh.

furnishings, with the Ferrers and Ufford arms quartered, together with a bed of double worsted and half a room with blue curtains and hangings for her marriage.[71] I bequeath to the aforesaid Margaret one gilt cup with a cover 'tourdechalis'. And if it should happen that Margaret should die before her marriage, then I wish that the said bed with all its equipment and the aforesaid cup with cover should be distributed for the salvation of my soul according to the disposition of my executors.

Item, I bequeath to Lady Philippa de Beauchamp my sister one silver-gilt goblet with cover standing on three lions, two silver pots, and one silver salt-cellar. Item, I bequeath to Lady Elizabeth Athol my sister the better plate for spices and one silver-gilt and enamelled tablet of three leaves decorated in the niche with the Assumption of the Blessed Mary.

To superintend this will I appoint the venerable father Lord John [Buckingham], by grace of God bishop of Lincoln, Lady Philippa de Beauchamp my sister, Sir Ralph Basset of Sapcote, and Simon Pakeman.

Item, I leave to Margaret my wife all rings, brooches and rosaries not bequeathed.

71 William's first wife was Margaret daughter of Robert Ufford earl of Suffolk, and his second wife Margaret Percy, the widow of Sir Robert de Umfraville; his daughter Margaret married Thomas earl of Warwick (d. 1401); his sister Philippa was the widow of Guy Beauchamp, and his sister Elizabeth the wife of David earl of Athol.

III: Land

The crucial importance of land as the source of wealth for noble and gentry society has been underlined in the discussion of both marriage and the family. As far as women's landholding is concerned, the significance of land is emphasised by the sheer amount of surviving evidence, although the nature of the sources varies over time. Women as landholders are found in the Domesday Survey, although the picture of women's estates and interests is by no means complete.[1] For the twelfth century, charters throw considerable light on women's *maritagia*, inheritances and dower. Because an increasing number of families came to hold at least part of their lands in chief of the king, much information is derived from the Pipe Rolls of the royal Exchequer, and Henry II's desire to be informed of his rights over wards and widows underlies the *Rotuli de Dominabus*.[2] The greatest increase in material began towards the end of the twelfth century as the royal government began to keep copies of letters and charters, and as the demand for royal justice and the practice of recording led to the survival of a mass of material, much of it related to landholding.[3] Free litigants found a growing range of actions available to them, and the royal courts, especially through the device of the final concord, gave greater security to landholding. From the thirteenth century, the growth of central authority and the changes in county government, together with further legal developments, increased documentation. Moreover the nobility and gentry themselves were increasingly aware of the value of the written word.

Women were always considered to have rights to land throughout the period 1066 to 1500. Yet women were far more restricted than their male kinsmen in how they could acquire land; it was very rare for a woman to be able to gain land as a result of service. This means that women's landholding has to be seen in the context of the family. A woman's estates comprised her *maritagium* and later her jointure, both secured at marriage, her dower, and, for some women, her inheritance, and all these had implications for her family. The estates also have to

1 P. Stafford, 'Women in Domesday', in *Medieval Women in Southern England*, Reading Medieval Studies, XV, Reading, 1989, pp. 75-94.

2 J. H. Round, ed., *Rotuli de Dominabus, passim.*

3 Clanchy, *From Memory to Written Record*, pp. 29-59.

be considered in the context of lordship and of the law of the land, and in both these areas the Crown was often involved. Although there are wide differences in the amounts of land held and in the degree of wealth, all these considerations applied across the whole spectrum of noble society throughout the period.

Maritagium and jointure have already been discussed in the context of marriage settlements.[4] It was accepted that a widow needed to be provided for in the event of her husband's death, and in his coronation charter Henry I promised widows both their dower and their marriage-portion.[5] The proportion of the husband's land held as dower varied in the Domesday Survey,[6] and this continued to be the case as long as dower was the subject of a specific endowment by the husband, often made at the church door at the time of the marriage; examples of this form of endowment are found into the early fourteenth century.[7] By the late twelfth century, however, dower could comprise one-third of the husband's lands that he held at the time of the marriage, and Magna Carta of 1225 was more generous in specifying that the widow should receive as her dower one-third of all her husband's land that had been his in his lifetime, unless she had been dowered with less at the church door.[8] This subsequently became the norm, and the widow was entitled to receive dower for her lifetime, provided that the marriage had taken place in public (and was therefore widely known), and that there had been no annulment nor adultery by the wife.[9] The widow lost her jointure and dower if she remarried without permission of the king or lord, but was able to recover them on payment of a fine. According to the 1225 Magna Carta, dower should be allocated within forty days, during which time the widow was allowed to remain in her husband's house. The allocation was carried out by royal officials in the case of tenants-in-

4 See above, nos. 10-15.

5 D. C. Douglas and G. W. Greenaway, eds, *English Historical Documents 1042-1189*, p. 401.

6 Stafford, 'Women in Domesday', p. 84.

7 E.g. Edmund Mortimer, son and heir of Roger Mortimer of Wigmore, dowered his wife Elizabeth at the church door in 1316, but the deed laid down that this did not preclude her from seeking common dower of one-third of her husband's lands; Public Record Office, London, DL27/93.

8 J. S. Loengard, '"Of the gift of her husband": English dower and its consequences in the year 1200', in J. Kirshner and S. F. Wemple, eds, *Women of the Medieval World*, Oxford, 1985, pp. 218-20; J. C. Holt, *Magna Carta*, pp. 503-4; H. Rothwell, ed., *English Historical Documents 1189-1327*, p. 342.

9 See above, nos. 30, 43.

chief, or by the officials of the husband's lord; the widow's dower together with the prospect of remarriage was a lucrative source of patronage and revenue. This allocation was not necessarily straightforward and the practice of remarriage and the existence of step-families undoubtedly presented complications.[10] The need for an estate to support one or more dowagers certainly straitened the circumstances of the heir, and could cause grievance; however, the woman's right to dower was unquestioned.[11] In contrast to dower which had to be allocated, Magna Carta laid down in 1215 that the widow was to have her *maritagium* and inheritance immediately after her husband's death and without hindrance.[12] As has been seen, it was the heiress who was most attractive as a marriage partner, and rights of succession through the woman were always accepted in law. An heiress was invariably married at least once; it was most unlikely that she would become a nun. It would have been regarded as a pointless waste to leave a single woman in charge of an inheritance, although later in life it was accepted that a widow could act as *femme sole*; according to Henry I's coronation charter, in the event of a daughter being left as heiress on the death of a baron, the king would bestow her with her land with the advice of his barons.[13] The development of primogeniture in the eleventh and twelfth centuries put emphasis on descent through the eldest son, but in the absence of sons, daughters were regarded as preferable to more distant male kinsmen, and by 1150 thirty baronies had descended through the female line.[14] Changes took place, however, as to how the law of female succession operated. Until the 1130s it was usual for a single heiress to succeed even when there was more than one daughter, but from the 1130s it became usual for the lands to be divided among the daughters, and this remained the

10 Loengard "'Of the gift of her husband'", p. 232.

11 For the higher nobility political circumstances could long delay dower, e.g. Eleanor Neville, widow of Richard Despenser, was formally granted her dower by the Crown in 1415 but did not receive it until 1447. A widow with jointure possibly did not receive an additional one-third of her husband's lands in dower; Wright, *Derbyshire Gentry*, p. 33. The problem of dowagers burdening an estate is discussed by Archer, 'Rich old ladies', pp. 15-35.

12 Holt, *Magna Carta*, pp. 452-3; H. Rothwell, ed., *English Historical Documents 1189-1327*, p. 318.

13 D. C. Douglas and G. W. Greenaway, eds, *English Historical Documents 1042-1189*, p. 401.

14 Holt, 'The heiress and the alien', p. 5. J. Hudson, *Land, Law and Lordship in Anglo-Norman England*, Oxford, 1994, p. 111, points out that in the 1160s both parties to the Anstey case accepted that a daughter was preferable to a nephew for inheriting from the father.

rule for the rest of the Middle Ages. The evidence suggests that this
was a deliberate step taken by the king's court,[15] reference being made
in a charter of 1145 to a 'statutum decretum' governing the practice of
female succession. However, the operation of female succession cannot
be regarded as having been automatic; as far as tenants-in-chief were
concerned, especially among the higher nobility, the king always had
the last word, and could manipulate inheritance in his own interests or
in those of powerful favourites.[16]

The woman who was an heiress and had dower (and in the later
Middle Ages jointure) from one or more husbands was a formidable
figure. During the later Middle Ages the definition of dower as one-
third of the husband's lands and the practice of jointure meant that she
was often wealthier than earlier on, and the development of royal
justice meant that in most cases she was more secure. It was usual for
the widow to keep her inheritance and for it to pass to her heir after
her death, and this added to her own power and to her attractiveness
to suitors. In addition to these types of landholding, a woman with
access to royal patronage might well secure additional grants, whether
of lands, wardships or annuities. She could also make purchases of land
on her own account. As a result, women with substantial estates are
found throughout the Middle Ages.

The tenures found between the late eleventh and thirteenth centuries
were tenures in fee simple, tenure of land by a vassal of a lord in return
for service, usually knight service. These tenures continued in the later
Middle Ages, but the whole picture of tenures then became more
complex. Conditional fees, laying down specific conditions of tenure,
particularly in relation to inheritance, are found in the thirteenth
century before the statute *De Donis Conditionalibus* of 1285 which was
designed to prevent alienation by holders of conditional fees.[17] The use
of entails and the putting of lands into the hands of feoffees to uses
became increasingly common among the nobility from the middle of
the fourteenth century, and among the gentry from the late fourteenth
century. Such arrangements made for greater flexibility over the

---

15 Holt, 'The heiress and the alien', pp. 8–14, considers that this move was a sudden
and deliberate change of policy; J. Hudson, *Land, Law and Lordship*, p. 112, suggests
that it may represent a royal decision between two current customs. The question
has also been considered by S. F. C. Milsom, 'Inheritance by women in the twelfth
and early thirteenth centuries', pp. 60–89.

16 See above, nos. 6, 49, for the inheritance to William earl of Gloucester in 1183, and
the delay in partitioning the Clare estates in 1314–17.

17 H. Rothwell, ed., *English Historical Documents 1189–1327*, pp. 428–9.

transfer of land both within and outside the family, and kept lands in the hands of the family and deprived the king or lord of rights to wardship; continuity of administration during a minority was secured. Joint enfeoffment undoubtedly benefited the wife who would hold the lands for life if her husband predeceased her; such arrangements were not only created at marriage, but could be added to at any point during the marriage. However, the use of the entail for securing male succession, even of a distant relation in the absence of a son, meant that in some families daughters lost the right to inherit. Therefore at a time when jointure tended to give a woman additional lands, she might well be denied her ultimate inheritance.

In view of the wife's subordinate legal position, the question arises as to whether the husband could do as he liked with his wife's land. Certainly he was responsible for the land during the marriage, and according to the custom of 'curtesy of England' he was entitled to keep the lands for life if his wife predeceased him, provided that a living child had been born.[18] The greatest problem centred on the alienation of land, and the law became increasingly concerned to prevent alienation which would damage the heir, and the misuse of rights over property by either husband or widow.[19] Charters of the twelfth century and later show the wife associated with and consenting to the husband's grant of her land, and making her own gifts from her *maritagium*, dower and inheritance. These grants were usually confirmed by other members of the family; in the case of gifts to religious houses it was usual for a lord to confirm the charters of his predecessors, whether male or female. However, as the husband was responsible for his wife's land, he might take action without her agreement, and it was to meet this danger that the widow was granted a remedy in the royal courts to recover alienated land; there was also an action by which heirs could reclaim lands granted away by dowagers, a necessary action as the barons protested in 1258 that widows were alienating their *maritagia*. From about 1200, any permanent alienation over which the wife as widow would have no right of dower had to be made by final concord, and the wife had to give her consent in the royal court.[20]

18 This custom was described by Glanville in the late twelfth century, although he did not give it a name.

19 Plucknett, *Legislation of Edward I*, pp. 122-4.

20 Pollock and Maitland, *History of English Law*, pp. 409-26; Harding, *England in the Thirteenth Century*, pp. 200-1.

Landholding has to be seen in the context of the law of the land as well as of the family. The royal courts provided protection for both widow and heir over dower, ensuring in the late twelfth century that the widow could secure her dower, and enabling the heir from the thirteenth century to secure a new assignment if he was dissatisfied. Some of these cases probably derived from family tension; in others it is possible that the publicity of the royal courts was sought for the dower settlement.

Although women were normally secure in their landholding, times of rebellion undoubtedly brought problems, even if the ostensible rebel was the husband rather than the wife. The penalty for treason was the forfeiture of estates; according to 'Bracton', this included loss of goods and the perpetual disinheritance of the heirs. His opinion was however regarded as too harsh, and *De Donis Conditionalibus* exempted entailed estates from forfeiture (but not lands held in fee simple). As a result the widow lost her dower, but not her inheritance and jointure because they predated her husband's treason; however, she could only claim these after her husband's death when she became a *femme sole*. In 1388 and 1398, during the troubles of Richard II's reign, lands held to the use of a traitor were liable for forfeiture, together with entailed estates in 1398, and it was this position which was adopted in the fifteenth-century acts of attainder; the woman's inheritance and jointure remained exempt.[21] Speaking generally, and bearing in mind that many acts of attainder were reversed, it was to a woman's advantage if her traitor-husband died, always provided that she had jointure or inheritance, but looking at the political troubles of the later Middle Ages there was great variety in the treatment of women, and much depended on individual political circumstances, as seen with Elizabeth de Burgh and Elizabeth countess of Oxford.

Apart from the very exceptional case, no man or woman of the nobility could do just what he or she wanted with the land, although the more complex tenures of the later Middle Ages gave more scope than the earlier arrangents. Within these parameters women played a role in helping members of their family, not just the heir, whether by making grants or using their wealth and power to support them. They also used their land to exercise power, as will be seen in the next chapter.

---

21 C. D. Ross, 'Forfeiture for treason in the reign of Richard II', *English Historical Review*, LXXI, 1956, pp. 560-75; J. R. Lander, 'Attainder and forfeiture, 1453-1509', *Historical Journal*, IV, 1961, pp. 119-51, and reprinted in *Crown and Nobility, 1450-1509*, London, 1976, pp. 127-58; A. Crawford, 'Victims of attainder: the Howard and de Vere women in the late fifteenth century', in *Medieval Women in Southern England*, Reading Medieval Studies, XV, Reading, 1989, pp. 59-74.

70. Extracts from the description of the lands held by Azelina, the widow of Ralph Taillebois, in Bedfordshire, showing instances of landholding derived from her *maritagium* and dower, 1086; altogether she held land in ten places in the county [From A. Farley and H. Ellis, eds, *Liber Censualis vocatus Domesday Book*, 4 vols, Record Commission, London, 1783–1816, I, fo. 218; in Latin]

Brodo holds one hide of Azelina in Eyeworth. There is land for one plough which is there with one bordar, and there is enough meadow for one plough-team. It has always been worth 10s.[22] This land is part of Azelina's *maritagium*. Brodo held it [before the Conquest] and could sell it to whom he wished.

Azelina holds as part of her *maritagium* five hides and $1\frac{1}{2}$ virgates in Cockayne Hatley. There is land for eight ploughs. There are one hide and one virgate in demesne and on it are two ploughs. There are eight villeins and four bordars with six ploughs. There are one serf and one mill valued at 18s, enough meadow for two plough-teams, woodland for four pigs, and rendering 3s. Altogether it is worth £6, when received 100s, and in the time of King Edward £6. Ulmar, King Edward's thegn, held this manor, and there were two of his sokemen there. They had $2\frac{1}{2}$ virgates, and could give and sell them to whom they wished.

Widrus holds one hide and three virgates of Azelina in Henlow. There is land for two ploughs which are there. There are two villeins, two bordars and two serfs, and enough meadow for two plough-teams. It is worth 30s, and was worth 20s when received, and 30s in the time of King Edward. Anschil held this land, and it was a berewick of Stotfold in the time of King Edward. Hugh de Beauchamp claims this land from Azelina, saying that she holds it wrongfully and it was never part of her dower.[23]

Bernard holds one hide of Azelina in the same vill. There is land for one plough which is there. There are three villeins, and enough meadow for one plough-team. When received and now it is worth 23s, and 28s in the time of King Edward. Two sokemen, the men of Anschil, held this land [before the Conquest] and could give it to whom they wished.

22 This value applies to the time of King Edward the Confessor, when the land was received after the Norman Conquest, and to 1086.

23 Hugh de Beauchamp had succeeded Ralph Taillebois on his estates. A berewick was an outlying part of the manor.

Three sokemen hold three hides of Azelina in Chicksand, of her dower land. There is land for two ploughs; there is one there and could be another. There is enough meadow for two plough-teams, and woodland for twenty pigs. When received and now it is worth 20s, and in the time of King Edward 25s. Four sokemen held this manor [before the Conquest] and could give and sell to whom they wished.

Walter holds one hide of Azelina in the same vill, and this belongs to her *maritagium*. There is land for one plough which is there, enough meadow for one plough-team, woodland for fifty pigs, and one mill valued at 10s. When received and now it is worth 20s, and 30s in the time of King Edward. Sueteman, the man of Ulmar of Eaton Socon, held this land [before the Conquest] and could give it to whom he wished.

71. Two women's holdings from *Rotuli de Dominabus*, 1185, showing how their land was derived from *maritagium* and dower [From Public Record Office, London, E198/1/2, rolls 3 and 3d (Northamptonshire), and 9d (Essex); in Latin]

Emma who was the wife of Hugh son of Robert and previously the wife of Robert de Sancto Paulo and the daughter of Henry Tiart is in the lord king's gift and is forty years old. She has dower in Oxfordshire of the gift of Robert de Sancto Paulo which is worth 50s. The land of her *maritagium* in Brington [Northamptonshire] is worth 63s, and is stocked with two ploughs, 100 sheep and three sows. Moreover she holds in dower in Northampton one house, of the gift of Robert de Sancto Paulo, which is worth £8 a year. The lord king gave her to Hugh son of Robert together with the aforesaid house, to be held of the lord king for 2s a year, for which she has the king's charter, as the jurors say. Her eldest son is aged twenty; she has a married daughter aged eighteen, a daughter aged sixteen, two daughters who are nuns, and two other younger daughters.

Alice of Essex is in the lord king's gift and is sixty years old. She is the aunt of Earl William [de Mandeville] and the sister of Earl Aubrey [de Vere], and she has two sons who are knights and one daughter married to John [fitz Eustace] constable of Chester. She holds her manor of Aynho [Northamptonshire] of Earl William, and it is worth £30 a year if it is stocked with four ploughs, 400 sheep, six sows and seven hogs, but because it lacks 300 sheep it is only worth £27.

Alice of Essex is in the lord king's gift and is eighty years old, and she holds Clavering [Essex] as her dower of the fee of Henry of Essex, and it is worth £40 with the following stock: six ploughs, 100 sheep, four cows, one bull, six sows and one boar, and two harrows. Alice has two sons who are knights, and in Northamptonshire she has thirty librates of land of the fee of Earl William.[24]

72. Grant by Hawise, wife of William earl of Gloucester, c. 1150–83; the reference to the gift from her husband probably means that this property formed part of her dower [From W. de G. Birch, 'Original documents relating to Bristol and the neighbourhood', *Journal of the British Archaeological Association*, XXXI, 1875, p. 292; in Latin]

Men both present and future should know that I Hawise countess of Gloucester have given to God and the church of St James of Bristol in perpetual alms one last burgage in the new borough of the meadow, namely the last one on the east side, free and quit of all service and custom as the earl my lord gave it to me.[25] Witnessed by my lord himself and with his consent. Witnessed by Robert de Maisi, Robert Dameri, Richard de Cardi, Simon his brother, Hervey the clerk, Ailward the young man.

73. Grant by Matilda of St Hilary, wife of Roger de Clare earl of Hertford, to the priory of Stoke by Clare, 1152–73; the land formed part of her St Hilary inheritance [From British Library, London, Cotton MS. Appendix xxi, fo. 31v; in Latin]

Countess Matilda, wife of Roger earl of Clare, greets all men French and English.[26] You should know that I have given and confirmed by this my charter to God and St John of Stoke and the monks serving God there in perpetual alms half a mark every year from the mill of Carbrooke, whoever should hold or have that mill, for the soul of my lord Roger earl of Clare and my soul, and for the souls of my children

---

24 J. H. Round, 'The families of Mandeville and de Vere', in *Geoffrey de Mandeville: A Study of the Anarchy*, London, 1892, pp. 388-96. Estimates of age in the Middle Ages were necessarily approximate.

25 The new borough, an expansion of the existing town, was situated between Bristol castle and St James's church; R. B. Patterson, ed., *Earldom of Gloucester Charters: The Charters and Scribes of the Earls and Countesses of Gloucester to AD 1217*, Oxford, 1973, p. 56.

26 The title earl of Clare was frequently used, but the official title of the family was earl of Hertford. For Matilda, see above, nos. 27, 57.

and all my ancestors. Witnessed by Richard brother of the earl of Clare, Conan his nephew, Matthew the butler, and others.

74. Grant by Alured de Bendeville and his wife Sibyl to the Knights Hospitallers of the church of Chaureth in Broxted, Essex, 1151 [From British Library, London, Cotton MS. Nero E VI, fo. 205r; in Latin]

Alured de Bendeville and his wife Sibyl greet all their friends and men and all the sons of holy mother Church. Be it known to you that we have given and granted to the hospital of Jerusalem in free and perpetual alms the church of Chaureth and the land which was held by Roger Picot, with all the appurtenances belonging to the said church and land, for the soul of Gilbert fitz Richard and for the soul of Richard fitz Gilbert and for the soul of Earl Gilbert and for the souls of our fathers and mothers, relations and friends and of our sons, William, Roger and Gilbert, and for the salvation of our lord Earl Gilbert de Clare, and for the salvation of our own souls, since Jesus Christ our Lord makes us and them sharers in all the good things which were done in Jerusalem from the days of the apostles or are to be done until the end of time.[27] The witnesses of this gift are Baldwin fitz Gilbert, Maurice the sheriff, Ranulf de Chauria, Godfrey de Chauria, William his son, Robert the priest, William de Fanna, Hugh the reeve, Aylmar the reeve. This gift was made in AD 1151.

75. Grant by Robert the butler of the church of Thurlow, Suffolk, to the priory of Stoke by Clare, with the consent of his wife and family, 1138–c.1150[28] [From British Library, London, Cotton MS. Appendix xxi, fo. 102r; in Latin]

Be it known to men present and future that when Robert the butler became a monk at Stoke he gave to the monks of the same place the church of Thurlow with all its appurtenances and also land in the said vill which rendered 5s 4d every year, to possess by perpetual right, with the consent of Mabel his wife and his sons. Witnessed by Rainald the priest and others.

---

27 Alured and Sibyl made this grant for the benefit of their lords, living and dead, as well as of their own family. Gilbert fitz Richard (d. 1117) and Richard fitz Gilbert (d.1136) were both lords of the honour of Clare; Richard's eldest son, Earl Gilbert de Clare, was the first Clare earl of Hertford. The first Earl Gilbert referred to is Richard's younger brother, Gilbert Strongbow earl of Pembroke.

28 Stoke by Clare was an alien priory of the abbey of Bec. It was the honorial priory of the honour of Clare, and Robert was the butler of the lord of Clare.

76. Grant by Amicia countess of Hertford to Silvester the chaplain of one messuage in Sudbury, Suffolk, 1198–1223[29] [From British Library, London, Cotton MS. Appendix xxi, fo. 29; in Latin]

Men present and future should know that I Amicia countess of Clare, daughter of William earl of Gloucester, have given and granted and by this my present charter have confirmed to Silvester the chaplain in return for his service one messuage with its appurtenances in the vill of Sudbury lying between Sudbury bridge and the house of William Piteman towards the north, to hold and have of me and my heirs to him and to whomsoever he wishes to assign it, freely and quietly, well and in peace, by rendering two pence yearly at Michaelmas to the. house of St Sepulchre of Sudbury for all services, customs and exactions, and for all things. And I the aforesaid Amicia and my heirs will warrant the aforenamed messuage with all its appurtenances to the said Silvester and his assigns against all people. And so that this my gift and grant may remain firm and stable I have confirmed this present writing by the affixing of my seal. Witnessed by Walter de Lanlee, William de Bridebec and others.

77. Grant by Hawise countess of Gloucester of part of her *maritagium* at Pimperne, Dorset, to Nuneaton priory during her widowhood (she intended to be buried at Nuneaton); 1183–97[30] [From British Library, London, Additional Charter 47,517; in Latin]

Hawise countess of Gloucester greets all the sons of holy mother Church to whom the present writing shall come. You should all know that I have given and granted and by this my present charter have confirmed for the salvation of my soul, and that of William earl of Gloucester my lord and those of my children and all my ancestors and successors, to God and the church of St Mary, Nuneaton, and to the nuns of the order of Fontevrault serving God there, 100 shillings worth of land in my manor of Pimperne together with my body, namely the mill of 'Nutfort' with the multure[31] from the men of the

---

29 This land was part of the honour of Gloucester, and was assigned to Amicia when the bulk of the inheritance passed to her younger sister Isabella, who married John, youngest son of Henry II; see above, no. 6. It is not clear if Amicia made this grant before or after the death of her husband, Richard de Clare earl of Hertford, in 1217.

30 R. B. Patterson, ed., *Earldom of Gloucester Charters*, p. 73, suggests that the grant may have been made towards the end of her life; Hawise paid 300 marks for the seisin of Pimperne, Dorset, in 1194. Nuneaton priory was founded by her father Robert earl of Leicester, and belonged to the order of Fontevrault.

31 Multure was the payment made in return for the grinding of corn.

whole of the aforesaid manor of Pimperne, and with all its other appurtenances, to make up 50s worth but the brothers of St Lazarus are to have half a mark from the same mill every year. And [I have granted] the land of Hamelin son of Ralph Barnage with all its appurtenances for 20s, and the land that was held by Master Roger with all its appurtenances for 20s, and the land of Ralph Palmer and his service and whatever belongs to that land for 10s, and the land which was held by Edmund the reeve with all its appurtenances for half a mark. I wish also that they should have and hold the aforesaid lands and rents freely and quietly, peacefully and honourably, in pure and perpetual alms, as my lord William earl of Gloucester ever held them or my father who gave that manor to me in free marriage, in meadows and pastures, roads and paths, waters and ponds and mills, wood and plain, and in all places, with all liberties and free customs. Witnessed by William abbot of Keynsham, John abbot of St Augustine [Bristol], Henry abbot of Bindon, Robert prior of Wareham, Roger Waspail, William of St Leger, Richard son of Hugh, Henry de Karentuem, Stephen de Edmodesham, Alan de Baieus, Gregory the chaplain, Gilbert de Dena, Richard de Petraponte, Master Andrew, Richard the chamberlain, Roland the butler.

78. **Confirmation by Alice de Gant, wife of Roger de Mowbray, to Fountains abbey of property they were holding which was part of her dower, 1176** [From W. Dugdale, *Monasticon Anglicanum*, ed. J. Caley, H. Ellis and B. Bandinel, 6 vols, London, 1817-30, V, p. 310; in Latin]

Alice de Gant, wife of Roger de Mowbray, greets the archbishop of York and all sons of holy mother Church. You should know that of my good and free will and without any compulsion from any man I have granted and by this my charter have confirmed to God and to the monks of St Mary of Fountains in perpetual alms whatever they have of my dower, in wood and plain, meadows and waters, pastures, assarts and ploughlands, which belongs to the honour of Kirkby Malzeard and to Nidderdale and to Azerley and also the whole of Brimham, with all the appurtenances and easements, in wood and plain and in all other places and appurtenances, as quietly, freely, wholly and fully as is contained in the charters of my aforenamed lord Roger de Mowbray, and in the charters of my sons Nigel and Robert. And know that the church of Fountains received me in all its prayers and benefits, and it will do fuller service for me after my death in masses and psalters, as is accustomed to be done for a monk of the same house. I have made

this grant and confirmation to the aforesaid church after Easter
namely on 10 April 1176, in the year when the towns of Thirsk and
Kirkby Malzeard were destroyed.[32] And in testimony and remem-
brance the aforesaid monks gave me a gold ring.

79. Grant by the abbot of Ramsey to William Pecche, providing for his wife to continue to hold the land if she survived him, 1088 [From *Chronicon Abbatiae Rameseiensis*, ed. W. D. Macray, Rolls Series, London, 1886, p. 233; in Latin]

Herbert by grace of God abbot of the church of Ramsey to the sons of
the catholic faith. I wish you to know and to give testimony to the
truth that we are giving William Pecche fraternity with us and our
congregation, and we grant that under his custody he should have the
land of Over for his profit and ours, on the condition that he should
pay us now one mark of gold for our grant, and every year hereafter
six pounds of pennies for the use of the land, and after his death he
should have a burial-place in the cemetery of the church of St Benedict,
and 100s or a mark of gold should be given from his property to the
church for his soul. If the wife whom he has today, named Aelfwynn,
shall survive him, she shall hold the land for life on the same condition,
but after her death it shall revert to the abbot's hands, either mine or
my successor's, without any claim or obloquy, and as well stocked as
it shall be on the day when mortal illness seizes Aelfwynn. By our
testimony and that of the whole congregation, and of Rodulf and
Ausger chaplains of King William the younger, and of Alfgar the
reeve, Turkil the steward, and Folquin. Given at Ramsey AD 1088, in
the eleventh indiction, on 17 June.

80. Charter of Roger de Valognes to the priory of Binham, Norfolk, referring to the decision that inheritances should be divided among co-heiresses, c. 1145[33] [From British Library, London, Cotton MS. Claudius D XIII, fo. 49; in Latin]

Roger de Valognes greets all his friends and men, French and English.
It has been noted and promulgated among many people that before

---

32 This is a reference to events connected with the 1173–74 rebellion against Henry
   II in which Roger de Mowbray was involved.

33 The charter is discussed by Stenton, *First Century of English Feudalism*, pp. 38–41,
   260–1; Holt, 'The heiress and the alien', pp. 8–14; Milsom, 'Inheritance by women',
   pp. 77–9; Hudson, *Land, Law and Lordship*, pp. 111–13.

Walter de Valognes, my kinsman, became a monk he solemnly gave
Barney with the land of Thursford, with everything in it and
belonging to it, in wood and outside wood, for my and his salvation
and the salvation of all our family both living and dead, to the church
of the blessed Mary of Binham for ever, for the needs of the monks
who serve or will serve God there, with the consent and in the
presence of Rohaise his wife, and in the presence of the abbot of St
Albans and of clerks and knights. We know also that Agnes his
daughter, with the same Walter her father, placed that land on the
altar by means of a knife in the presence of all the bystanders.[34] Agnes
was Walter's heir to Barney according to the decision enacted[35] that
where there is no son the daughters divide the father's land by the
distaffs, and the elder by birth cannot take away half of the inheritance
from the younger except by force and wrongdoing. I myself, Roger de
Valognes, compelled by love of God and of the blessed and glorious
Virgin Mary mother of our Lord Jesus Christ, have therefore also
granted that this gift should be made at the request and prayers of
Walter himself, and I grant and confirm it for the service of one-third
of a knight only, for the soul of my father who first gave Barney to the
church of Binham ordering Walter that this should be done, and for
the soul of my mother, and for my own soul, and for the salvation of
my wife Agnes, and of my sons who are in agreement with me over
this and join in the grant, and for the common salvation of all our
family both living and dead, and by the admonition and recommenda-
tion of many wise men, but especially by the exhortation, prayers and
advice of Lord Theobald archbishop of Canterbury and primate of all
England who showed me by the reason and truth of his arguments
that it is very just for a noble and honourable man who has a fee of six
knights to bestow not only the land of one-third of a knight but also
his whole fee or more on God and holy Church for the salvation of
himself and his family, adding also that, if his heir tries to take away
the alms which are placed between the father and paradise like a bridge
which the father can cross, he also, as much as in him lies, disinherits
his father from the kingdom of heaven, and therefore the heir should
not obtain the rest of his inheritance by right, since he shows that he
is no son when he has killed his father. The archbishop declared these
things to us with diligent argument, and on account of this Walter's
gift of Barney with all its appurtenances is to remain firm by perpetual

34 The seisin or possession of the land was transferred visually by means of the knife.
35 The charter describes this in the Latin as 'statutum decretum'. The distaffs or
   spindles referred to subsequently are symbolic of female inheritance.

right in the possession of the church of the blessed Mary of Binham as freely, well and honourably as Walter held it in the time of my father or my time. May anyone who wishes to take these alms away from the church of Binham have his place in the depths of hell with Dathan and Abiron and Judas the betrayer, but may the soul of him who confirms, supports and maintains this be among the elect and enjoy eternal life. Amen. Witnessed by Agnes de Valognes, Fulk de Munpunzun, Geoffrey the priest of Hertingfordbury, Ralph son of Robert, Ralph son of Turgis, Gilbert son of William de Roinges, Godfrey the chaplain, Robert de Valognes, Winemar, Geoffrey de Mannaville, Simon son of William, Robert son of Ralph.

81. A division among co-heiresses which may date back to the reign of Henry I, 1199–1216 [From G. Rose and W. Illingworth, eds, *Placitorum in Domo Capitulari Westmonasteriensi Asservatorum Abbreviatio*, Record Commission, London, 1811, pp. 79–80; in Latin]

Robert son of Hamo seeks against Simon de Kime whom Walter de Ribof and Isabella his wife call to warranty and who warranted him the fee of half a knight with appurtenances in Bilborough as his right and as that whereof Ivicia his grandmother was seised as of fee and right in the time of King Henry, grandfather of King Henry, father of the lord king, and from her the right to that land descended to her son Robert, and from Robert to Ralph his brother, Robert's father. Simon says that Ivicia through whom he claims had an elder sister named Emma who had a son called Robert, and Robert had a son, Ivo de Heriz, who is still alive, and he does not wish to answer without him. Robert recognised that Ivicia had an elder sister named Emma, but when their inheritance was partitioned Gonalston and Kelmarsh were assigned to Emma's pourparty, and Emma's heirs were seised of them. He also says that Ivicia was assigned 'Molintun' and Bilborough in her pourparty, to which the aforesaid fee of half a knight belongs, so that Ivicia was seised of it as of her pourparty. It was decided that Simon should reply. Simon therefore came and proffered the charter of Henry the king's father which stated that he granted and confirmed to Simon son of William, grandfather of Simon de Kime, all the tenements which he held of him in chief, namely Bilborough which he holds of him in chief. And Simon offers him thirty marks to warrant that land to him. And Robert says that he himself claims to hold that land of the lord king and he offers the lord king twenty marks that he will let the action proceed according to the custom of the realm. The lord king receives the twenty marks.

82. Richard I's confirmation of the division of the inheritance of William de Say, 1198[36] [From Public Record Office, London, DL10/ 47; in Latin]

Richard by the grace of God king of England, duke of Normandy and Aquitaine, and count of Anjou, greets the archbishops, bishops, abbots, earls, barons, justices, sheriffs, and all his bailiffs and faithful men. You should know that we have granted and confirmed by our present charter the agreement written below made with the assent and by the will of the lord king H[enry] our father and in his presence, between Beatrice de Say and Matilda her sister, daughters of William de Say, concerning the partition of their whole inheritance, as the chirograph made between them testifies. Namely that 'Bruninton' with its appurtenances should remain for ever in the hands of Matilda the younger and her heirs, together with the service of William de Reigny and the service of Ralph son of Bernard. From the first conquest or escheat of their inheritance Matilda ought to have ten librates of land to remain to her and her heirs by hereditary right. By this aforesaid agreement the rest of all their inheritance has been given up by Matilda and her heirs, and she has quitclaimed everything to her elder sister Beatrice and her heirs – demesnes, services, homages, and tenements – and all right and hereditary claims which their father or their other predecessors held at any time without any reservation. Wherefore we wish and strictly order that the above agreement be firmly and constantly observed, as when, after their marriage, the agreement between them and their husbands, Geoffrey fitz Peter husband of Beatrice, and William de Buckland husband of Matilda was recorded and granted in the court of the lord king H[enry] our father both by the husbands and by the wives, and pledged to be kept faithfully without any claim which they or their heirs could make in the future, saving to Beatrice her right as the elder daughter, according to what is contained in the chirograph made between them, and as the charter of the lord king H[enry] our father testifies. Witnessed by S[avaric] bishop of Bath, G[eoffrey] [arch]bishop of York, Master Roger Richemund, Master Mauger of York, Simon de Camera archdeacon of Wells, J[ohn] count of Mortain our brother, the earl of Arundel, W[illiam] Longespee earl

36 This was an unequal partition, probably influenced by the fact that the elder daughter was married to the Geoffrey fitz Peter who was justiciar between 1198 and 1213, and they received the bulk of the inheritance. The claim by women of the de Say family to the Mandeville inheritance and the political considerations involved are discussed by R. V. Turner, 'The Mandeville inheritance, 1189-1236: its legal, political and social context', *Haskins Society Journal*, I, 1989, pp. 147-72.

of Salisbury, William Marshal, Hugh Bard', William fitz Ralph
seneschal of Normandy, John de Preaux, Peter his brother, Robert de
Harecort, Robert de Tresgoz, Baldwin our chaplain. Given by the
hand of E[ustace] bishop of Ely our chancellor at Chateau Gaillard at
Andeli, 15 June, in the ninth year of our reign.[37]

83. Division among co-heiresses in the Peverel and Pecche families in the twelfth and thirteenth centuries [From *Liber Memorandorum Ecclesie de Bernewelle*, ed. J. W. Clark, Cambridge, 1907, pp. 47–8; in Latin]

After the death of William Peverel [*c.* 1130–33], the whole barony of
Pain Peverel was divided among four sisters. The eldest was called
Matilda de Dovre [d. 1185], and she died without an heir of her body.
And so the inheritance devolved on three sisters and Matilda's share
was divided among them. One was the wife of Hamo Pecche senior [d.
1178–85] and was called Alice. She had sons and daughters. Hamo's
eldest son was called Gilbert Pecche I [d. 1212], and the second was
called Geoffrey Pecche [d. 1188]. Geoffrey gave the canons the church
of Harston for their clothing. Gilbert had a son Hamo Pecche [d.
1241] who married a wife named Eva, born overseas, who bore him
five sons and daughters. The eldest, Gilbert Pecche [d. 1291], was our
last patron of that line. The second sister was called Rose, and she had
a daughter, Albreda de Harecurt, who was the mother of Geoffrey
Trussebut, and Roger, William, and Richard Trussebut. After all these
people had died without an heir of their bodies, three sisters remained,
namely Rose, Hilary and Agatha. Rose's son, Robert de Ros the elder,
had a son William de Ros, and these three, namely William, Hilary and
Agatha are heirs in part. The third sister was called Ascelina de
Waterville, and she had two daughters, Ascelina de Waterville [d.
1220] and Matilda de Diva. Ascelina's son was Roger de Torpel [d.
1225] and Matilda's Hugh de Diva.

84. Partition among co-heiresses, 1206 [From T. D. Hardy, ed., *Rotuli de Oblatis*, p. 353; in Latin]

William de Mulum and Avicia his wife give twenty marks to have their
reasonable share which appertains to Avicia of the land that was held
by Richard son of Roger, her father, and Margaret her mother and

---

37 The place of issue is given as 'Bellum Castrum de Rupe Andel'.

which is in the lord king's hands. The sheriff of Lancaster is ordered to take security and let them have full seisin. A similar order was made to the sheriff of Leicester to let them have full seisin of this land in his bailiwick.

Thomas de Bothun and Amur' his wife give forty marks to have their reasonable share which appertains to Amur' of the land that was held by Richard son of Roger, her father, and Margaret Banastre, her mother, and which is in the lord king's hand. The sheriff of Lancaster is ordered to take security for those forty marks, and to let them have full seisin of the aforesaid land. A similar order was made to the sheriff of Leicester to let them have full seisin of this land in his bailiwick.

85. Grant of her inheritance to Margaret de Chesney, 1214[38] [From T. D. Hardy, ed., *Rotuli Chartarum in Turri Londinensi asservati, 1199–1216*, Record Commission, London, 1837, p. 203; in Latin]

John by the grace of God etc. Know that we have granted to Margaret who was the wife of Robert son of Roger all her inheritance of which her husband, Robert son of Roger, was seised on the day he died, on condition that she should answer in court if anyone wishes to make any claim against her. We have also granted to the same Margaret that she should have her right in our court concerning her inheritance which her father had on the day he died, and all the lands which her husbands gave to others, and that she should not be distrained to marry; if however she should wish to marry this should be with our consent. Moreover we have granted to the same Margaret that she should have peace all the days of her life from the debts of the Jews which her father owed in his lifetime, and that she should have her dower according to the custom of our realm of England, but the castle of Norwich is to be kept in our hands as long as it pleases us. Wherefore we wish and firmly order that the said Margaret should have and hold all her said inheritance with all its appurtenances and that she should not be distrained to marry, and that she should have peace all the days of her life from the debts of the Jews which her father owed in his lifetime as aforesaid. Witnessed by William Marshal earl

---

38 According to the Pipe Roll she owed £1,000 for this grant, and the Pipe Roll summary of the charter adds that she was to have her dower according to the custom of the realm of England if her son was not willing to give it to her; P. M. Barnes, ed., *The Great Roll of the Pipe for 16 John, Michaelmas 1214*, Pipe Roll Society, new series, XXXV, 1959, p. 175. Holt, *Magna Carta*, pp. 199–200 comments that the size of the sum due from Margaret was due to the circumstances after the king's defeat in France in 1214.

of Pembroke, R[anulf] earl of Chester, W[illiam] earl Warenne, W[illiam] earl of Arundel, W[illiam] earl Ferrers, S[aer] earl of Winchester, Robert Fitzwalter, William de Albini. Given by the hand of Master Richard Marsh our chancellor at the New Temple London, 22 December, in the sixteenth year of our reign.

86. Homage performed by Ela, the widowed countess of Salisbury, for her inheritance, 1226 [From T. D. Hardy, ed., *Rotuli Litterarum Clausarum in Turri Londinensi asservati 1204–27*, 2 vols, Record Commission, London, 1833–44, II, p. 103; in Latin]

The king greets the sheriff of Dorset. You should know that we have taken the homage of our beloved Ela countess of Salisbury for the lands in your bailiwick which belong to her by inheritance from her father and which you took into our hands on account of the death of our beloved uncle and faithful man William earl of Salisbury, formerly her husband.[39] So we order you to let the countess have full seisin of all the aforesaid lands, reserving to the executors of the earl's will the goods he had in those lands in order to carry out his will. Witnessed by the king at Westminster on 19 March.

The same orders were sent to the sheriffs of Somerset, Wiltshire, Berkshire and Surrey.

87. Partition of the lands of Richard Sergeaux and Philippa his wife among their four daughters, 1400 [From Public Record Office, London, C60/206, m. 22; in Latin]

The king greets his escheator in Oxfordshire. We have recently taken the homage and fealty of William Marny knight who married Elizabeth, one of the sisters and heirs of the late Richard, son of Richard Sergeaux and his wife Philippa, and one of Philippa's daughters and heirs, for Elizabeth's pourparty both from all the lands and tenements held in chief on the day of his death by her father Richard of the former king Richard II, and which came into that king's hands and then into ours by reason of Richard's death and the death of his son Richard while a minor and in the former king's custody, and from all the lands and tenements which Philippa held of us in chief on

---

39 On her father's death in 1196, Richard I arranged for Ela, heiress to the earldom of Salisbury and then aged about six, to marry his illegitimate brother William Longespee who thus became earl of Salisbury by right of his wife. He died on 7 March 1226.

the day she died. According to the law and custom of our realm of
England, because of the offspring born to William and Elizabeth, we
have delivered that pourparty with its appurtenances to William and
Elizabeth. By our writ we have ordered you to take security from
William and Elizabeth for their reasonable relief to be paid to us at our
exchequer, and to make a lawful partition into four equal parts of all
the lands and tenements with appurtenances of which Richard the
father and Philippa were seised in their demesne as of fee or in entailed
fee, and of those lands and tenements which Philippa held in dower or
for the term of her life, of the inheritance of the said Elizabeth; and of
the inheritance of Philippa, another of the daughters and heirs of the
said Philippa and sister and heir of Richard the son, who is of full age
and married to Robert Passele; and of the inheritance of Alice, third of
the daughters and heirs of the said Philippa and third sister and heir
of Richard the son, whom Guy de Seyntaubyn married; and also of the
inheritance of Joan, fourth of the daughters and heirs of the said
Philippa and fourth sister and heir of Richard the son, who is under
age. The partition is to be made of the lands in your bailiwick·
according to the survey which has been made, or according to another
if it should be necessary to make it again, in the presence of William
and Robert, and of the nearest friends of Alice and Joan, who are to be
given notice by you, or in the presence of their attorneys, if they wish
to be present. You are to let William and Elizabeth have full seisin of
Elizabeth's pourparty of all the lands and tenements in your bailiwick
which by the death of her father Richard and Philippa his wife and by
the minority and death of Richard the son while in the former king's
custody came into the hands of the former king and then into ours,
according to law and custom, saving the right of anyone else. The
pourparties of Philippa, wife of Robert, and of Alice and Joan are to be
kept in our hands according to law and custom until we shall order
otherwise, provided always that any of the aforesaid heirs and
parceners should have her pourparty of the said lands and tenements
held of us in chief and be our tenant, as is fully apparent by inspection
of our chancery rolls. We for one mark paid to us in our hanaper have
postponed until the next quindene of St Hilary Robert's homage due
to us for the pourparty of Philippa his wife by reason of the offspring
born to Robert and Philippa, and we have handed over to Robert and
his wife all Philippa's pourparty with appurtenances. So we order you
to take Robert's fealty due to us according to the form of a certain
schedule which is enclosed, and to take security from Robert and
Philippa his wife for their reasonable relief to be paid to us at our

exchequer, and let Robert and Philippa have full seisin of Philippa's pourparty with its appurtenances in your bailiwick without delay, saving the right of anyone else. Witnessed by the king at Westminster on 6 November.

A similar order was sent to the escheator of Cornwall concerning Robert and Philippa.

88. Action for dower in the king's court, 1209 [From G. Rose and W. Illingworth, eds, *Placitorum Abbreviatio*, p. 63; in Latin]

Matilda who was the wife of Alured de Oirri seeks half a virgate of land with appurtenances in Hardwick against the prior of St Neots as her dower of the gift of her husband. The prior says that her husband gave that half virgate of land to his church, and he produces his charter. And William de Augo his son ought to warrant this.

89. Extracts from the action for dower in the king's court by Alice, widow of Ralph son of Hugh, 1199, showing the right to dower in alienated land; she brought actions against her son and eleven other men. [From F. Palgrave, ed., *Rotuli Curiae Regis*, Record Commission, London, 1835, 2 vols, I, pp. 406–9; in Latin]

Alice, who was wife of Ralph son of Hugh, seeks her reasonable dower against Hugh her son which pertains to her from the free tenement of Ralph, sometime her husband, in Camps and Horseheath. Hugh comes and agrees to give her a reasonable share of the tenement he holds.

Similarly, Alice seeks against Adam son of Gerard one-third of nine acres with appurtenances in Horseheath, and Adam comes and says that Gerard his father held them of Ralph son of Hugh her husband and he was his man. He says that he is under age and seeks verification of this, and she says that his father put himself into that land after she was married, and she places herself on a jury of the neighbourhood. Because Hugh recognised his father's charter and gift, let her have seisin of the nine acres as her one-third share, and let him make an exchange.

Alice seeks against Robert Walensis one-third of one virgate of land with appurtenances as her dower, and Robert comes and says that he has Ralph's charter and is Hugh's man. Hugh was summoned to warrant him, and he came and recognised that he ought to warrant that land. Let her have one-third.

90. Legal action in the royal court taken by Roger Mortimer against his mother, 1292[40] **[From Public Record Office, London, Just 1/740, m. 48d; in Latin]**

Matilda Mortimer was summoned to answer Roger Mortimer in the plea that she should return to him a charter which she detains from him unjustly. He complains that on Monday after the feast of St George in the forty-seventh year of the reign of King Henry [1263], father of the present lord king, at Wigmore, he handed over to Matilda a charter of feoffment, which Roger Mortimer, Roger's father, had issued to Roger concerning the manor of Presteigne, to be kept and handed back when required, and Matilda ever afterwards detained the charter, and refuses to give it back to him. Wherefore he says that he has suffered damage and losses to the value of £500, and on this he produces his suit.

Matilda comes and defends the force and injury etc. She says that there was a bargain between Roger the father and Roger the son, namely that Roger the father should give the aforesaid manor to Roger the son to hold until Roger the father should provide 100 librates of land elsewhere for Roger the son. She says furthermore that Roger the father had drawn up a charter of feoffment of the aforesaid manor for Roger the son, but never delivered it to Roger, but always kept it by him during his life. She says also that Roger the father afterwards assigned to Roger the son 200 marks worth of land elsewhere, namely in Marden and 'Wynfryton', of which Roger the son is now in seisin. Therefore she says that Roger never had the aforesaid charter, so he could neither hand it over to her, nor did he hand it over to her to keep. On this she puts herself on the country.[41]

Roger says that he handed over the charter to Matilda, as said above, and that after the death of Roger Mortimer, formerly her husband, she had the charter in her custody. He asks for an inquiry by jury that this is so. Matilda makes the same request. So the sheriff was ordered to arrange for twelve men to appear before the justices in eyre at Lichfield in Staffordshire on the octave of St Hilary [20 January].

40 I would like to thank Dr Paul Brand for drawing my attention to this case. Other accounts of the litigation are found in British Library, London, Additional MS. 31,826, fo. 215v, and A. V. Horwood, ed., *Year Books 20-21 Edward I*, Rolls Series, London, 1866, pp. 188-91. Matilda's husband, Roger Mortimer of Wigmore, died in 1282; the Roger in this case was her third son, known as Roger Mortimer of Chirk which he was granted by Edward I in 1282.

41 Matilda was asking for the issue to be decided by a jury of local men.

91. Claim to hold by curtesy of England, 1200–01 [From G. Rose and W. Illingworth, eds, *Placitorum Abbreviatio*, p. 30; in Latin]

William son of Walter seeks against Herbert son of Alan one hide of land with appurtenances in 'Thuotekelawe' by writ of the assize of mort d'ancestor on behalf of Richolda his mother and one hide of land with appurtenances held by her in Whittingslow. Herbert calls to warranty Walter, William's father, who came and said that he married Richolda, William's mother, by whom he had children, namely William and several other sons and a daughter named Matilda whom he gave in marriage to Herbert with the aforesaid land. William countered by saying that his father was not permitted to give his mother's inheritance with his daughter. Walter countered by saying that he married Richolda with her *maritagium* and she died, and by the custom of England he ought to hold her inheritance for the whole of his life and he seeks the judgment of the court.

92. Order for the allocation of dower to Cecily de Morley, 1379[42] [From Public Record Office, London, C54/218, m. 4; in Latin]

The king greets his beloved William Berard, escheator in Norfolk and Suffolk. We have taken an oath from our beloved Cecily, who was the wife of the late William de Morley knight, tenant-in-chief, that she will not marry without our licence, and we order you to assign to her her reasonable dower of all the lands and tenements in your bailiwick which were held by William, formerly her husband, on the day he died, and which by reason of William's death were taken into our hands according to the law and custom of our realm of England, according to the survey which has been made, or according to another to be made again if necessary, and in the presence of Thomas de Morley knight, William's son and heir, or his attorney, if they wish to be present, who are to be given notice by you. After you have made the assignment, you are to send it under your seal to us in our chancery without delay, so that we can have it enrolled on our chancery roll, as is customary. Witnessed by the king at Westminster on 1 June.[43]

---

42 A similar procedure for the allocation of dower was followed by lords in the fourteenth century; after an inquisition *post mortem* had been taken, dower was allocated to the widow, and the heir admitted to the fee if he was of age. The widow had to give security that she would not remarry without licence. E.g Public Record Office, London, SC2/212/39, m. 7d, 8, 14d.

43 A similar writ was sent on the same day to Roger Keterich, escheator of Essex and Hertfordshire.

93. The use of the entail to exclude female inheritance; arrangements made by Thomas de Beauchamp earl of Warwick and his eldest son Guy, 1344[44] [From Public Record Office, London, CP25/1/287/41, no. 334; in Latin]

This is the final concord made in the lord king's court at Westminster in the octaves of Holy Trinity, in the eighteenth year of the reign of Edward III king of England and the fifth year of his reign as king of France, in the presence of John de Stonor, William de Shareshull, Roger Hillary, Richard de Kelleshull and Richard de Willoughby, justices, and others of the lord king's faithful men who were then present there, between Thomas de Beauchamp earl of Warwick and Guy his son, plaintiffs, and John de Melbourn and Roger de Ledebury, clerks, deforciants, concerning the castle of Warwick with its appurtenances, and the manors of Warwick, Brailes, Claverdon, Tanworth, Sutton Coldfield, Berkswell and Lighthorne with their appurtenances in Warwickshire, and of Barnard Castle with appurtenances and the manor of Gainford with appurtenances in Northumberland, and of Castle Maud with appurtenances and the manor of Elfael with appurtenances in Herefordshire, and of the manor of Flamstead with appurtenances in Hertfordshire, and of the manor of Kirtling with appurtenances in Cambridgeshire, and of the manor of Walthamstow with appurtenances in Essex, and of the manor of Cherhill with appurtenances in Wiltshire, concerning all of which a plea of covenant was brought in the same court. According to the agreement, the earl acknowledged the said castles and manors to be the right of John and Roger as those which John and Roger have of the earl's gift. In return for this acknowledgement, fine and agreement, John and Roger have granted to the earl and Guy the aforesaid castles and manors with appurtenances and have given them to them in the same court to have and to hold to the earl and Guy and the male heirs begotten of Guy's body of the lord king and his heirs by the services due from the said castles and manors for ever. If it should happen that Guy should die without begetting a male heir, then after the deaths of Guy and the earl the said castles and manors with their appurtenances shall remain to Thomas, Guy's brother, and the male heirs begotten by him to hold of the lord king and his heirs by the services due from the aforesaid

---

44 This is one of a series of documents creating entails on the estates of the earldom of Warwick. They are discussed by G. A. Holmes, *Estates of the Higher Nobility in Fourteenth-Century England*, Cambridge, 1957, pp. 48-9. Guy died in 1361, predeceasing his father.

castles and manors for ever. If it should happen that Thomas should
die without begetting a male heir, then after Thomas's death the said
castles and manors with their appurtenances shall remain wholly to
Reynbrun, Thomas's brother, and the male heirs begotten by him to
hold of the lord king and his heirs by the services due from the said
castles and manors for ever. If it should happen that Reynbrun should
die without begetting a male heir, then after Reynbrun's death the
aforesaid castles and manors with their appurtenances shall remain
wholly to the male heirs begotten by the earl and to the male heirs
whom they beget to hold of the lord king and his heirs by the services
due from the aforesaid castles and manors for ever. If the male heirs
begotten by the earl should die without begetting male heirs, after
their deaths the said castles and manors shall wholly remain to John
de Beauchamp, the earl's brother, and the male heirs begotten by him,
to hold of the lord king and his heirs by the services due from the said
castles and manors for ever. If it should happen that the same John de
Beauchamp should die without begetting a male heir, then after John's
death the aforesaid castles and manors shall wholly remain to the right
heirs of the earl to hold of the lord king and his heirs by the services
due from the said castles and manors for ever. This agreement was
made by order of the lord king.

94. Arrangements for the inheritance of Katherine Wingfield to be
restored to her eldest son, Michael de la Pole, earl of Suffolk, after the
death of his father, 1389 (his father had forfeited the lands after being
appealed in the Merciless Parliament of 1388) [From Public Record
Office, London, C66/329, m. 29d; in Latin]

The king greets his beloved and faithful men, Robert Carbonnell
knight, George Felbrigg knight, Hugh Fastolf, Robert Hotot and
Robert Asshefeld. Our beloved and faithful Michael de la Pole, son and
heir of Michael de la Pole late earl of Suffolk, has petitioned us alleging
that his father, the late earl, on 1 October in the tenth year of our reign
[1386] and for a long time before was seised for life after the death of
Katherine his wife and Michael's mother, whose son and heir he is,
according to the law of England,[45] of the manors of Wingfield,
Stradbroke, Syleham, Fressingfield, Sternfield, and Saxmundham, and
of the manor of Wingfield called 'Oldhall', with their appurtenances,
and of the advowsons of the churches of Stradbroke and Saxmundham,

45 This is a reference to tenure by curtesy of England.

and of the chantry of Wingfield, and of 700 acres of arable land, twenty acres of meadow, 100 acres of pasture, twenty acres of wood, 100 acres of heath, 100 acres of marsh, and 100s rent with appurtenances in Wingfield, Syleham, Easham, Fressingfield, Weybread, Mendham, Hoxne, Sternfield, Saxmundham, Benhall, Farnham, Rendham, Freston, and Snape with appurtenances in Suffolk, and of the manor of Nether Hall of Saxlingham with appurtenances, and of the advowson of the church of Saxlingham Thorp, and of two messuages, 400 acres of arable land, ten acres of meadow, twenty acres of pasture, and 42s rent with appurtenances in Saxlingham and Newton Flotman, Brockdish and Harleston with appurtenances in Norfolk of Katherine's inheritance. The late earl had his title to those lands until the above manors, lands, tenements and rents, with appurtenances, and the aforesaid advowsons were taken into our hands by virtue and authority of the judgment against him in our parliament held at Westminster held on the morrow of the Purification of the Blessed Virgin Mary in the eleventh year of our reign [3 February 1388]. The late earl died on Sunday 5 September last, as we have heard. Michael de la Pole has entreated that we should be willing graciously to order that all the aforesaid manors, lands, tenements and rents, with appurtenances, together with the issues and profits received and arising since his father's death, and also the above advowsons should be delivered to Michael as his right and inheritance. Wishing to do what is just and right, and wanting to be more fully informed, we have appointed you (or four, three or two of you) to enquire by means of sworn statements of honest and lawful men of the said counties, from whom the truth of the matter may be better known, whether the late earl on 1 October and earlier was seised in the aforesaid way of all these manors, lands, tenements and rents, with appurtenances, and of the advowsons, and continued to have his title until the same manors, lands, tenements and rents, with appurtenances, and the advowsons were taken into our hands, or not; if so, then of whom these manors, lands, tenements and rents, with appurtenances, and the advowsons of churches are held, and by what service, and how much the said manors, lands and tenements, with their appurtenances, and the advowsons are worth yearly altogether in addition to the aforesaid rent, and on what day the late earl died, and whether Michael, Michael's son, is Katherine's next heir, and how old he is; so as to tell the truth more fully on each and every of the above items and of other articles and circumstances concerning them by whatever right. So we order you to attend diligently to all this at appointed days and in appointed places and carry it out in the above form. The inquisitions, which are to be made clearly and openly, you are to send to our chancery without delay under your seals and the seals of those by whom they were made, and we have sent our writ to the sheriff of the said counties that he may summon the jurors before you on set dates and places. Witnessed by the king at Westminster on 7 November.

95. The effects of the joint enfeoffment of Andrew and Alice de Bures, 1392 (Andrew died in 1360, but Alice held the lands for life and thus enriched her second husband) [From Public Record Office, London, C60/196, m. 29; in Latin]

The king greets his beloved John Wynter, escheator in Suffolk. We have learned from the inquiry that you carried out that the late Alice, wife of John de Sutton knight, was jointly enfeoffed with the late Andrew de Bures knight, formerly her husband, and therefore held for life the manor of Acton in the aforesaid county of us in chief as of the honour of Hatfield Peverel by the service of two-thirds of a knight's fee, of the gift and grant of Edmund le Botiller to Andrew and Alice and Andrew's heirs; and a manor with appurtenances in Raydon together with the advowson of the church there which was formerly held by Robert de Reydon knight; and also a manor in Wherstead with appurtenances in the same county held of lords other than us, of the gift and grant of Michael de Poynings and Thomas le Boteler to Andrew and Alice and the heirs of their bodies by a fine levied in the court of Lord E[dward], formerly king of England and our grandfather. We have found that Alice de Brian, daughter of Robert de Bures knight, Andrew's son, is Andrew's kinswoman and next heir, and is of full age. In return for half a mark paid in our hanaper we have postponed Alice de Brian's homage and fealty due to us until the quindene of Easter next. So we order you to take security from Alice de Brian for her reasonable relief to be paid to us at our exchequer, and to let her have full seisin without delay of the aforesaid manors with appurtenances and of the above advowson in your bailiwick which were taken into our hands because of the death of Alice, wife of John [Sutton], saving the right of anyone else. Witnessed by the king at Oxford on 22 September.[46]

---

46 A similar order was sent to Thomas Coggeshale, escheator of Essex, concerning lands at Middleton and Bulmer.

96. The use of feoffees by the Morley family to deal with the tenure of lands within the family, 1380 (this document should be compared with no. 92) [From Public Record Office, London, C66/307, m. 13; in Latin]

The king greets all those to whom these letters will come. You should know that Cecily, who was the wife of William de Morley knight, held of us in chief one-third of the manor of Swanton Morley with appurtenances as her dower after the death of her late husband William, of the inheritance of Thomas de Morley, William's son and heir, and she surrendered the title which she had in the aforesaid land to Thomas. Afterwards Thomas gave and granted both the one-third with appurtenances, on the pretext of the above surrender, and the rest of the two-thirds of the aforesaid manor, with appurtenances, and the advowson of the church of that manor which he similarly held of us in chief, to Roger de Wylesham knight, William Hastyng of Aylsham, Roger de Wolfreston, and John Muriell, parson of the church of Wortham, to have and to hold to them and their heirs for ever. Both the aforesaid Thomas, and the said Roger, William Hastyng, Roger and John entered the one-third and the whole of the above manor, with appurtenances, and the said advowson successively, but our licence for this had not been obtained. Of our special grace, and in return for forty marks paid to us by Thomas, we have pardoned the trespasses done, and have granted for us and our heirs, as far as in us lies, to the same Roger, William Hastyng, Roger and John that they should have and hold the aforesaid manor, with appurtenances, and the advowson to them and their heirs of us and our heirs by the services due and accustomed for ever. We have also granted to the said Roger, William Hastyng, Roger and John that they can enfeoff the aforesaid Thomas and Elizabeth his wife of the said manor with appurtenances and the advowson, to have and to hold to Thomas and Elizabeth and the heirs of their bodies of us and our heirs by the aforesaid services for ever. So that if Thomas and Elizabeth should die without an heir of their bodies, the manor with appurtenances and the advowson should remain to the right heirs of Thomas to hold of us and our heirs by the aforesaid services for ever. Similarly we have given special licence to Thomas and Elizabeth that they can receive the manor and appurtenances and the advowson from Roger, William Hastyng, Roger and John, and hold them to the same Thomas and Elizabeth and the heirs of their bodies of us and our heirs by the aforesaid services for ever. So that if Thomas and Elizabeth should die without an heir of their bodies, that manor with appurtenances and that advowson should remain to the right heirs of Thomas to hold of us and our heirs by the aforesaid services for ever, as has been said above. We do not wish that the aforesaid Cecily, Thomas and Elizabeth or their heirs, or the aforesaid Roger, William Hastyng, Roger and John or their heirs should be interfered with, molested or in any way troubled by reason of the above matters by us or our heirs or by our justices, escheators, sheriffs or other of our bailiffs or officials. In testimony of this we have had these our letters patent drawn up. Witnessed by the king at Westminster on 10 June.

97. The use of feoffees which ultimately allowed Joan de Mohun to grant her husband's inheritance to Elizabeth Luttrell, 1374[47] [From Public Record Office, London, C66/373, m. 27]

Edward, by grace of God king of England and France and lord of Ireland, greets all to whom the present letters will come. You should know that we recently by our letters patent granted and gave licence for us and our heirs, as far as in us lies, to John de Mohun of Dunster knight and Joan his wife that they could enfeoff Simon bishop of London, Richard earl of Arundel, Aubrey de Vere knight and John de Burghersh knight of the castle of Dunster and the manors of Minehead and Kilton with appurtenances which are held of us in chief, to have and to hold to them and their heirs of us and our heirs by the services due and accustomed for ever. By other letters patent we granted and gave licence for us and our heirs to the same bishop, earl, Aubrey and John de Burghersh that they could give and grant the same castles and manors with appurtenances to any lay persons that Joan wished to nominate or assign them to. Afterwards the same earl remitted, relaxed and quitclaimed all the right and claim that he had in the aforesaid castle and manors by reason of the said enfeoffment to the bishop, Aubrey and John de Burghersh without our licence. Of our special grace and for half a mark that the bishop, Aubrey and John de Burghersh have paid to us we have pardoned the earl's trespass. We do not wish that the said bishop, Aubrey and John de Burghersh or those

47 The background to Joan de Mohun's actions and the other documents which were drawn up are discussed by H. C. Maxwell Lyte, *A History of Dunster*, 2 vols, London, 1909, I, pp. 49-53. Joan de Mohun was the daughter of Bartholomew de Burghersh. Soon after her husband's death in 1375, the feoffees conveyed the lands to her for life, with remainder to Elizabeth Luttrell, thus bypassing any rights of her three daughters to the estates; however, these inherited part of the Mohun property from their father. It is not known why the earl of Arundel ceased to be a feoffee.

to be enfeoffed by them of the aforesaid castle and manors, or their heirs should be interfered with, molested in any way or troubled by reason of that trespass by us or our heirs, our justices, escheators, sheriffs or other of our bailiffs or officials. In testimony of this, we have had these our letters patent drawn up. Witnessed by the king at Westminster on 12 November in the forty-eighth year of his reign in England and the thirty-fifth year of his reign in France.

98. Final concord by which Joan de Mohun granted Dunster and other lands to Elizabeth Luttrell after her death, 1376 (John de Mohun died in 1375; Elizabeth Luttrell paid 5,000 marks for the grant)[48] [From Public Record Office, London, CP25/1/200/27, no. 90; in Latin]

This is the final concord made in the lord king's court at Westminster in the octaves of St Martin in the fiftieth year of the reign of Edward III as king of England and the thirty-seventh year of his reign as king of France, in the presence of Robert Bealknap, William de Skipwyth, William de Wichyngham, Roger de Kirketon and Roger de Fulthorp, justices, and other faithful men of the lord king then present there, between Joan, who was the wife of John de Mohun of Dunster, plaintiff, and Simon archbishop of Canterbury, formerly bishop of London, Aubrey de Vere knight, and John de Burghersh knight, deforciants, concerning the castle of Dunster and the manors of Kilton, Minehead and Carhampton and the hundred of Carhampton, with appurtenances, for which there was a plea of covenant brought between them in the same court. According to the agreement, the archbishop, Aubrey and John granted the castle, manors and hundred with appurtenances to Joan and surrendered them to her in the same court, to have and to hold to Joan of the lord king and his heirs by the services due and accustomed for Joan's whole life. After Joan's death the castle, manors and hundred with appurtenances are wholly to remain to Elizabeth Luttrell and John Wermyngton and Elizabeth's heirs, to hold of the lord king and his heirs by the services due and accustomed for ever. In return for this grant, surrender, fine and agreement, Joan gave the archbishop, Aubrey and John de Burghersh £1,000 sterling. This agreement was made by order of the lord king.

48 *Ibid.*, p. 53.

99. Grant by Ela countess of Salisbury of land from her inheritance to her son Nicholas Longespee, 1226-36[49] [From British Library, London, Harley Charter 53 B12; in Latin]

Present and future men should know that I, Ela countess of Salisbury in my widowhood and liege power have given and granted and by this my charter have confirmed to Nicholas Longespee my son in return for his homage and service the manor of Edgware with all its appurtenances, and whatever can fall into my hands in the vill of Cowlinge, with all appurtenances, to hold and to have of me and my heirs to him and the heirs born to him and his wedded wife well and in peace, freely and quietly, by rendering one sparrowhawk a year to me and my heirs at the feast of St Peter which is called *ad vincula* [1 August] for all service and secular demand pertaining to me or to my heirs, saving the service of the lord king. If however the aforesaid Nicholas Longespee dies without an heir born to his wife, the manor of Edgware and whatever can accrue to me in the vill of Cowlinge, with their appurtenances, shall revert fully to me or to my heirs. I, Ela and my heirs will warrant the aforesaid manor and the land of Cowlinge with all their appurtenances to Nicholas and his heirs born to his wedded wife, held by the aforesaid service, against all people. Witnessed by Master Geoffrey penitentiary of Salisbury, Sirs John Dacus, Henry de Albinyaco, Roger de Derneford, Philip de Depeford, Robert de Holta, Thomas, clerks, Peter Salcetum, Matthew de la Mare, and others.

100. Exercise of royal patronage by Richard II, granting to Joan de Mohun the manor and hundred of Macclesfield, 1385[50] [From Public Record Office, London, C66/320, m. 19; in Latin]

The king greets all to whom this letter comes. You should know that we recently granted by these our letters patent to our dearest kinswoman Joan Lady Mohun, for the whole of her life 100 marks to be received every year from the manor and hundred of Macclesfield in Cheshire, and the custody of the aforesaid manor and hundred, rendering to us the true value over and above the aforesaid 100 marks, as is more fully contained in the same letters. The manor and hundred

---

49 The charter was granted between the death of Ela's husband William Longespee, earl of Salisbury, and Ela's entry early in 1237 into Lacock priory. Nicholas entered the Church and was bishop of Salisbury between 1291 and his death in 1297. It appears that at this time he was destined for a lay career. See also no. 146n.

50 Two years later Richard II granted Macclesfield to Joan for life rent-free; *Calendar of Patent Rolls, 1385-89*, p. 372. Richard II's mother died in 1385.

are valued at £170 a year. Because our aforesaid kinswoman has returned to our chancery to be cancelled our letters patent issued to her previously concerning £100 a year to be received by her for life from the stannary of Devon and Cornwall, we, wishing to act graciously towards her, have given and granted to her for life the aforesaid manor and hundred, to hold from the date of the death of our dearest lady and mother, in return for rendering to us 100 marks a year and for maintaining the houses and buildings of the manor and bearing all the charges incumbent on the manor and hundred during her life. In witness of this we have had these our letters patent drawn up. Witnessed by the king at Westminster, 17 November.

101. Grant by Henry III to Sibyl, widow of John de Dyve, for the support of herself and her children, 1266 [From Public Record Office, London, C66/84, m. 32]

The king greets all to whom these letters come. You should know that by way of grace and humanity we have granted for us and our heirs to Sibyl who was the wife of John de Dyve our enemy that, out of the lands and tenements held by John in Deddington, Wicken and Ducklington which we recently gave to our beloved and faithful Osbert Giffard, Sibyl should have for life the manor of Ducklington together with the park and everything else belonging to the manor for the maintenance of herself and her children by the title of free tenement. Sibyl may take reasonable estovers in the park without waste and destruction. However, concerning the knights' fees and the advowson of the church belonging to the manor we shall ordain what we shall see should be done with the advice of our council. In testimony of this we have had these our letters patent drawn up. Given at Westminster on 30 January.

102. Elizabeth de Burgh's protest at her treatment by Edward II and Hugh le Despenser the younger, especially concerning the exchange of the lordship of Usk for the lordship of Gower, 1326[51] [From British Library, London, Harley MS. 1240, fos 86v–87r; the beginning and end of the document are in Latin, and the main text in French.]

In the name of God, amen. On 15 May, AD 1326, in the ninth indiction and the tenth year of the pontificate of the most holy father and lord

---

51 G. A. Holmes, 'A protest against the Despensers, 1326', *Speculum* XXX, 1955, pp. 207-12, shows that Elizabeth's allegations were genuine and can be corroborated from other sources. Hugh le Despenser the younger was Elizabeth's brother-in-law.

John XXII, pope by divine providence, the noble woman Lady Elizabeth de Burgh, one of the sisters and heirs of Lord Gilbert de Clare, late earl of Gloucester, and formerly wife of the late Roger Damory knight, exhibited and recited word for word a parchment schedule written in French, of the tenor and contents written below, in her oratory in the small chapel next to her chamber in Clare castle in Norwich diocese in the presence of the discreet men, Sir Thomas de Cheddeworth, rector of the church of Lutterworth, and Sir John Diccus of London, clerk of the diocese of London, her close advisers, specially summoned, and witnesses to those matters written below which were personally drawn up, and in the presence of my public notary.[52] In the name of God, I Elizabeth de Burgh, one of the sisters and heirs of Sir Gilbert de Clare late earl of Gloucester, and formerly wife of Sir Roger Damory, wish that it be known by all people that, when certain disagreements occurred between our Lord, Edward king of England, son of King Edward, and several great men of his land in the fifteenth year of his reign [1321-22] on account of certain oppressions which caused them grievance, contrary to the law of the land, my lord Sir Roger was one of those great men and was harried and oppressed so that he died.[53] While he was still alive I was captured in the castle of Usk, part of my inheritance, by power and command of the king, and taken to the abbey of Barking where after my lord's death I remained imprisoned more than half a year, and all my lands were taken into the king's hands. During that time, the king sent three letters of credit by Master Richard de Clare, Sir John Lestourmy and Piers Mareschal in turn, the condition for the credits being that I should agree to exchange the land of Usk and all my inheritance in Wales with Sir Hugh le Despenser the younger in return for the land of Gower. In that the land of Gower was worth less than the land of Usk and my Welsh inheritance, the king promised fully to make up the difference at the true value with other lands more convenient to me, and to give me back all my inheritance of the earldom of Gloucester, my dower, all my lands purchased jointly with my lord, all my castles, jewels, vessel and wardrobe.[54] If I would not agree, I would never hold in peace the land of my inheritance, dower or joint purchase during the lifetime of our lord the king. I Elizabeth was distressed at these threats, and, seeing the great oppression done from day to day to the

52 This is the end of the Latin preamble; the document continues in French.

53 This is a reference to the Marcher rising of 1321 and the battle of Boroughbridge the following year. Damory died shortly before the battle.

54 The term 'vessel' denotes silver plate.

good people of the land, the danger to myself and my children who were imprisoned with me, and our disinheritance, agreed under protest to make the exchange, and this was done before Sir John de Bousser, justice of our lord the king, Sir William de Clif, clerk of the chancery, and most of my household, and in return I was to receive suitable lands at their true value, and all my inheritance, dower and joint purchase, together with all my castles, jewels, vessel and wardrobe, as had been promised. After the exchange our lord the king delivered to me the rest of my inheritance and my dower, and retains the lands of joint purchase and all the other things promised except the manor of Holton in Oxfordshire. Then the king ordered me by letter to be with him at York at Christmas in the sixteenth year of his reign [1322], and put me in hope that at my coming I should have grace and the residue. On hearing this command I took the road to York. On arrival the king kept me as it were under guard, ousting my council and household, until I sealed a quitclaim against my will of the land of Usk and all my inheritance in Wales, and over and above this he ordered me to seal another writing, namely a letter obligatory binding me by my body and lands, contrary to the law of the land.[55] Because of the argument I put up over sealing this writing, some of my councillors were taken and imprisoned for a long time, and I left the court to great ill will. When I had travelled five days on my way back to my castle of Clare, the king ordered me back, threatening that, if I did not return and seal the writing, all the land which I held of him would be taken away and I would never hold a foot of land of him. In order to avoid this great evil, I returned, and sealed that writing against my will, and the king has never carried out his promises. Soon after I was seised of Gower, Sir William de Braose through the abetting, help and maintenance of the aforesaid Sir Hugh brought a writ of novel disseisin against me naming the land of Gower,[56] contrary to the law of the land which does not allow the king's writ concerning any free tenement to run in Wales. Sir Hugh, through his lordship and the royal power usurped by him, made the assize go against me and made me lose that land in the presence of Sir John de Bousser and Sir William de Clif, the king's justices assigned to the case, although Sir Hugh was obliged to provide warranty to me and my heirs. After he had recovered that land, Sir William de Braose gave it to Sir Hugh le Despenser the elder who

55 This letter obligatory probably contained the promise that she would not marry or make grants of her lands without the king's agreement; this is referred to in *Rotuli Parliamentorum*, II, p. 440, where the letter was cancelled on 1 March 1327.

56 This writ was brought against Elizabeth in April 1324.

gave it to his son, Sir Hugh the younger, who still holds it. To injure me more, the king has taken back from me by his will and detains and distrains all the wood of my inheritance in the chace of Tonbridge. I Elizabeth have sued on this at all the parliaments these three years by bill asking for the king's grace and redress of the above wrongs, and I could have no remedy, reply, nor have the bill endorsed, nor find a sheriff who was willing to make execution according to law of the writ of warranty that I have carried and prosecuted against Sir Hugh the younger for the land of Gower thus lost. Now Sir Hugh the younger, seeing the great scandal of the aforesaid wrongs, and in order to blind the people, and deceive and injure me more, offers me lands in recompense for Gower which are less than half the yearly value of Gower. In this I Elizabeth clearly see my disinheritance, the oppressions done by the king and the royal power which is in the hands of Sir Hugh the younger, the disgrace to myself to be thus disparaged or put in danger, the loss of my children, and all my lands and property, and, in view of all this and for fear of being reputed or surmised to be among those whom the king holds to be his enemies, I make the protest before you Notary and the witnesses who are here present that, if any lands should be delivered to me in recompense for Gower, I do not and will not accept them of my free will, nor will I receive them for any other reason than for fear of the king by the malice of Sir Hugh the younger who opposes me, and to avoid the above dangers, restore my goods and secure my right to the lands that are wrongly detained until the time that grace may be more open and the law of the land better maintained and common to all. I make the statement that I would wish to make this protest openly and publicly as civil law demands if fear of royal power with the peril that could follow did not stop me.[57] I, John de Radenhale, clerk of the diocese of Hereford, public notary by apostolic authority, was present with the above witnesses while Lady Elizabeth recited each and every of the items mentioned above written in the French language, and thus made her declaration as stated above, and I saw, heard, wrote and recorded those things done, recited and carried out by the aforesaid Lady Elizabeth in this public form, and being asked I signed it with my accustomed mark, in the aforesaid year, indiction, pontificate, month, day and place. I wrote this French word, reputed, between the lines in the fifth line from the end.[58]

---

57 The reference to civil law denotes Roman law. The document then resumes in Latin.

58 The protest survives as a copy in the Black Book of Wigmore, so this interlineation is not now apparent.

103. Measures taken to provide land for women after the Merciless Parliament, 1388 [The first example is taken from Public Record Office, London, C54/229, m. 44, and the second and third from *Rotuli Parliamentorum*, III, p. 245; the first is in Latin, and the second and third in French]

The king greets his beloved Robert de la Lee, his escheator in Staffordshire. We have learned by the inquisition that you carried out that the late John Salisbury knight held on the day he died of the inheritance of Joan his wife who is still living the manor of Chebsey with appurtenances in the aforesaid county of other lords than ourselves. We therefore order you to withdraw immediately from the manor, with appurtenances, which was taken into our hands because of John's death, and not to interfere with it in any way, provided that it was for that reason and none other that it was taken into our hands, saving the rights of us and of anyone else, and delivering the issues, if any, from the time of John's death to Joan, as is just. Witnessed by the king at Westminster, 13 July.[59]

Our lord the king granted in this parliament to Lady Anne who was the wife of Sir James Berners knight the manor of West Horsley with appurtenances in Surrey which is in the hands of our lord the king because of James's forfeiture, to have in aid of her maintenance until she marries or is otherwise helped or advanced, without rendering anything.[60]

Grant to Lady Katherine, daughter of the earl of Stafford, on whose soul may God have mercy, and to Sir Michael de la Pole the son, her husband, of certain manors in Lincolnshire and Nottinghamshire of which Sir Michael de la Pole the father, formerly earl of Suffolk, long before his forfeiture enfeoffed Lady Katherine and her husband to have to them and the heirs of their bodies, and which by virtue of the judgment on Sir Michael the father in this parliament were taken into the hands of our lord the king. This our grant of the lord king was made at the request of the earl of Warwick and certain other lords, cousins and allies of Lady Katherine.

---

59 John Salisbury was a household knight who suffered forfeiture. Similar orders were sent to the escheators of Warwickshire and Worcestershire concerning Joan's lands in those counties.

60 West Horsley had belonged to her husband. Ross, 'Forfeiture for treason', p. 569, points out that Anne had neither inheritance nor jointure.

104. Margaret Paston's preparations for Lord Moleyns' attack on the manor-house at Gresham, 1448 (the attack took place on 28 January 1449) [From J. Gairdner, ed., *Paston Letters*, I, no. 67; in English]

Most worshipful husband, I recommend myself to you, and ask you to get some crossbows and windlasses to bend them with, and crossbow-bolts, because your houses here are so low that no man can shoot out with a longbow, however great the need. I suppose that you could have such things from Sir John Fastolf if you would send to him. Also I wish that you would get two or three short poleaxes to keep by the doors, and also many jacks if you can.[61]

105. Extract from the parliamentary petition of John de Vere earl of Oxford, 1485, relating to his mother's conveyances of land to Richard duke of Gloucester in 1473-74[62] [From *Rotuli Parliamentorum*, VI, p. 282; in English]

Furthermore, the late Elizabeth countess of Oxford, mother of the aforesaid John de Vere, whose heir he is, because of the true and faithful allegiance and service which she like the same John de Vere owed and performed to the most blessed prince King Harry [Henry VI], was so threatened, put in fear of her life and imprisoned by Richard III, the late king of England by deed and not by right, while he was duke of Gloucester, at the time when John de Vere was not at liberty but in prison. Because of her fear the countess to save her life was compelled to make, and cause her feoffees to make, such estate, releases and confirmations and other things to the late duke of Gloucester and to others to his use of divers manors, lordships, lands, tenements and hereditaments of inheritance, as she was advised by the late duke and his council, as is notoriously and openly known, against all reason and good conscience. As a result the aforesaid John de Vere is likely to be disinherited of a great part of his inheritance unless some remedy is provided by the authority of parliament on his behalf.

---

61 The jack was a leather coat worn by footsoldiers.

62 John de Vere consistently supported the Lancastrians. As a result of this petition, the earl secured the reversal of the acts of attainder passed against members of his family, and recovered his mother's lands. The case is discussed by A. Crawford, 'Victims of attainder: the Howard and de Vere women in the late fifteenth century', in *Medieval Women in Southern England*, Reading Medieval Studies, XV, 1989, pp. 59-74, and by M. A. Hicks, 'The last days of Elizabeth countess of Oxford', *English Historical Review*, CIII, 1988, pp. 76-95. M. A. Hicks prints the earl's petition and the depositions of 1495 which throw light on the details of the case.

IV: Wealth and lordship

Women's landholding is well documented, the amount of land in their hands varying according to the accidents of birth and fortune. Land, however, had to be managed if it was to yield as good an income as possible, and wealth was essential for any member of the nobility to maintain a conspicuous lifestyle, to play a part in local and possibly central politics through the exercise of influence and patronage, and to support and further family interests. In looking at the way in which women ran their estates, much of the evidence applies to widows who as *femmes soles* were legally in charge. During their married lives, wives certainly took over in their husbands' absence, and there are cases where a wife who was an heiress or a wealthy remarried dowager ran her estates in her own name.[1] Much of the evidence for land exploitation comes from the wealthier members of the nobility, as fewer accounts have survived for less notable families.[2]

Women running estates had their own officials who were responsible to them; absentee husbands like John Paston I gave advice and made it clear that the officials answered to him. Patterns and methods of administration were those adopted by fathers, husbands and brothers: the use of the household in the twelfth century; the moves towards professional administration and direct exploitation of demesne land from *c.* 1200; the adoption by *c.* 1300 of increasingly complex and bureaucratic methods including auditors and, on large estates, a council;[3] and the development of a *rentier* economy in preference to direct exploitation of the manors from *c.* 1370. There was some variation within these broad parameters, depending on the needs of the lady and the nature of the lands, as is brought out once estate officials began to produce their own accounts, surveys and valors from *c.*1250. For the earlier period, information has to be derived from Crown records, notably Domesday Book, the Pipe Rolls, and the *Rotuli de Dominabus.*

1 E.g. Anne Neville, dowager duchess of Buckingham, was named as being in charge during her second marriage to Lord Mountjoy; British Library, London, Latin Egerton 2822; Additional MSS. 29608, 34213.

2 R. H. Britnell, 'Minor landlords in England and medieval agrarian capitalism', *Past and Present*, no. 89, 1980, p. 3, comments on the inadequate number of manorial accounts from small estates.

3 An illustration of professional administration is seen in no. 129, Elizabeth de Burgh's wardrobe account of 1350-51.

It is difficult to calculate the amount of wealth which women had. Some indications are provided by the Domesday survey and the twelfth-century Crown records, but there are difficulties over the interpretation of Domesday values, and most figures have to be regarded as approximate. The estate accounts from the thirteenth century onwards, whether those for individual manors or for whole bailiwicks,[4] are much more detailed, but were designed to give information on the accountability of the official, rather than on the lady's income. Surveys of estates were drawn up by the officials themselves, or by the Crown in connection with the inquisition *post mortem* into the lands of a tenant-in-chief, the allocation of dower or partition among co-heiresses. Many of these surveys are detailed, but vary in reliability. For this reason the valors, such as that of Anne Stafford, which were drawn up on certain estates in the fourteenth and fifteenth centuries, are particularly valuable, since they provide a breakdown of receipts and expenses, and can show how income varied over the years.[5] The income taxes of the fifteenth century throw some light on the wealth of the nobility, although it has to be stressed that they provide minimum rather than maximum figures.[6]

Certainly estates needed to be well managed, but there were times when even good management was unable to boost wealth. Many factors were outside the lady's control. According to Elizabeth de Burgh's valors, her income dropped in the 1330s, and this was due to low prices rather than to weak management. Ankaret Talbot was a conscientious manager who devoted personal attention to the estate, but she found that she was up against adverse circumstances in the early fifteenth century.[7]

4 A bailiwick was a grouping of estates, often on a geographical basis, for purposes of administration and exploitation.

5 Another example is given in Holmes, *Estates of the Higher Nobility*, pp. 143–4, who provides the figures from Elizabeth de Burgh's two valors of 1329–30 and 1338–39 which covered all her estates. The importance of valors as a source for baronial income is discussed by C. D. Ross and T. B. Pugh, 'Materials for the study of baronial incomes in fifteenth-century England', *Economic History Review*, second series, VI, 1953–54, pp. 192–3, and by R. R. Davies, 'Baronial accounts, incomes and arrears in the later Middle Ages', *Economic History Review*, second series, XXI, 1968, pp. 214–18.

6 T. B. Pugh and C. D. Ross, 'The English baronage and the income tax of 1436', *Bulletin of the Institute of Historical Research*, XXVI, 1953, pp. 1–28; Gray, 'Incomes from land in England in 1436', pp. 607–39.

7 A. J. Pollard, 'Estate management in the later Middle Ages: the Talbots and Whitchurch, 1383–1525', *Economic History Review*, second series, XXV, 1972, pp. 561–2.

What is very difficult to see from the records is what the level of the lady's management abilities really were;[8] this applies equally to lords. They received advice from treatises on management, such as 'The Rules of St Robert', said to have been written by Robert Grosseteste for Margaret countess of Lincoln. Here the Paston Letters are particularly valuable, since Margaret sent John Paston I news of what was happening locally, while he sent her advice. Where the lady was in charge, officials and others regarded her as ultimately responsible, as seen with petitions on matters to be redressed, such as that sent to Anne Neville dowager duchess of Buckingham. It was up to the lady to choose officials who were honest and efficient when those whom she inherited left office. Decisions were issued in the lady's name, although the emphasis on counsel during the Middle Ages made it likely that wide consultation took place. It was important that she should be seen to be taking an active role, and the supervision of the estates provided a major reason for travel. It was essential for women to be aware of their rights and the need to maintain them, and vigilance over rights can be seen as a sign of energetic management, as in the case of Margaret de Brotherton. The section entitled Foreign Expenses in Elizabeth de Burgh's household account of 1350-51 also points to a high level of activity.[9]

Landholding involved service which had to be met by the lady in the absence of a lord. The land of the nobility and gentry was normally held by knight service, either of the Crown (as became increasingly usual in the twelfth and thirteenth centuries), or of a lord, whether ecclesiastical or lay. Such tenure in the late eleventh and twelfth centuries necessitated the provision of active service by knights in the host and for castleguard, or the payment of scutage. Women were occasionally recorded as holding fees in the *Carte* of 1166 when Henry II required his tenants-in-chief to make a return of the knights enfeoffed on their honours before and after 1135, the date of the death of Henry I. The reduction in feudal knight service by means of the quota in the early thirteenth century, and the subsequent use by the Crown of different ways of raising an army meant that military service

8 This problem is addressed by R. E. Archer, 'The estates and finances of Margaret of Brotherton, *c.* 1320-1399', *Historical Research*, LX, 1987, pp. 264-80; R. E. Archer, '"How ladies ... who live on their manors ought to manage their households and estates": women as landholders and administrators in the later Middle Ages', in P. J. P. Goldberg, ed., *Woman is a Worthy Wight: Women in English Society c. 1200-1500*, Gloucester, 1992, chapter 6; Ward, *English Noblewomen*, pp. 110-16.

9 See no. 129.

gradually became obsolete.[10] Lords' rights over wardship and marriage continued and were a useful source of occasional profit and patronage, but they came to be at least partially evaded through joint enfeoffments of husband and wife, and the use of feoffees. Obligations to defend the realm by provisioning and garrisoning castles continued in the later Middle Ages, especially on the borders of the realm, and here women were expected to play their part.

Ladies of the higher nobility gained additional profits from their exercise of various forms of jurisdiction. As the lady of feudal tenants, she had the right to levy feudal incidents and to conduct feudal business in her honour court. Although many honour courts had become less active by the thirteenth century, the evidence for the court for the Isle of Wight of Isabella de Forz countess of Aumale shows that it was still an asset worth having. Feudal business in these courts was often combined with other forms of jurisdiction, and the Clare court had always catered for free as well as military tenants.[11] The right to hold the view of frankpledge and to exercise leet jurisdiction was widespread, and the court of Isabella de Forz combined this with feudal business. Women with estates in Wales exercised much greater jurisdiction, since the king's writ did not run there in spite of Edward I's attempts to make it do so. A few women like Isabella de Forz exercised greater franchisal jurisdiction on their English estates, a matter tackled by Edward I in his Hundred Roll inquiries and the subsequent pleas of *quo warranto*. Occasionally women are found holding a royal office which was hereditary or had frequently been held in their family, or were appointed to custodies and local commissions. Usually there were special reasons for these appointments, as in the cases of Ela countess of Salisbury and Joan de Bohun countess of Hereford. Margaret de Brotherton was the only noblewoman to be granted a title in her own right.

The concept of reward in return for service was deeply ingrained in the medieval world, and women rewarded their servants and officials throughout the Middle Ages. The evidence for this in the late eleventh and twelfth centuries is mainly derived from charters.[12] From the

10 A lord who produced his quota of knight service in the thirteenth century provided a smaller number of knights for the feudal host. By the Hundred Years War the Crown was raising companies of knights by making indentures with individual captains who were often members of the higher nobility.

11 Ward, *English Noblewomen*, p. 130.

12 E.g. no. 76.

thirteenth century, the recording of the bestowal of fees and robes in receivers' accounts, valors, and household and livery rolls shows that ladies were building up their own affinities. The evidence is reinforced by the frequent giving of bequests in wills. This practice of giving fees enabled the lady to reward her own servants and officials and at the same time to extend her political network so as to reward those useful to her in royal government and the courts as well as in the locality.[13] Great ladies took up the cause of their retainers with the king. In times of political uncertainty the affinity could be mobilised against the king, as the countess of Oxford tried to do in 1404. All such activity gave the lady an involvement in politics; although women were not to be found attending council or parliament, their officials were summoned to special councils and were known to be active at time of parliament.

Land was the basis of wealth, and there is every sign that most noblewomen appreciated and made the most of their riches. Wealth was not to be hoarded; it had to be put to use. Its support of the lady's lifestyle and its use for religious purposes will be considered in the following chapters, and conspicuous consumption and piety are well-known themes in the medieval world. However, wealth was also essential for the exercise of power and influence, and, although noblewomen did not play a formal role in the world of politics, there is little doubt that some of them made their influence felt.

106. Confirmation charter of Adeliza de Clermont, widow of Gilbert of Tonbridge, to the abbey of Thorney, 1138–48; two of her household officials were among the witnesses [From Dugdale, *Monasticon Anglicanum*, II, p. 603; in Latin]

Adeliza mother of Earl Gilbert [of Pembroke] greets all her friends and men, French and English. You should know that Ralph son of Nigel and Amicia his wife have given and granted to the church of St Mary and St Botolph at Thorney with my consent the land at Raunds which they held of me and four shillings yearly which they had from it from rent of the aforesaid church, and all the customs, and whatever belongs to them there. Be it known that this was done in the presence of Earl Gilbert and Walter his brother, and in the presence of many of my men, clerks and lay, at Melchbourne. Afterwards I gave and

13 Ward, *English Noblewomen*, pp. 135-6; J. R. Maddicott, *Law and Lordship: Royal Justices as Retainers in Thirteenth- and Fourteenth-Century England*, Past and Present Supplement 4, 1978, pp. 20-3.

granted in alms to the same church twelve shillings, with all the customs and services belonging to me from the aforesaid land. Witnessed by Robert my chaplain, Robert my knight of Barton, Robert my steward, Mabel my daughter, Aderiz Heaved.[14]

107. Letter of Roger de Clare earl of Hertford to his grandmother, Adeliza de Clermont, her steward and men, soon after 1152[15] [From British Library, London, Cotton MS. Appendix xxi, fo. 22r; in Latin]

Roger earl of Clare greets Adeliza de Clermont his grandmother and Peter her steward and her men of Norfolk. I am greatly displeased that you are demanding from my monks of Stoke or from their men customs or other gelds which they had in the time of my grandfather or the customs which it is proper to claim as free alms. Therefore I order you to allow my aforesaid monks and their men and all their possessions to be at peace in all things as they ever were in the time of Gilbert my grandfather or in the time of Richard my father, and not to lay hands on them or their property, but to allow them to sue for all their possessions as of their free alms.

108. Fees paid by Isabella Lady Morley to household servants, estate officials and others, 1463-64[16] [From British Library, London, Additional MS. 34,122A, m. 3; in Latin]

Domestic fees

Paid to Isabella Wryghte, gentlewoman of the lady, for her pay this year, 26s 8d.
Paid to Alice Povy, gentlewoman of the lady, at Christmas for her pay, 10s.
Paid to Matilda Wynter for her pay from the feast of All Saints [1 November] within the period of the account to the feast of All Saints after the account finished, 26s 8d.[17]

14 Ralph son of Nigel and his wife had been involved in an earlier confirmation charter by Adeliza to Thorney; here the wife was named Avicia; Dugdale, *Monasticon Anglicanum*, II, p. 601; F. M. Stenton, ed., *Facsimiles of Early Charters from Northamptonshire Collections*, no. XVIII.

15 As the letter was addressed to his grandmother, the letter was presumably sent soon after 1152; it is not known when Adeliza died.

16 Because of the overlap between the section entitled domestic fees and the one entitled fees, both have been translated in full. Isabella spent this year in the household of her son-in-law John Hastings, and paid him £80 for her maintenance.

17 As was usual with accounts, this account ran from Michaelmas to Michaelmas.

Paid to John Multon for his pay this year, 26s 8d.

Paid to Inge Pygot for his pay this year, 20s.

Paid to Edmund Harsyk for his pay this year, 26s 8d.

Paid to John Boteler for his pay this year, 26s 8d.

Paid to Alice Chyrche, laundress of the lady, for her pay this year, 6s 8d.

Paid to Simon Parker for his pay this year, 10s.

Paid to Henry Chapman, yeoman of the lady, for his pay this year, 26s 8d.

Paid to John Dyton, yeoman of the lady, for his pay this year, 33s 4d.

Paid to friar John Norewych celebrating mass for the lady and for the soul of her lord, Lord Morley, and all her benefactors, £4.[18]

Paid to William Stather, clerk, steward of the lady's household and receiver of the lady's money this year, £6 13s 4d.

Paid to Richard Brandon, Augustinian friar, for celebrating a trental for the soul of Thomas Lord Morley, 10s.

Sum total: £23 3s 4d.

Fees

Fee of John Heydon, chief steward of the lady, 66s 8d.

Fee of Edmund Bokyngham esquire of the lady for this year, £4.

Fee of William Jeneye retained legal expert of the lady's council this year, 26s 8d.

Fee of Thomas Spyrk attorney of the lady for procuring writs this year, 13s 4d.

Fee of Robert Brampton surveyor of the lady this year, 40s.

Fee of Robert Pynnes auditor of accounts of the lady's manors and steward of the courts of the same manors, 53s 4d.

Sum total: £14.

109. The management of lands in the mid-thirteenth century, according to 'The Rules of St Robert', said to have been written by Robert Grosseteste, bishop of Lincoln, for Margaret countess of Lincoln, c. 1241[19] [From E. Lamond, ed. and trans., *Walter of Henley's Husbandry*, Royal Historical Society, London, 1890; in French]

The first rule teaches how a lord or lady shall know in each manor all

18 Thomas Lord Morley died in 1435. Isabella was the daughter of Michael de la Pole earl of Suffolk, and Katherine Stafford; she died in 1467; C. Richmond, 'Thomas Lord Morley (d. 1416) and the Morleys of Hingham', *Norfolk Archaeology*, XXXIX, 1984-86, pp. 1-12.

19 'The Rules of St Robert' concern the household as well as the estates. Extracts from the Rules covering the lands are given here, and extracts concerning the household in the next chapter, no. 127.

their lands by their parcels, all their rents, customs, usages, services, franchises, fees, and tenements.

Touching your foreign lands;[20] to begin with, buy the king's writ, to inquire by the oath of twelve free men in each manor all the lands by their parcels, all the rents, customs, usages, services, franchises, fees, and tenements, and let this be carefully and lawfully inquired into by the most loyal and wisest of the freeholders and villeins, and distinctly enrolled, so that your chief steward may have one whole roll, and you another, and let each bailiff have what belongs to his bailiwick. And if plaintiffs come to you because of a wrong that anyone has done them, or making a petition, first look yourself at the rolls of that manor to which the plaintiff belongs, and according to them give answer and maintain justice.

The second rule teaches how you may know by common inquisition what there is on each manor, movable or not movable.

Next, cause to be made without delay right inquiry, and enrol distinctly in another roll every one of your manors in England, each by itself, how many ploughs you have in each place, small or great, and how many you can have; how many acres of arable land, how many of meadow, how much pasture for sheep, and how much for cows, and so for all kind of beasts according to their number; and what movables you have in each place of live stock;[21] and keep this roll by you, and often look at the first roll, and this also that you may quickly know how to find what you ought to do. Let all your servants on the manors be set at a fixed sum of money; and after August let your granges be closed.

The third rule teaches the discourse that the lord or lady ought to have with their chief steward before some of your good friends.

When the aforesaid rolls and inquests have been made, and as soon as you can, that the work of your people be not hindered, call your chief steward before any of your people in whom you trust, and speak thus to him: 'Good sir, you see plainly that to have my rights set forth clearly, and to know more surely the state of my people, and of my lands, and what I can henceforth do with what belongs to me and what leave, I have caused these inquiries and enrolments to be made; now I

20 The term 'foreign lands' was probably used to denote manors other than the lady's residence.

21 Movables were personal property, goods and chattels, as distinct from property in land.

pray you, as one to whom I have committed trust, as many as I have under me guard and govern. And strictly I command you that you keep whole and without harm all my rights, franchises, and fixed possessions, and whatever of these said things is withdrawn or diminished by the negligence of others, or by wrongdoing, replace it as far as you are able. And my movable goods and livestock increase in an honest and right way, and keep them faithfully. The returns from my lands, rents, and movables, without fraud and with lawful diminution, bring to me and to my wardrobe to spend according as I shall direct,[22] that God may be satisfied, and my honour and my profit preserved by the foresight of myself and you and my other friends. Further, I strictly command that neither you nor any of your bailiffs under you in any way, by unlawful exactions, or fear, or accusations, or receipt of presents or gifts, vex or hurt or ruin those who hold of me – rich or poor; and if in any of these said ways they are by anyone vexed, hurt, or ruined, by fixed inquiry which I will that you make in your eyre wherever it can be attained, quickly make amendment and redress.'

The fourth rule teaches how a lord or lady can further examine into their estate, that is to say, how he or she can live yearly of their own.

In two ways by calculation can you inquire into your estate. First this, command strictly that in each place at the leading of your corn there be thrown in a measure at the entrance to the grange the eighth sheaf of each kind of corn, and let it be threshed and measured by itself. And by calculating from that measure you can calculate all the rest in the grange. And in doing this I advise you to send to the best manors of your lands those of your household in whom you place most confidence to be present in August at the leading of the corn, and to guard it as is aforesaid. And if this does not please you, do it in this way. Command your steward that every year at Michaelmas he cause all the stacks of each kind of corn, within the grange and without, to be valued by prudent, faithful, and capable men, how many quarters[23] there may be, and then how many quarters will be taken for seed and servants on the land, and then of the whole amount, and of what remains over and above the land and the servants, set the sum in writing, and according to that assign the expenses of your household

22 The wardrobe was here being used as a financial office. The reference to the wardrobe in the fourth rule saw it as a household department responsible for some of the provisioning.

23 The quarter was used as the measure for grain; it usually contained eight bushels, although there could be local variations.

in bread and ale. Also see how many quarters of corn you will spend in a week in dispensable bread, how much in alms. That is if you spend two quarters a day, that is fourteen quarters a week, that is seven hundred and fourteen quarters a year.[24] And if to increase your alms you spend two quarters and a half every day, that is seventeen quarters and a half in the week, and in the year eight hundred and fifty-three quarters and a half. And when you have subtracted this sum from the sum total of your corn, then you can subtract the sum for ale, according as weekly custom has been for the brewing in your household. And take care of the sum which will remain from sale. And with the money from your corn, and from your rents, and from the issues of pleas in your courts, and from your stock, arrange the expenses of your kitchen and your wines and your wardrobe and the wages of servants, and subtract your stock. But on all manors take care of your corn, that it be not sold out of season nor without need; that is, if your rents and other returns will suffice for the expenses of your chamber and wines and kitchen, leave your store of corn whole until you have the advantage of the corn of another year, not more, or at the least, of half [a year].

The fifth rule teaches you how prudently you ought to act when wards or escheats fall to you.

If a ward or escheat fall to you, at once send your letters to two of the most prudent and faithful of the country, with one of your own [people] in whom you have confidence, who in no way desire to have this thing; and cause the survey of the wardship or escheat to be made in all the things, and make them send you the survey under their seals, and according to what he who counsels you shall say and yourself direct, either keep it or give it whole to one of your people, or to two or three, according as more or fewer of them shall have been in your service, and have undergone much toil about you and for you, and you ought always especially to regard this reason. And on no advice be too hasty in giving the thing until you are most sure what it is and what it is worth.

The sixth rule teaches you how and when you ought to command your granges to be shut and opened.

Command your steward that your granges everywhere be entirely closed after August, that no servant may open them without special

---

24 Grosseteste was reckoning on a year of less than fifty-two weeks.

command or letter from you or him until threshing-time come. And then let there be sent a faithful man or servant whom the reeve shall take from that place, and another true man from the township, and all the time let them be present at the opening of the granges, and at the close, at threshing, at winnowing, at the delivery, at the survey by tally. And take care that no servant or bailiff receive the money of the returns, but only the reeve and another who shall have wherewithal to be answerable to you.

The seventh rule teaches you how you may know to compare the accounts with the estimate of the survey or the fault of your servants and bailiffs of manors and lands.

At the end of the year when all the accounts shall have been heard and rendered of the lands, and the issues, and all expenses of all the manors, take to yourself all the rolls, and with one or two of the most intimate and faithful men that you have, make very careful comparison with the rolls of the accounts rendered, and of the rolls of the estimate of corn and stock that you made after the previous August, and according as they agree you shall see the industry or negligence of your servants and bailiffs, and according to that make amendment.

110. Examples of accounts of the demesne lands of Isabella de Forz countess of Aumale: Little Humber, 1276–77; Lymington, 1280–81[25] [From Public Record Office, London, SC6/1078/16, m. 2d; SC6/984/9, m. 3; in Latin]

The account of Alan Anstyby, reeve of Little Humber from the morrow of Michaelmas in the fourth year of the reign of King E[dward] to the morrow of Michaelmas in the fifth year of the same reign.

Receipts. The same man renders account for £4 17s 1¼d of the arrears of the last account. 33s 4d of the same Alan's arrears from the time he was stockman. 3s 6d from the sale of manure from the cattle-shed. 48s

25 A considerable collection of the ministers' accounts for the estates of Isabella de Forz survives. For general consideration of her household, administration and economic resources, see N. Denholm-Young, *Seignorial Administration in England*, Oxford, 1937, pp. 13-21, 32-85, and 'The Yorkshire estates of Isabella de Fortibus', *Yorkshire Archaeological Journal*, XXXI, 1934, pp. 388-420; M. Mate, 'Profit and productivity on the estates of Isabella de Forz, 1260-92', *Economic History Review*, second series, XXXIII, 1980, pp. 326-34. As accounting methods became more sophisticated, the sections for receipts and expenses were subdivided into separate paragraphs according to subject. Isabella's estates were being farmed directly, as was usual in the thirteenth and first half of the fourteenth century; the transition to a *rentier* economy came after *c.*1370, as exemplified by the valor of Anne Stafford.

6d from the sale of 2 oxen and 3 pigs. £32 3s 2d from the sale of 61 quarters of wheat, 25 quarters and 6 bushels of beans, and 77 quarters and 5 bushels of oats. 9s 2d from the sale of plough-service of eleven acres of land. 7d from the sale of the hide of one mare which died of murrain. 8s from the agistment of pasture of eight horses in summer.[26] Nothing this year from stubble. 43s 5$^1/_2$d from 1 quarter and 3 bushels of wheat, and 4 quarters and 6 bushels of oats which were sold on account.[27] Sum total of the receipts: £43 21$^3/_4$d. [£44 6s 9$^3/_4$d]

Expenses. The same accounts for acquittance of rent of the reeve in return for his service, 6s 8d. Iron bought for the ploughs, 2 ploughs bought new accounted for below, wages of the blacksmith with 4 yokes and other things bought for the ploughs, 7s 2d. Wax-silver at Easter, 2d. Purchase of horseshoes for three cart-horses and three halters, 9$^1/_2$d. Tithe of one colt of issue for last year, 1d.[28] One waggon with all its equipment bought new, binding three pairs of wheels with iron, cart-clouts and nails and other things, with tallow and grease bought for the same, 6s 7d, and so more this year, because of carting for the mill at 'Lod'.[29] Making half a granary new, all costs included, 3s 10$^1/_2$d. For thirty-two perches of embankment at 'Herdcroft' next to the River Humber newly made, and mending seventy-two perches of embankment with completing the moving of Westgot, 48s 10d.[30] Know that the aforesaid Alan has to maintain all embankments against the Humber belonging to the manor of Little Humber, and he will receive 10s from the countess for this. Threshing and winnowing 118 quarters and 3 bushels of wheat, 27 quarters and 3 bushels of beans, and 137$^1/_2$ quarters of oats, 36s 11d. 3 oxen and 5 pigs purchased, 71s. Hoeing and earthing up all the corn, 5s 4d. Mowing, spreading, tossing and gathering in 7 acres of hay, 2s 3d. Reaping, collecting and binding 75$^1/_2$ acres and 1 rod of wheat and 67$^1/_2$ acres of beans and oats, 63s 2d. In aid of carting and stacking corn in the yard, 2s 1d. Pay of four oxherds, 12s. Pay of one harrower at each sowing, 2s 3d this year on account of the variety of the weather.
Sum total: £13 9s 2d.

26 This was the payment for pasturing other men's horses on the lady's land.

27 This term was used when an item had to be written off.

28 The term 'of issue' was used to denote an item produced on the manor, not purchased or brought from elsewhere.

29 The construction of the windmill at 'Lod' is entered on m. 1.

30 The perch measured 5$^1/_2$ yards, just over 5 metres; there was however local variation.

Deliveries. The same accounts for delivery to Robert Hyldeyerd of £13 6s 10d by one tally. Item, delivered to the same by Robert Cayr, £9 by one tally. Hay bought for the stallions of the countess, 18d. Item, delivered to the same by the same man, 60s by one tally.

Sum total: £25 8s 4d.

Sum total of expenses and deliveries: £38 17s 6d.

So the countess is owed £4 4s 3³/₄d. [£5 9s 3³/₄d] Of this, Peter de Northyby owes 67s 1¹/₄d, and the aforesaid A[lan] owes 17s 2¹/₂d.

Grange.

Wheat. The same renders account of 124¹/₂ quarters and ¹/₂ bushel of wheat of issue. Of this, used as seed on 84¹/₂ acres, 24¹/₂ quarters and ¹/₂ bushel. For maslin, as below, for servants' livery, 17 quarters. Delivered to William the reeve of the park, 3¹/₂ quarters by one tally. Item, sold as above, 61 quarters. Profit on the aforesaid sale, 2¹/₂ quarters and 3 bushels.[31] Delivered to the reeve of Keyingham, 14 quarters and 2 bushels, and sold on account, 1 quarter and 3 bushels. And he is quit.[32]

Beans. The same renders account of 28¹/₂ quarters and 2 bushels of issue. Of this, sown on 6 acres, 1 quarter and 6 bushels. Sold, as above, 25 quarters and 6 bushels. Profit on the same sale, 1 quarter and 2 bushels. And he is quit.

Oats. The same renders account of 150 quarters of oats of issue. Of this, by estimate in the sheafs, 5¹/₂ quarters. Sown on 76 acres, 46 quarters and 3¹/₂ bushels. Provender for draught-animals, 2 quarters. Provender for oxen by estimate in the sheafs, 5¹/₂ quarters. Provender for the stallions, 5 quarters and 5¹/₂ bushels. Delivered to William the reeve of the park, 4¹/₂ quarters. Sold as above, 77 quarters and 5 bushels. Profit on the same sale, 3¹/₂ quarters. Sold on account, 4 quarters and 6 bushels. And he is quit.

Maslin.[33] The same renders account of 17 quarters of wheat as above, all used in the livery of four ploughmen, each taking 1 quarter for 12 weeks. And he is quit.

Stock.

Mares. The same renders account of 2 mares remaining [from the

---

31 The term *avantagium*, translated as profit, denoted the difference between a heaped and a razed measure of grain.

32 The reeve was quit if he owed nothing more to the lady and if his account for stock tallied.

33 Maslin was mixed corn, usually a mixture of rye and wheat.

previous year̄], 2 additions as below, and 1 from the reeve of the park. Sum total: 5. 1 died of murrain. There remain 4 mares.

Fillies. The same renders account of 2 fillies remaining, and 1 addition as below. Sum total: 3. Of these, additions were made, as above. There remains 1 filly, aged $2\frac{1}{2}$.

Foals of issue. The same renders account of 1 filly remaining, and 2 colts of issue. Sum total: 3. Of these, 1 filly was added, as above. There remain 2 colts.

Oxen. The same renders account of 25 oxen remaining, and 3 purchased as above. Sum total: 28. Of these, sold as above, 2. There remain 26 oxen.

Pigs. The same renders account of 5 pigs purchased as above. Of these, sold as above, 3. There remain 2 pigs.

Hide. The same renders account of the hide of one mare which died of murrain. Sold as above. And he is quit.

The account of Roger le Bel, reeve of the borough of Lymington, from the morrow of Michaelmas in the eighth year of the reign of King Edward to the morrow of Michaelmas in the ninth year of the same reign.

Receipts. The same man renders account of 32s 8d of the arrears of the last account. £4 9s 9d from rent of assize per year.[34] 30s from the farm of the toll and the market there. 13s $2\frac{1}{2}$d from the toll of the fair this year. 55s 10d from pleas and perquisites of the court this year and so less by reason of the eyre of the [royal] justices in the county. £4 6s 4d from the sale of $2\frac{1}{2}$ tuns of wine from wreck.[35] 45s from Geoffrey le Palmer, formerly reeve of Old Lymington, by one tally.
Sum total of receipts: £17 12s $9\frac{1}{2}$d.

Expenses. The same accounts for acquittance of rent of the reeve and bedel for the year, 12d. Expenses of the constable and others keeping the fair, with the expenses of Roger Clerk and his ferry-passage towards Hursley for providing for the countess's larder, 5s 4d. Salvaging the aforesaid wines and for the part of the same bought from the merchant, 45s.
Sum total of expenses: 51s 4d.

Deliveries. The same accounts for the delivery made to Philip de Perham, receiver of the countess, of $2\frac{1}{2}$ tuns of wine, with the carriage

34 These were fixed rents.

35 Certain lords, including Isabella, held the franchise of wreck, entitling them to any wrecks of ships on their shores.

towards St Denys, 73s.[36] Item, delivered to the same by Robert Clerk, formerly reeve, and William de Rodeston, 8s by one tally. Item, delivered to William de Monte, reeve of Bowcombe, £7 9s by four tallies. Item, delivered to the same by Robert Clerk, 10s 9^{1}/$_{2}$d. Item, delivered to William Gest, reeve of the old vill, 21s 8d by one tally. Item, delivered to the same by Robert Clerk, 10s by one tally.
Sum total: £13 12s 5^{1}/$_{2}$d.

Wine. The same renders account of 2^{1}/$_{2}$ tuns of wine from wreck. Sold as above. And he is quit.
Sum total of all expenses and deliveries: £16 3s 9^{1}/$_{2}$d.
Thus 29s is owed to the countess. Of this, Robert Clerk, formerly reeve, owes 3s 10^{1}/$_{2}$d, and the aforesaid Roger 25s 1^{1}/$_{2}$d.

The account of William Gest, reeve of Old Lymington.

Receipts. The same man renders account for 31s ^{1}/$_{4}$d of the arrears of the last account. £4 10s 8^{1}/$_{2}$d from rent of assize for the year, with the increment of rent of the previous year. 4s 7d a year from a custom called 'fonyltol'. 2s from a custom for the carriage of salt remitted this year. 6s 8d for having the first purchase of all salt in the name of the countess. 32s 5^{1}/$_{2}$d from customary aid this year. 10s from chevage this year.[37] 13s 4d from the fine at the view of frankpledge. 6s 8d from the fine of William le Barettur to have entry on his father's land. 45s 5d from pleas and perquisites of the court, and so less this year by reason of the eyre of the [royal] justices in the county. From pannage of wood, dead wood, and crop and lop of trees, nothing this year. 7s 8^{1}/$_{2}$d from customary pannage this year. 5s from herbage and fruit of the garden sold this year.[38] 10s from the sale of herbage of the meadow. 16s 6d from the sale of 1 ox and 36 hens. 5s 4^{1}/$_{2}$d from the custom of mowing the meadow and carting the hay which was remitted this year. 7s 4^{1}/$_{2}$d from 29^{1}/$_{2}$ carrying services sold this year. 13^{1}/$_{2}$d from the sale of one pound of pepper and one pound of cumin of rent. £102 3s 3d from 1,149 quarters and 1^{1}/$_{2}$ bushels of salt sold by divers men as below. £10 2s from 113^{1}/$_{2}$ quarters and ^{1}/$_{2}$ a bushel of salt sold on account.
Sum total of receipts: £127 14^{1}/$_{2}$d.

---

36 The receiver was the financial official for the honour. The priory of St Denys was outside Southampton.

37 Chevage was paid at the view of frankpledge by the capital pledges for the other men in their tithings, usually at the rate of 1d a head.

38 Herbage denoted the right to pasturage which was sold by the lady.

Foreign receipt.[39] The same renders account for 31s 8d from Roger le Bel, reeve of the borough of Lymington.
Sum total: 31s 8d.

Expenses. The same accounts for the acquittance of rent of the reeve, one hayward, and one collector, 3s. 1 axle bought for the cart and fitted, with horseshoes for the mares, 8¹/₂d. 12 sacks purchased, 3s, and these will be answered for in the following year. Wages of one carter carrying salt this year, 3s. Repairing hedges in places round the garden, 3d. Allowance by grace of the countess made to divers reeves in the previous year for expenses concerned with the sale of salt this year, 11s 7¹/₂d, and this should not be taken as a precedent.
Sum total of expenses: 21s 6¹/₂d.

Deliveries. The same accounts for the delivery made to Philip de Perham, receiver of the countess, by Robert Edmund, £21 2s by one tally. Item, delivered to William del Hylle, reeve of Bowcombe, £10 12s 11¹/₂d by one tally. Item, delivered to the same by Robert Edmund, £4 12s 8d by two tallies. Item, delivered to the same by Geoffrey le Palmer, £17 8s by two tallies. Item, delivered to the same by Ralph de Blakedon £37 13s 8d by three tallies. Item, delivered to the same by Richard Colebronde £20 6s by one tally. Item, delivered to Roger le Bel, reeve of the borough of Lymington, by Geoffrey le Palmer, 45s by one tally.
Sum total: £114 3¹/₂d.
Sum total of all expenses and deliveries: £115 22d.

Thus the countess is owed £13 11s ¹/₂d. Of this, Richard Colebronde owes 44s, Lucy, widow of Richard de Blakedon, 103s 3d, Geoffrey le Palmer 16s 6d, Robert Edmund 47s 2¹/₄d, and the aforesaid William owes 60s 1¹/₄d.

Stock

Oxen. The same renders account of 2 oxen from heriot of Ralph at the well and John Botte.[40] Of these, 1 was delivered to William, reeve of Bowcombe, and 1 sold as above.

Bullocks. The same renders account of 1 bullock remaining which was delivered to William reeve of Bowcombe. And he is quit.

---

39 The term 'foreign' was used to denote a receipt or item of expenditure outside the estate.

40 On the death of a villein, the lord took his best beast as heriot. Ralph's surname was entered on the roll as *ad fontem*.

Hens. The same renders account of 36 hens of rent. Sold as above. And he is quit.

Pepper. The same renders account for 1 lb. pepper of rent. Sold as above. And he is quit.

Cumin. The same renders account of 1 lb. cumin of rent. Sold as above. And he is quit.

Salt. The same renders account of 1,687 quarters and $3^1/2$ bushels of salt remaining. And for $157^1/2$ 'wythewerk', $1^1/2$ bushels of salt of rent, making 354 quarters and $5^1/2$ bushels. Sum total: 2,042 quarters and 1 bushel. Of this, in acquittance of the rent of the reeve for the year, 4 quarters. Alms of the countess to the priory of Christchurch, 4 quarters.[41] Allowance made to the same for the rent of John de Fonte, by charter of the countess, 4 quarters. Gift of the countess to Henry de Schenholt, clerk, $4^1/2$ quarters, by Ralph de Blakedon. Delivered to Henry Bereward for the expenses of the castle in the eighth year from the issues of salt of the seventh year by Geoffrey le Palmer, 28 quarters, and in the ninth year by the same Geoffrey, $3^1/2$ quarters. Sold as above, 1,149 quarters $1^1/2$ bushels. Sum total: 1,197 quarters, $1^1/2$ bushels. Thus there ought to remain 844 quarters, $7^1/2$ bushels. Of this, there lack $113^1/2$ quarters and $^1/2$ bushel which are sold on account. Thus there remain 731 quarters, 3 bushels. Of this, there have been suspended 368 quarters, $5^1/2$ bushels, of which there are debited against Laurence de Wadeforde from 3 storehouses 143 quarters; against Richard Colebronde from 1 storehouse 42 quarters and 1 bushel; against Ralph de Blakedon from 2 storehouses 84 quarters, $3^1/2$ bushels; against Geoffrey le Palmer $44^1/2$ quarters and 16 quarters of the alms of the countess to the abbot of Quarr;[42] against Robert Edmund 22 quarters and 5 bushels, and 16 quarters of the alms of the countess to the abbot of Quarr; and against William Gest 362 quarters $5^1/2$ bushels, with twenty quarters delivered to Henry Bereward for the expenses of the countess, as he says, and 16 quarters of the alms of the countess to the abbot of Quarr.

Mowing and the carriage of hay, sold as above. And he is quit.

Carrying services. The same renders account for $29^1/2$ carrying services of the issues of the customary peasants. Sold as above. And he is quit.

---

41 Isabella was born into the Redvers family, and was heiress to their earldom of Devon. Christchurch priory was a Redvers foundation.

42 The abbey of Quarr was a Redvers foundation.

111. Extracts from the valor of the lands and lordships of Anne, countess of Stafford, 1435–36[43] [From Public Record Office, London, SC11/816, m. 1, 3, 8; in French]

The county of Hereford

The fee of the county of Hereford is worth £20 a year.[44]

The county of Gloucester

Newnham. Net value this year, 28s 1d.[45]

Thornbury: the office of reeve there. Net value of rent, not counting £4 13s 1d of rent repaid and 8s 6d in decay, £121 16s 8¹/₂d. Farms of demesne land, mills, and other small farms, £12 12s 11d. Annual casual issues, namely, sale of herbage in the meadow and pasture (£13 15s 5d), avesage and pannage of pigs (14s 6d),[46] agistment of pasture this year (18s), heriots and strays this year (78s 6d), hay sold this year (56s 8d), herbage of the garden this year (nothing), £22 3s 1d. Sum total of value: £156 12s 8¹/₂d.

Of this, spent on the repair of the houses of the manor (108s 6d), mills (31s 6¹/₂d), the dovecote of 'Wolford' (58s 9d), fencing of 'Callecroft' and 'Crowley' with the repair of the ponds (30s 8d), fencing of the parks with the chase of the beasts on the heath (30s 8d), payment of a hayward of 'Fylnore' (13s 4d), payment of a tiler (20s), expenses on the sea walls this year (nothing), expenses of the steward with parchment and other necessary expenses (45s 1d), £16 18s 6¹/₂d.
Wages of the parkers of 'Estwode' (60s 8d) and 'Morlewoode' (40s), 100s 8d.

43 The valor distinguished between the overall value of the lands, and the amount which accrued to the lady. In contrast to Isabella de Forz, Anne's wealth was largely derived from rents and farms. Anne was described in the heading of the valor as countess of Stafford, Buckingham, Northampton and Hereford, and lady of Brecon and Holderness; her first title was derived from her first two husbands, Thomas and Edmund earl of Stafford; the second from her father Thomas of Woodstock; and the third and fourth from her mother, Eleanor de Bohun, as she succeeded to half of the Bohun inheritance; C. Rawcliffe, *The Staffords, Earls of Stafford and Dukes of Buckingham, 1394–1521*, Cambridge, 1978, pp. 12–18. Brecon was not included in the valor, and, although Anne claimed Holderness, she did not secure it until the year before she died. The extracts give the whole valor entry for Herefordshire and Northamptonshire, selected entries for Gloucestershire, and the whole of the final summary.

44 This payment, due to the comital family, was originally the third penny, representing one-third of the profit of the county court.

45 The document uses the term 'clear value' for the net amount received by Thomas Laurence, Anne's receiver-general.

46 Avesage was a payment for pasture.

Annuity paid to John Hake, 40s a year.

Total deduction from profits: £23 19s 2¹/₂d.

Net value this year: £132 13s 6d.

Thornbury: the office of bedel. Net value of rent (5s 1d) not counting 4s a year allowed to the bedel to do his office, ploughshares[47] and customs commuted and sold this year (£49 8s 7d), £49 13s 8d. Perquisites of courts there this year, £15 7s 4d.

Sum total of value: £65 12d.

Of this, in fencing the park of 'Estwoode' this year (48s 4¹/₂d), making hay for the deer in the parks, with the carriage, and payment for officials of my lady there this year (7s), carrying letters of my most honoured lady and of the receiver-general this year (4s 6d), 59s 10¹/₂d.

Fee of the steward in the county of Gloucester, 100s.

Deduction from profits: £7 19s 10¹/₂d.

Net value this year: £57 13¹/₂d.

Thornbury: the borough. Yearly value of rent of assize, not counting 29s in decay, £6 3s 8d. Toll of fairs and markets with the issues of the Shambles, £7 15s.[48] Perquisites of courts this year, £4 2s 2d.

Sum total of value: £18 10d.

Of this, in repair of the Shambles there this year, 4s 7d.

Net value this year: £17 16s 3d.

Little Marshfield. Net value of rent, not counting rent repaid to the manor of Thornbury and rent in decay, £10 14s 6¹/₂d. Sale of pasture (4d) and pannage of pigs (21d), 2s 1d. Perquisites of courts this year, 2s 6d.

Sum total of value: £10 19s 1¹/₂d.

Rendcomb. Net value of rent this year, £4 18s 7d. Farms of demesne land, meadows and pastures, 55s 2d. Annual casual issues, namely, issues of wool and store sheep, with sheepskins sold, £4 9s 4d. Perquisites of courts this year, 117s ¹/₂d.

Sum total of value: £18 0s 5d. [£18 0s 1¹/₂d]

Of this, in store sheep purchased this year (62s 4d), mowing and making hay for the sheep (7s 4d), repair of one house called 'le Shepinne' (£9 4s ¹/₂d), wages of the bailiff (6s 8d), expenses of the steward with parchment for the courts (7s), £13 8s 10¹/₂d [£13 7s 4¹/₂d].

Deductions from profits: £13 8s 10¹/₂d. [£13 7s 4¹/₂d]

Net value this year: £6 11s 6¹/₂d. [£4 12s 9d]

---

47 Rents in kind, like ploughshares, were commuted by this time.

48 The Shambles were butchers' shops and slaughterhouses.

Office of the feodary of the honour of Gloucester. Net value of rent as described this year, 34s 4¹/₂d. Annual casual issues, namely avowries, 12d,⁴⁹ perquisites of courts this year, 46s 1d.

Sum total of value: £4 17¹/₂d.

Of this, in wages of the bailiff there, 60s 8d.

Net value this year: 20s 9¹/₂d.

The county of Northampton

Rothwell: the manor. Net value of rent and ploughshares, not counting 74s 7¹/₄d in decay, £35 17s 11¹/₄d.

Farm of the borough (£14 10s), and of demesne land (£13 6s 8d), and of pastures of 'Litilwoode' (60s) and 'del Hay' (66s 8d), and other small farms this year (73s 11d), £37 17s 3d.

Farm of the mills there a year, £11.

Annual casual issues, namely, chevage, and the sale of underwood, 37s 1d.

Perquisites of the hundred and courts this year, £8 4s 6d.

Sum total of value: £94 16s 9¹/₄d.

Of this, spent in repair of the houses and mills this year (44s), expenses of the steward together with parchment (15s 8d), wages of the bailiff of the manor (20s), and of the collector of rent (20s), and fencing of the great wood (23s 8d), £6 3s 4d.

Fee of the steward there a year, £4.

Annuity granted to Thomas Laurence, £10.

Deductions from profits: £20 3s 4d.

Net value this year: £74 13s 5¹/₂d.

Rothwell: the hundred. Value of the farm this year, 40s.

Issues of escheated lands, 53s 4d. Perquisites of courts this year, 76s 5d.

Sum total of value: £8 10s 2d [£8 9s 9d]

Glapthorn. Value of the farm this year, £15.

The fee of the county of Northampton is worth £20 a year.

Sum of the total value of all the manors and lordships of my most sovereign lady of Stafford in England, except the lordship of Holderness, as described fully and individually specified: £2,186 15s 10³/₄d. [£2,185 15s 10¹/₂d]

Of this, in rent, £815 7s 11¹/₄d.

Of this, in farms, £1,132 17s 9³/₄d.

Of this, in annual casual issues, £123 15s 11d.

Of this, in perquisites of courts, £113 14s 2¹/₂d.

Of this, spent on repairs of castles, houses, mills, parks and other items

---

49 Avowries were legal payments for warranty and protection.

as described in divers lordships individually and clearly specified,
£164 4s 2¹/₂d.

Fees of stewards and other officials described and specified individually, £48 12s 4d.

Wages of bailiffs, parkers and other officials as described and specified,
£79 16s 6d.

Annuities granted by my most sovereign lady of Stafford to divers
persons in divers manors and lordships as fully described and
individually specified, £128 13s 4d.

Sum total of all the above deductions from profits and annual charges:
£421 6s 4¹/₂d.

Sum remaining of net annual value this year: £1,765 9s 6¹/₄d. [£1,764
9s 6d]

Of this sum, there is delivered to Thomas Laurence, receiver-general,
of this year's issues for which he has accounted, as fully appears in the
receiver's certificate of account delivered to my lady, £1,751 22d.

And so of the aforesaid annual value there lacks £14 7s 8¹/₄d [£13 7s
8d], and there are in the hands of divers ministers and officials £208
7s 7³/₄d, with divers sums of desperate debts as fully appears in an
indented roll of arrears of which one copy remains with my lady for
her information, and the other with the receiver-general for levy to be
made for my lady.

**112. Extract from a letter of John Paston I giving instructions to his
wife Margaret, John Daubeney and Richard Calle, 15 January, 1465
[From J. Gairdner, ed., *Paston Letters*, Introduction, no. LIX; in
English]**

I pray you to see to the good governance of my household and the
guidance of other things concerning my profit. I ask you, Daubeney
and Richard Calle, with those of my friends and servants who can
advise you according to what the matter requires, to have a discussion
of what is to be done once a week, or more often if necessary. Take the
advice of the master, the vicar and Sir James, both concerning the
provision of stuff for my household and for the collection of the
revenues of my livelihood or grain, or for setting my servants to work,
and for the best way of selling and carrying my malt, and for all other
things which need to be done. So when I come home I do not have the
excuse that you spoke to my servants, and that Daubeney and Calle
excuse themselves that they were too busy to attend to the matter. I
will have my business so managed that, if one man cannot act, another

shall be ordered to do the job. If my servants fail, I would rather pay wages to some other man for a day or a season than that my business should not go forward.

113. A receiver's account signed by Anne Neville, duchess of Buckingham, 1467 [From British Library, London, Egerton Roll 2210; in English]

To the high and noble princess, the duchess of Buckingham. John Harcourt esquire, receiver in Staffordshire, meekly beseeches your good ladyship to command your auditor to discount and allow divers items written below for which he was given respite in divers years ending at Michaelmas, the seventh year of King Edward.[50]

First 2s 8d paid for the expenses for four days of William Barbour of Stafford riding from Stafford to Welshpool in Wales in March, the fifth year of King Edward [1465], with your letter of discharge to Lord Powys of occupying the lordship of Caus.[51] 40s for the expenses for ten days of the receiver riding with five others from Stafford to Writtle in July, the said fifth year, on your orders sent to him by letter, on the same business, staying there and returning. 16s for the expenses for four days of the receiver riding with five others from Stafford to the castle of Caus in August the same year on your orders to inquire into waste, extortions and other faults done within the lordship there by virtue of your commission sent to the receiver, staying there and returning. 6s 8d for the expenses for ten days of Ralph Hilton, the receiver's servant, riding from Stafford to Writtle in September the same year with the receiver's letter of certification of the aforesaid inquiry to your good grace. 16s for the expenses for four days of Humphrey Barbour, son of John Barbour, sent to you by the receiver on your orders from Stafford to London in November the same year. Also for the expenses of William Barbour and a boy of the same Humphrey on the same journey, taking four days, staying for two days, and home again, taking four days, in all amongst them twenty-four days. 6s 8d for the hire of two horses at Stafford for ten days for the same Humphrey Barbour and his boy on the same journey there and back. 6s 8d for the expenses for six days of Roger Clerk and his boy with William Warde riding from Stafford to Marshfield to

50 John Harcourt was receiver of Caus in 1466, and of Staffordshire from 1465 until at least 1476; Rawcliffe, *The Staffords*, pp. 208, 215.
51 Richard Lord Powys was steward of Caus in 1465-66.

supervise the lordship and repairs, staying there and returning in November the same year.

Sum total: £4 14s 8d.

Also for the money paid to Sir John Stanley knight, sheriff of Staffordshire, in the aforesaid fifth year, for rent paid to the king in his exchequer at Westminster for the farm of a pool in Stafford called the 'kyngespoole' for the same year, 26s 8d.

Also for money paid to Sir John Stanley, former sheriff of Staffordshire, for green wax paid by you in the king's exchequer, 70s.[52]

Also for money paid to him as former sheriff of Staffordshire for the king's use for green wax, 46s 8d.

Also for money paid to William Basset esquire, former sheriff of Staffordshire, for green wax, 33s.

Also for money paid to Lady Shrewsbury for half a year on your orders, £30.[53]

Also for money paid to Cicely Doughty on your orders, 40s.

Sum total: £45 11s.

May it please your most noble grace to sign this bill with your hand and sign manual as warrant and discharge to your auditor.

Anne duchess of Buckingham, countess of Hereford, Northampton and Stafford, greets our trusty and well-beloved Thomas Rogers, our auditor in Staffordshire, willing and charging you that if these above items have not been allowed in any earlier account you should then make full and clear allowance of them to our most trusty and well-beloved John Harcourt esquire, our receiver in the aforesaid shire.

[Signed] Anne b

114. Petition of Margaret de Brotherton to parliament, pointing out that her tenants were not liable to contribute to the building of the bridge at Huntingdon, 1377 [From *Rotuli Parliamentorum*, III, p. 30; in French]

To our lord the king and to the noble lords of parliament. Margaret countess of Norfolk and Lady Segrave shows that she holds the vills of Everton and Fenstanton in the county of Huntingdon as part of the earldom of Norfolk and the lordship of Segrave. The earldom and

---

52 The seal of green wax was used on documents issued by the exchequer.

53 The sum of £30 was originally written, but crossed out and £15 substituted. Anne Neville's daughter, Katherine Stafford, married John Talbot, earl of Shrewsbury.

lordship with all the vills and tenants belonging to them are quit of toll, pontage, passage and all other customs in the kingdom of England, and have been so since time immemorial. An action has been brought in King's Bench against the tenants of the above vills to distrain them to make a contribution to the building of Huntingdon bridge, contrary to the aforesaid quittance and franchise, to the disinheritance of the countess and her heirs, and the injury of the tenants of the above vills. May it please our lord the king and the aforesaid noble lords to ordain remedy in this case, and may the action cease until another remedy be provided.

115. *Carta* of Margaret de Bohun, 1166 [From H. Hall, ed., *Red Book of the Exchequer*, 3 vols, Rolls Series, 1897, I, pp. 293–4; in Latin]

Margaret de Bohun has these knights who were enfeoffed in the time of King Henry [I] in the fee of Miles of Gloucester, her father, and whom she holds in chief of the king.[54]

Hugh the small owes four knights.[55]
Philip son of Ernulf, two knights.
Othuer de Sunewrthe, two knights.
Almaric de Lokintona, one knight.
Ralph Cokerel and Elias his brother, one knight.
William de Pinkeini, one knight.
Richard de Blenchendone and Walter son of Robert, one knight.
Richard de Sancto Quintino, $\frac{1}{2}$ knight.
Richard Canut and Walter, one knight.
Walter de Esseleia, one knight.
William Picard, two knights.
Gilbert de Mineriis[56] and Hugh de Cundicote $\frac{1}{2}$ knight.
Of these, Isabella the wife of Henry de Hereford has five knights in dower.[57]

---

54 Henry II asked his tenants-in-chief to distinguish between the knights of the old enfeoffment who were enfeoffed before the death of Henry I in 1135, and those of the new enfeoffment who were enfeoffed subsequently. He also asked how many knights were needed to make up the service due to the king over and above those who had been enfeoffed. Margaret de Bohun was the daughter of Miles of Gloucester earl of Hereford (d. 1143); her four brothers succeeded in turn, but left no heirs, and Margaret succeeded to the inheritance in 1165, the same year as her husband, Humphrey de Bohun, died. She did not remarry, and died *c.* 1197.

55 Hugh's name was given in Latin as *parvus.*

56 The Latin word *mineria* means 'a mine'.

57 Henry de Hereford was the third son of Miles of Gloucester, and died in 1165.

Margaret also has the following knights enfeoffed of her demesnes after the death of King Henry [I]; her father and brothers enfeoffed them.

William de Cernay, ¹/₂ knight.

William Torel, in 'Cernay', ¹/₄ knight.

Elias Cokerel, ¹/₂ knight.

Roger son of Alan, 1¹/₂ knights.

Richard Murdac, one knight.

116. Letter sent by Edward III to Margaret, widow of Edmund earl of Kent, concerning the defence of the realm, 1335 [From A. Clarke, J. Caley, J. Bayley, F. Holbrooke and J. W. Clarke, eds, *Rymer's Foedera*, *1086–1383*, 4 vols, Record Commission, London, 1816–69, II, p. 916; in Latin]

The king greets Margaret who was the wife of Edmund, formerly earl of Kent. As we have learned for certain, divers fleets of warships, strongly armed, and with men at arms and others from foreign parts, are now massed on the sea. The same men and ships have the hostile intention of invading our kingdom, attacking and oppressing us and our people, and perpetrating other evils if possible both by land and sea. Desiring to meet their cunning and presumptuous villainy, and to provide for the salvation and defence of our realm and people, with the Lord's inspiration, and fully trusting in the maturity of your counsel and of other prelates and magnates in your region, we firmly order you in the faith and love in which you are bound to us that, leaving everything else, you should send some of the more discreet of your close advisers to London.[58] They are to be there on Friday, the morrow of the feast of St Bartholomew the apostle next [25 August], along with some of our faithful men whom we are going to send there on that day, and with certain other prelates, magnates and other faithful men who are going to gather there on our orders. They are to treat and ordain on the safe custody and secure defence of our realm and people, and on resisting and driving out the foreigners; and also on certain other matters concerning us and the state of the realm to be more fully explained to you by our aforesaid faithful men whom we are sending, and you are to give your counsel and advice on the aforesaid business. Notwithstanding this, you should meanwhile arm and array your people, so that they are well arrayed and may set out promptly with other of our faithful men for the defence of the realm and people, and

58 The corresponding orders to magnates summoned them in person to London.

of you and yours, to repel powerfully and courageously the presumptuous boldness and malice of our same enemies, with God's help, if
those enemies invade. You and the rest of our realm are bound in every
possible way to give help for the defence of the kingdom against
hostile invasions of this kind, especially as we are in remote parts for
the realm's defence, and we are heartily assuming that you would not
deservedly be blamed for any negligence or lukewarmness in so great
and so arduous a business, but rather be commended for showing
strength and mature counsels. Witnessed by the king at Perth on 7
August.

The same orders were sent to:
Marie who was the wife of Aymer de Valence, late earl of Pembroke.
Joan who was the wife of Thomas Botetourt.

**117. The honour court of Isabella de Forz for the Isle of Wight, 1280–
81**[59] [From Public Record Office, London, SC6/984/9, m. 3d; in Latin]

The account of William and Roger de Rugrigge, serjeants of the
liberty from the morrow of Michaelmas in the eighth year of the reign
of King Edward to the morrow of Michaelmas in the ninth year of the
same reign.

Receipts. The same render account of 118s 10¹/₂d from the arrears of
the last account. 53s 4d from the fine at the view of frankpledge. 7s 8¹/₂d
from the relief of John the goldsmith for his tenement in Upper
Clatford. 13s 4d from the abbot of Titchfield for scutage of one-third
of a knight's fee in Cadnam. 13s 4d from the same abbot for making the
eldest son of the countess a knight, due from the same tenement.[60] £15
14d from the pleas and perquisites of the court this year, and so less
this year because of the eyre of the [royal] justices in the county. 56s
2d from the sale of one tun and one pipe of wine at Yarmouth and one
piece of mast and boards coming from wreck of the sea at Newtown
and Chale. 4s from Adam Osbern, formerly reeve of Yarmouth for his
arrears.
Sum total of receipts: £28 7s 11d.

Expenses. The same account for the expenses of William the serjeant
at Winchester for the eyre of the [royal] justices in the county, with
his ferry-passage on divers occasions, 8s 5¹/₂d. Expenses of Roger de

59 Isabella de Forz's administration of justice in the Isle of Wight is discussed by
   Denholm-Young, *Seignorial Administration*, pp. 99-108.

60 Isabella's son Thomas died before 6 April 1269.

Rugrigge, bailiff, at the county court at Winchester and before the justices of gaol delivery there, with his ferry-passage several times, and for making distraint for the scutage of the abbot of Titchfield 13s 4^1/$_2$d, and henceforth they ought not to have an allowance for expenses. Sum total of expenses: 21s 10d.

Deliveries. The same account for delivery made to William de Monte, reeve of Bowcombe by William, £8 15s by three tallies. Item, delivered to the same man by Roger de Rugrigge, £10 18s 4^1/$_2$d by four tallies. Item, delivered to the same by the same from the arrears of Nicholas Crey, 17s 6d.
Sum total: £20 10s 10^1/$_2$d.
Sum total of all expenses and deliveries: £21 12s 8^1/$_2$d.
Thus £6 15s 2^1/$_2$d is owed to the countess. Of this, Nicholas Crey, formerly serjeant, owes £4 4s 5^1/$_4$d, William the serjeant 14s 5^3/$_4$d, and the aforesaid Roger 36s 3^1/$_2$d.

118. Instances of feudal business at the honour court of Clare, 1326–27 (the lady was Elizabeth de Burgh) [From Public Record Office, London SC2/212/43, m. 2, 7, 10d; in Latin]

Norfolk, 33s 4d.[61] From Roger Gyney for respite of suit of court until Michaelmas, ^{1}/$_2$ mark. From Richard de Boylond for the same, 4s. From John de Boylond for the same, 6s. From William de Brethenham for the same, 40d. From John de Brokedisch, 40d. From William de Brunne for the same, 40d. From John de Broughtone for the same, 40d. From John Howard for the same, 40d.

Essex, memorandum. William FitzRalph makes fine for the guard of the castle of Clare, one mark for each fee, to be paid at Christmas if his peers do the same, by the pledges, Thomas rector of the church of Little Wendon, Nicholas de Noers and Robert de Shangh.

Suffolk, Essex. Relief £6 5s [sic]; assigned by letter of the lady, 100s. Richard de Cornerde who held of the lady certain tenements in Finchingfield, Bulmer, Cavendish, Clare and elsewhere in return for the service of 1^1/$_2$ fees and a quarter of a knight's fee and suit of court and 4d yearly rent etc. has died. Thomas, his son and next heir who is of age, now comes, and asks to be admitted to the inheritance. He is admitted, and did homage and fealty to the lady. He pays his relief of

---

61 The opening statement of each entry is taken from the margin of the manuscript.

which 100*s* is assigned to Edward de Monthermer by the lady's letter.[62]

Petronilla de Nerford who recently died held of the lady certain tenements in Bodham, Letheringsett, Holt and Bayfield and elsewhere by the service of 1½ knights, and she died in the homage of the lady. John her son and heir who is of age comes and pays £7 10*s* relief.

119. Arrangements for wardship made by Alina la Despenser countess of Norfolk, 1280[63] [From Public Record Office, London, E40/5480; in Latin]

Agreement made in the eighth year of King Edward at Fastern [in Wootton Bassett] on the feast of Holy Trinity [16 June] between Lady Alina la Despenser countess of Norfolk on one side and Robert fitz John of Otley on the other, namely that Alina grants and demises to Robert the custody of the lands and tenements in Barningham with all appurtenances which used to be held by John Pond[64] and Lucy his wife, and were in the hands of the countess because of the custody of Isabella and Katherine, daughters and heirs of John and Lucy, except anything which can fall to the countess because of the custody or which ought to belong to her in 'Ighinton' and elsewhere in Hertford-shire, and saving to the countess the marriages of Isabella and Katherine. Robert, his heirs and assigns are to have and hold the custody until Isabella and Katherine come of age. In return for this grant and demise, Robert is bound to pay the countess or her appointed attorney in her manor of Wix ten marks a year of good sterling until Isabella and Katherine come of age, at these terms, namely five marks at Christmas and five marks at the Nativity of St John the Baptist, the first payment to be made at Christmas in the ninth year of King Edward [1280]. The countess also granted to the aforesaid Robert the portion appertaining to her of all the grain sown on the aforesaid land on the day of completion of the agreement, in return for six marks of good sterling which Robert is bound to pay to the countess or her appointed attorney in her manor of Wix at

62 Edward de Monthermer was Elizabeth de Burgh's half-brother. There are further payments of relief in no. 129.

63 Alina was the daughter and heiress of Philip Basset and the widow of Hugh le Despenser (d. 1265); Wix and Wootton Bassett were part of her inheritance. She was dealing with this matter in the lifetime of her second husband, Roger Bigod earl of Norfolk (d. 1306).

64 The surname is given in the Latin form, *de stagno*.

Michaelmas in the eighth year of the reign of King Edward [1280]. Robert and four good and suitable men with him will bind themselves, their heirs and executors by a writing of obligation as principal debtors for the ten marks a year and the aforesaid six marks to be paid to the countess, together with restoration and refunding of losses and expenses if any are incurred by the countess, her heirs or executors, or if they incur them by reason of not paying the aforesaid money at the said place and terms. The countess and her heirs will warrant the custody of the aforesaid lands and tenements to Robert, his heirs and assigns until Isabella and Katherine come of age. In witness of this, the countess and Robert have affixed their seals alternately to this present writing which has been made in the form of a chirograph. Given at Fastern on the above-named day and year.

120. Franchises claimed by Isabella de Forz in Cockermouth, 1292
[From W. Illingworth and J. Caley, eds, *Placita de Quo Warranto*, Record Commission, London, 1818, pp. 112–13; in Latin]

Isabella de Forz countess of Aumale and Thomas de Lucy were summoned to answer the lord king in the plea by what warrant they claim to have the return of the lord king's writs in Cockermouth and within the liberty of the honour of Cockermouth infangenetheof, utfangenetheof, and the right to hold pleas of withername; and to have the chattels of hanged felons who were condemned in their court at Cockermouth;[65] and to have a coroner to do their will in their aforesaid liberty; and to hold pleas of the Crown, make attachments of appeals of felony, and in the prosecution of appeals of this kind proceed to outlawry, all of which franchises belong to the Crown and the dignity of the lord king.

Isabella and Thomas come in the person of Isabella's attorney and say that a certain William fitz Duncan died seised of the aforesaid liberties between the waters of Cocker and Derwent as belonging to his lands as of old. The right descended from William to Cecily and Annabel as daughters and heirs. The right of Cecily's pourparty descended to Hawise as daughter and heir, and from Hawise to her son and heir, William de Forz, formerly Isabella's husband, whose lands are in the seisin of the lord king. Isabella holds what she now holds there in

---

65 The franchise of return of writs enabled its holder to exclude the sheriff from his lands; pleas of withername comprised cases of wrongful distraint or unjust detention of chattels. Infangenetheof and utfangenetheof gave the lord the right to exact justice on a thief caught red-handed on or off the demesne.

dower, and the lord king has the reversion. From Annabel daughter of William fitz Duncan, the right of her pourparty descended to Richard as son and heir, and from Richard to Amabel and Alice as daughters and heirs. Amabel's pourparty descended to Thomas de Multon of Egremont as son and heir. The right of Alice's pourparty descended to Thomas de Lucy as son and heir. Therefore they say that without Thomas de Multon of Egremont the parceners should not answer.

William Inge says on behalf of the lord king that the above-mentioned predecessor William fitz Duncan did not die seised of the aforesaid liberties. He asks for an inquiry on this on behalf of the king. He says also that Isabella and Thomas are not now in seisin of the liberties in the form in which they claim them, saying that although they claim to have return of writs in common, Isabella's bailiff, appointed there to do her will, received the returns of writs and made executions without Thomas being involved in any way. He asks for an inquiry on this on behalf of the king, and he asks for judgment.

As for infangenetheof and utfangenetheof, the same William says on behalf of the lord king that they used them improperly, and asks for an inquiry.

As for the chattels of felons the same William says that no one in the realm is allowed to receive these chattels without a special deed of one of the kings of England, and he asks that Isabella and Thomas should say from which felons they were in seisin of the chattels. They say that their predecessors had this type of chattels, namely from an Adam Rayfra, Henry Saurthone and Alan Locheyn hanged at Braithwaite.

William asks them to show if a liberty of this kind was ever allowed them in the lord king's court, and if they or any of their predecessors ever received chattels of this kind in the lord king's exchequer from the treasurer or barons there, or in any eyre from the itinerant justices. They show nothing, and they do not wish to call on any record as warrant. They make no answer except only that they and all their predecessors from time immemorial took all the chattels of felons which they could find in their fee immediately after those felons were condemned in their court and hanged in their fee, so that they never afterwards came to claim them.

William Inge says on behalf of the lord king that it is and used to be a general article of inquiry in every eyre to inquire concerning the chattels of felons wheresoever they were condemned. Inasmuch as Isabella and Thomas wish to appropriate this liberty and cannot say that they or any of their predecessors were ever allowed in any eyre to receive chattels of felons nor that these were ever allowed them in the exchequer, he asks for judgment on behalf of the lord king whether they can have any title to the aforesaid liberty through this kind of unjust usurpation and when the chattels were never allowed them. As for the other liberties he asks for an inquiry on behalf of the lord king as to how they and their predecessors exercised them. So let there be an inquiry.

The jurors say on oath that the common ancestor of the aforesaid Thomas and of William, formerly Isabella's husband, died in seisin of the aforesaid liberties, and they and all their ancestors exercised these liberties without any interruption. They say that after the death of the common ancestor the lands were partitioned between William, Isabella's husband, and Alice, mother of Thomas whose heir he is. William had the privilege as eldest co-heir, and therefore whoever was William's constable of the castle of Cockermouth was coroner of the whole of William's and Alice's land between the waters of Cocker and Derwent. When any plea of the Crown arose, Alice's steward sat with the coroner and they held the pleas in common and shared the profits between them equally. They say also that the bailiff appointed by William received the returns of writs, executed them and answered for them on behalf of William and Alice, so that if the bailiff was convicted before the justices of any transgression in returns of this kind both William and Alice would be amerced. If the bailiff received the return of a writ to be pleaded in the court of his lord, then William's bailiff and Thomas's bailiff held these pleas together, and the profits were divided as aforesaid, and thus they used the liberties for the whole lives of William and Alice, and after their deaths Isabella and Thomas similarly exercised them. Asked if the coroner or bailiff took an oath to Thomas or Alice, they say that he did not.[66]

121. Ela countess of Salisbury's right to be sheriff of Wiltshire, according to a case brought by her son, 1237-38[67] [From F. W. Maitland, ed., *Bracton's Note Book*, no. 1235; in Latin]

William Longespee sought against the lord king the custody of the castle of Salisbury and the county of Wiltshire in fee as that which

66 Isabella died before judgment was pronounced.

67 Ela was required to surrender Salisbury castle shortly after the death of her husband William Longespee in 1226, but she acted as sheriff in 1227-28 and between 1231 and the beginning of 1237; she accounted at the exchequer in person at Michaelmas 1236.

descended to him from his ancestors by right of inheritance, namely from Earl Patrick and William his son, and from Ela, William's daughter and the mother of William Longespee. He says that Patrick was seised of this as of his fee in the time of King H[enry II], grandfather of the lord king, and he seeks his seisin.

The lord king now as on another occasion replied that there was an inquisition by jury concerning this in the time of King John his father between the lord king John and William earl of Salisbury and Ela his wife. This found that Ela had no right to the custody. The lord king put himself on the record of his court.

William replied that if the inquisition was taken it should not damage him because at that time Ela was a minor and not married to William his father. On this he put himself on an inquiry by the neighbourhood. The record from the time of King John was sought and found, and it stated that the inquisition by jury was taken in the ninth year of King John [1207-08] between the lord king himself and William earl of Salisbury and his wife to find out whether she had the right to the county of Wiltshire as of fee or by royal grant. The jurors said that she had no hereditary right to it from her ancestors, but only by royal grant, and not in fee, and therefore John the lord king remained in seisin both of the castle and of the county. This is correct because after the death of William Longespee Ela came in her widowhood and received the castle and county by grant of the present lord king, and she drew up her charter to the lord king that she could claim or acquire nothing of right for herself from that grant.

122. Grant of the custody of Rochester castle by Henry IV to his mother-in-law Joan de Bohun countess of Hereford, 1399[68] [From Public Record Office, London, C66/355, m. 21; in Latin]

The king greets all to whom these present letters come. You should know that of our special grace we have granted to our beloved mother Joan de Bohun countess of Hereford that for the term of her life she should be able to stay in our castle of Rochester with free ingress and egress as often and when she pleases, and that she should have custody of the same castle in the absence of William Darundell knight, with her reliable deputy to occupy it for whom she is willing to be answerable.

68 For Joan de Bohun's role in foiling plots against Henry IV early in his reign, see A. Goodman, 'The countess and the rebels: Essex and a crisis in English society (1400)', *Transactions of the Essex Archaeological Society*, third series, II, 1970, pp. 267-79.

In testimony of this we have had these our letters patent drawn up. Witnessed by the king at Westminster on 5 November.

123. The creation of Margaret de Brotherton as duchess of Norfolk, 1397 [From *Rotuli Parliamentorum*, III, p. 355a; in French]

Item, our lord the king wishing to honour, enhance and increase the name and estate of his honourable cousin Margaret Marshal countess of Norfolk, on the same day in full parliament, in the absence of the countess, has made and created her a duchess, and has given her the style, title, honour and name of duchess of Norfolk, to hold for life. He sent her her charter of the creation.

124. The attempt by the countess of Oxford to rally support for Richard II, 1404 [From H. T. Riley, ed., *Thomae Walsingham Historia Anglicana*, 2 vols., Rolls Series, London, 1863–64, II, pp. 262-3; in Latin]

At the same time, the little old countess, formerly of Oxford, mother of Robert de Vere duke of Ireland, whom we have said was in exile and died at Louvain, had rumours spread throughout Essex by her and her household servants that King Richard was alive and that he would soon come to claim his former honour. She had made very many silver and gilt harts, the badges that King Richard used to confer on his knights, esquires and friends, so that, when these were distributed in place of the king, the knights and the rest of the powerful men of that region might be more easily enticed to go along with her wishes.[69]

At this time many gave credence to the words and writings of the countess to such an extent that they believed her lies. Some religious men, abbots of that region, were held on the king's orders and committed to prison because they were seen to have sided with the countess. The countess was committed to strict custody and all her goods were confiscated.

125. The annuities and fees of the retainers of Joan Beauchamp, lady of Abergavenny, who were members of her council or in her service, 1425–26 [From Public Record Office, London, SC11/25; in Latin]

John Lenche esquire, £6 13s 4d
Walter Hakeluyte esquire, £6 13s 4d
Thomas Hewster, 40s

---

69 Walsingham goes on to other subjects at this point, and returns to the countess on the next page.

Thomas Gower, £6 13s 4d
John Harewell esquire, £10
John Brugge esquire, £10
Edward Blondell esquire, £10
Thomas Harewell, £6 13s 4d
Thomas Besforde esquire, £10[70]
John Brace esquire, £6 13s 4d
William Buryton esquire, 100s
Hugh Harnage esquire, 40s
William Aubrey esquire, 100s
John Wysham esquire, £6 13s 4d
Thomas Stanley esquire, 100s
Nicholas Wylkes, £6 13s 4d
John Barton, 40s
John Burgoyn, 40s
Laurence Engle, 13s 4d
Lewis Robesart knight, £26 13s 4d
Oliver Groce esquire, 40s
William Newporte, 40s
John Leverer esquire, 66s 8d
William Faukener yeoman, 53s 4d[71]
Sum total: £137. [£147]

126. Letters patent issued by Edward III in favour of Andrew de Bures and Warin de Bassingburn at the request of Elizabeth de Burgh, 1345 (both men were among her officials and counsellors)
[From Public Record Office, London, C66/214, m. 12; in Latin]

The king greets all to whom the present letters come. You should know that of our special grace and because our beloved and faithful Andrew de Bures is attending to the business of our beloved kinswoman Elizabeth de Burgh, we have granted to Andrew at the request of our same kinswoman that he should not be compelled to set out with us in our service outside our kingdom of England against his will for one year after the date of these present letters, notwithstanding any commission or order made by us to the contrary. In testimony of this we have had these our letters patent drawn up. Witnessed by the king at Westminster on 8 October.

Warin de Bassingburn has similar letters of the same date.

70 Thomas Besforde received a bequest of 100 marks in Joan's will.
71 William Faukener was described as *valettus*, the only use of the term in the list.

V: Household

The household was the centre and hub of the lady's life and activities, and can be regarded as a community in its own right. Households varied considerably in size according to the lady's status and responsibilities. Wives of the higher nobility generally had their own mini-household, as in the case of Elizabeth countess of Hereford, and they took charge of the whole household in the absence of their husbands.[1] Much of the information about women's households, however, relates to the time when they were widows. The smooth running of the household enabled the lady to pursue her public and private activities, to offer hospitality, entertain friends and members of her and her husband's family, and maintain contacts with the court, great nobles, and gentry and local society, depending on her rank, connections and interests. The household constituted the administrative centre of her lands; here she met her officials and council, and sent out her orders. It provided her with the means to travel and moved residences with her, thus furthering her landed and business responsibilities and her social and religious interests. Much of the lady's life was lived in the public gaze, even at the end of the Middle Ages, although there was then greater privacy than earlier on. The household provided the setting of splendour, colour and display with which the lady impressed society. Certainly there were differences of degree depending on the lady's rank and wealth, but for women of both the nobility and the gentry the desire to put on a good show was universal, and all had similar concerns and responsibilities for family, dependants and land.[2]

Although the witnesses to twelfth-century charters throw light on women's servants and officials, much fuller information on the household is available from the thirteenth century. The importance of the household at that time is underlined by the 'Rules of St Robert', said to have been drawn up by Robert Grosseteste for the widowed countess of Lincoln in c. 1241; he emphasised that the tone of the household was set by the lady who was in overall charge. Most knowledge of the household is derived from household accounts and wills; household accounts are

1 Ward, *English Noblewomen*, pp. 50-2.
2 For detailed discussion on the nature of the household, see K. Mertes, *The English Noble Household, 1250-1600: Good Governance and Politic Rule*, Oxford, 1988.

first found in the 1180s and become more numerous after *c.* 1250. The term covers a wide variety of records, all throwing light on different aspects of household activity. Many came to be arranged according to household department, which aided the attempt to ensure the account-ability of officials, but can give a misleading impression, especially in smaller households, of the degree of bureaucratic departmentalisation.[3] Some accounts cover the provisioning of a household over the year; the accounts for the higher nobility, as for Elizabeth de Burgh in 1350-51, reveal an extremely complex operation, while those for Elizabeth Stonor point to a much smaller household. Some accounts survive which give details of the lady's personal expenditure; others referred to individual household departments or to particular occasions such as a journey. The majority of accounts to survive were diet accounts, showing the consumption of provisions on a daily or weekly basis, and often providing information as to the place of residence and visitors.[4] The fullest series of accounts to survive are those of Elizabeth de Burgh, dating from 1326 to 1359, who as a member of the higher nobility ran a complex business operation, as her wardrobe account for 1350–51 shows. Her use of her demesne manors to supply the household was combined with purchasing along the lines recommended in the 'Rules of St Robert'. At the end of the Middle Ages, the development of a *rentier* economy put more emphasis on purchase from local markets and from London.

Household accounts provide some information about the servants of the household, especially where references survive to wages and fees and where there are details about the provision of livery. However, fuller information is often provided in wills and some testators, such as Elizabeth countess of Salisbury, provided bequests for their entire household, naming them individually. What all the lists indicate is that the household was very much a male institution, with only a small number of female servants. The servants had their own hierarchy, a point made clear by both the livery lists and bequests.[5]

---

3 It also has to be borne in mind that the nature and work of individual departments varied between one household and another. As will be seen from the examples translated, most household accounts specified the pantry, buttery, kitchen and stables, but in a noble household the number of accounting departments could be much larger.

4 For detailed discussion of household accounts and for examples in the original language, see C. M. Woolgar, ed., *Household Accounts from Medieval England*, 2 vols, British Academy, Records of Social and Economic History, new series, XVII, XVIII, Oxford, 1992-93.

5 The hierarchy is apparent in no. 156, the rules for the household of Cecily duchess of York.

The lady's residence acted as the centre for hospitality, and here the diet accounts of the household are most informative. The exercise of hospitality by gentry, knights and nobility was regarded as an important social duty throughout the Middle Ages and later. Some household accounts, like those of Alice de Brian, show the range of people fed and entertained, from the poor and nameless strangers to relatives and neighbours of noble rank. The entertainment of one's peers occurred frequently, and quite apart from the element of enjoyment and pleasure, provided occasions for the exercise of influence and the discussion of business.

It was on occasions such as these that the element of display was all-important. The diet accounts give details of the food on offer, though not of its presentation. In view of the number of servants and retainers who belonged to the household or were visiting, the quantities were not necessarily excessive. Of more significance than the standard fare are the special items provided by the lady for her special guests, such as swan, heron, and boar's head, which were designed to impress. The setting for the lady also needed to be splendid. Most women inherited their residences, but some engaged in building activity, particularly if they wished to develop a new place of residence. Building work was sometimes recorded in both household and estate accounts, mostly with reference to wages and materials, rather than to the appearance of the new building. Wills are usually most informative on the colour and rich materials of the furnishings, and on the amount of silver and silver-gilt plate, although a few separate inventories survive.[6] The lady's dress and jewellery added to the overall impression of wealth, and here again much information is derived from wills, although the accounts of Mary de Bohun countess of Derby provide detail on the purchase of materials and the making of clothes.

The lady had her own pursuits in addition to her business and entertainment. Hunting and falconry were popular among noble-women, and sewing and embroidery were regarded as female pursuits. Many noblewomen were able to read, and romances were apparently enjoyed. Some are recorded in wills, though not in the same numbers as the devotional works to be considered later.[7] All these activities

---

6 E.g. the inventory of plate for Elizabeth countess of Hereford of 1304-05; Public Record Office, London, E101/367/1.

7 See no. 34, from the will of Eleanor de Bohun. In 1432 Joan Hilton made two bequests of romances, one to her sister and one to her niece; Borthwick Institute of Historical Research, York, Probate Register 3, fo. 347.

could be carried on wherever the lady was living. Although the changing of residences became less frequent than indicated in the 'Rules of St Robert', travel was often undertaken for a variety of purposes, the lady travelling by carriage, litter or on horseback. When the time came to move to another residence, the household packed up its belongings and moved on.

127. The governance of a noblewoman's household, *c.* 1241[8] [From 'The Rules of St Robert', in Lamond, *Walter of Henley's Husbandry*, pp. 132–7, 140–1, 144–5; in French]

The ninth rule teaches you what you ought to say often to small and great of your household, that all should do your commands.

Say to all small and great, and that often, that fully, quickly, and willingly, without grumbling and contradiction, they do all your commands that are not against God.

The tenth rule teaches you the particular command that you ought to give to the marshal of your household.

Command those that govern your house before all your household that they keep careful watch that all your household within and without be faithful, painstaking, chaste, clean, honest and profitable.

The thirteenth rule teaches you how by your commandment peace shall be kept in your household.

Command that in no way there be in your household any who make strife, discord, or divisions in the household, but all shall be of one accord, of one will as of one heart and one soul. Command that all those who are your yeomen[9] be obedient and ready to those who are over them in the things which belong to their occupation.

The fourteenth rule teaches you how your alms shall, by your commandment, be faithfully observed and gathered, and discreetly spent on the poor.

Command that your alms be faithfully gathered and kept, not sent from the table to the grooms, nor carried out of the hall, either at

---

8 See no. 109 for the 'Rules' for the governance of estates.

9 The French term used here, *seriaunz de mester*, means literally 'workers at a craft'. However, the term is used in other households (e.g. Public Record Office, London, E101/92/23) as an intermediate rank between esquires and grooms, and it is likely that this is the meaning here.

supper or dinner, by good-for-nothing grooms; but freely, discreetly, and orderly, without dispute and strife, divided among the poor, sick and beggars.

The fifteenth rule teaches you how your guests ought to be received.

Command strictly that all your guests, secular and religious, be quickly, courteously, and with good cheer received by the steward from the porters, ushers, and marshals, and by all be courteously addressed and in the same way lodged and served.

The sixteenth rule teaches you in what clothes your people should wait on you at meals.

Command your knights and all your gentlemen who wear your livery, that that same livery which they use daily, especially at your meals, and in your presence, be kept for your honour, and not old tabards and soiled surcoats, and imitation short hose.

The seventeenth rule teaches you how you ought to seat your people at meals in your house.

Make your freemen and guests sit as far as possible at tables on either side, not four here and three there. And all the crowd of grooms shall enter together when the freemen are seated, and shall sit together and rise together. And strictly forbid any quarrelling at your meals. And you yourself always be seated at the middle of the high table, that your presence as lord or lady may appear openly to all, and that you may plainly see on either side all the service and all the faults. And be careful of this, that each day at your meals you have two overseers over your household when you sit at meals, and of this be sure, that you shall be very much feared and reverenced.

The twenty-first rule teaches you how your people ought to behave towards your friends, both in your presence and absence.

Command that your knights and chaplains, and yeomen and your gentlemen, with a good manner and hearty cheer and ready service receive and honour, in your presence and out of it, all those in every place whom they perceive by your words or your manners to be especially dear to you, and to whom you would have special honour shown, for in so doing can they particularly show that they wish what you wish. And as far as possible for sickness or fatigue, constrain yourself to eat in the hall before your people, for this shall bring great benefit and honour to you.

The twenty-sixth rule teaches how at Michaelmas you may arrange your sojourn for all the year.

Every year, at Michaelmas, when you know the measure of all your corn, then arrange your sojourn for the whole of that year, and for how many weeks in each place, according to the seasons of the year, and the advantages of the country in flesh and in fish, and do not in any wise burden by debt or long residence the places where you sojourn, but so arrange your sojourns that the place at your departure shall not remain in debt, but something may remain on the manor, whereby the manor can raise money from increase of stock, and especially cows and sheep, until your stock acquits your wines, robes, wax, and all your wardrobe, and that will be in a short time if you hold and act after this treatise, as you can see plainly in this way. The wool of a thousand sheep in good pasture ought to yield at the least fifty marks a year, the wool of two thousand a hundred marks, and so forth, counting by thousands. The wool of a thousand sheep in scant pasture ought to yield at the least forty marks, in coarse and poor pasture thirty marks.

The twenty-seventh rule teaches you how much the return from cows and sheep is worth.

The return from cows and sheep in cheese is worth much money every day in the season, without calves and lambs, and without the manure, which all return corn and fruit.

The twenty-eighth rule teaches you at what times in the year you ought to make your purchases.

I advise that at two seasons of the year you make your principal purchases, that is to say your wines, and your wax, and your wardrobe, at the fair of St Botolph [Boston], what you shall spend in Lindsey and in Norfolk, in the Vale of Belvoir, and in the country of Caversham, and in that at Southampton for Winchester, and Somerset at Bristol; your robes purchase at St Ives.

128. Evidence for the household of Elizabeth countess of Hereford, 1304 (although the countess was with her husband, she was paying her own servants and had her own wardrobe)[10] [From Public Record Office, London, E101/365/20, m. 1; in Latin]

Edinburgh, Tuesday 28 July. For the buttery, kitchen, scullery, saucery and chamber, nothing, because with the earl of Hereford. Wages delivered to servants, 5s. Stable: pasture for 5 horses for the carriage, 5 palfreys, 6 pack-horses, 14 cart-horses, 2 hackneys, two horses of Gilbert de Bromle, 1 horse of Martin, marshal of the horses, and 1 horse of Roger de Markle, clerk of offices, 2s 4d. Oats for 10 carriage-horses and palfreys, taken together, and 26 horses at the allowance of $^1/_2$ bushel, $2^1/_2$ quarters and 1 bushel, costing 5s 4d a quarter, 14s. Wages of the grooms, with light, 3s $10^1/_2d$. Paid for 1 cart carrying the countess's wardrobe, 2s.
Sum total: 27s $2^1/_2d$.

129. The provisioning of Elizabeth de Burgh's household according to her wardrobe account of 1350–51[11] [From Public Record Office, London, E101/93/8; in Latin]

The account of Sir William de Manton, clerk of the wardrobe of Lady Elizabeth de Burgh, lady of Clare, from the morrow of Michaelmas in the twenty-fourth year of the reign of King Edward III to the same day in the twenty-fifth year.

Receipts[12]

Brandon. Sir William de Manton answers for 70s 1d received from

10 Elizabeth was starting her journey to Knaresborough where her son Humphrey was born; see nos. 50, 51. Of the household offices, the pantry was responsible for bread, the buttery for drink, the kitchen for meat and fish, the scullery for dishes, the saucery for sauces, and the chamber for the countess's personal expenses. The clerk of offices was the clerk who accounted for the kitchen.

11 Much of the account on the face of the roll has been given, although in certain places selected extracts have been chosen. The corn and stock account was entered on the dorse of the roll, and this has not been translated. The wardrobe was responsible for the overall provisioning of the household.

12 The receipts begin with eighteeen entries detailing money and provisions received from demesne manors and bailiwicks. The provisions were costed and the local reeve or other official would enter the amount among the receipts of his own account, and produce his acquittances for the auditors. In the wardrobe account, the provisions were entered again under expenditure, this section being arranged according to the type of goods supplied. All the accounts were audited. Six of these initial entries are given, to indicate the range of the provisions supplied, and the geographical extent of Elizabeth's estates.

Thomas Spink, serjeant of Brandon, namely for 29 pigs, price 2s a head, and for six days' expenses driving them from Brandon to Clare, 8s 1d. Expenses of 2 grooms driving them for 6 days, and returning in 3 days, 4s, by 1 acquittance. £10 3s 5¹/₂d received from Thomas Spink, serjeant of Brandon, namely for 1 quarter of peas, 3s; for 32 quarters and 1 bushel of oats, price 3s 4d a quarter; for hay bought for 756 horses kept there as if for one night, at ¹/₂d per horse per night, and for money delivered for the wages of 3 grooms and 3 pages looking after these horses for 84 days, with 9s 4¹/₂d for iron, and 61s 10¹/₂d for stable expenses, by another acquittance. £32 13s 7¹/₂d received from Walter de Caldecote, receiver of Brandon, namely, £24 in cash of which 60s was delivered by Robert de Stalyngton; for 4 bushels of peas, 18d; for 25 quarters of oats, price 3s 4d a quarter; for hay for 729 horses kept there as if for one night, at ¹/₂d per horse, and for money delivered for the wages of 3 grooms and 3 pages looking after these horses, with 7s 8¹/₂d for iron, and 58s 5d for stable expenses, by another acquittance. £15 10s received from Walter de Caldecote, receiver of Brandon, of which 22¹/₂d paid for the wages of one groom keeping the pigs there for 15 days, beginning on 15 September, by another acquittance. Sum total: £61 17s 2d.

Erbury.[13] Sir William answers for £78 18s 10¹/₂d received from John Parker, serjeant of Erbury, namely for 74 quarters and 4 bushels of wheat, price 6s a quarter; for 6 quarters and 4 bushels of maslin, price 4s a quarter; for 21 quarters of peas, price 4s a quarter; for 9 quarters and 7 bushels of barley, price 7s a quarter; for 13 quarters of dredge, price 5s 6d a quarter;[14] for 49 quarters of malt dredge, price 8s a quarter; for 4 cows, price 8s a head; for 252 sheep, price 12d a head; for 3 sticks of eels, price 6d a stick; for 1 swan, price 2s 6d; for herbage of 1¹/₂ acres of meadow, price 4s an acre;[15] for hay of 31 acres of meadow, price 5s an acre; for hay from 6¹/₂ acres rowen, price 2s 6d an acre,[16] and for 24 acres of pasture for the oxen of the larder, price 12d an acre, by one acquittance. 59s 10¹/₂d received from John Parker, serjeant of Erbury, namely for 4 acres of underwood in 'Alfidenheye', price 8s an acre; for 117 perches of one hedge, price 2¹/₂d a perch; and for 3

13 This name was given to the demesne manor of Clare.

14 Maslin and dredge were mixed grains; maslin was a mixture of wheat and rye, and dredge a mixture of barley and oats.

15 Herbage was a payment for pasture.

16 Rowen denoted the second crop of hay. The oxen of the larder were only slaughtered when needed by the kitchen; there was a preference for fresh meat.

cartloads of litter, price *3s 6d*, by another acquittance.[17]

Sum total: £81 18*s* 9*d*.

Clare. Sir William answers for £25 sterling received from Humphrey de Waleden, receiver of Clare, by one acquittance. £81 15*s* 6*d* received from Humphrey de Waleden, receiver of Clare, of which £24 7*s* 6*d* was from the relief of John de Rising for his share of the inheritance of Sir Richard FitzSimon, by another acquittance. £45 received from Humphrey de Waleden, receiver of Clare, of which 65*s* was from the relief of Sir Hamo de Felton for his share of the inheritance of Sir Richard FitzSimon, by another acquittance.[18] £6 16*d* received from John Curteis, former receiver of Clare, without acquittance.

Sum total: £157 16*s* 10*d*.

Cranborne. Sir William answers for £58 13*s* 4*d* received from Peter de Cutinden, receiver of Cranborne, of which £18 13*s* 4*d* was for 7 sacks of wool sold by him, by 1 acquittance. £37 sterling received from Peter de Cutinden, receiver of Cranborne, of the issues of his bailiwick, by another acquittance. £6 19*s* 6*d* received from Walter de Berdefeld, former receiver of Cranborne, without acquittance.

Sum total: £102 12*s* 10*d*.

Usk. Sir William answers for £92 19*s* 9½*d* received from Sir Henry Motelot, receiver of Usk, namely for £80 cash; for the expenses of Alexander Charman, John Harpin, John Motelot and others coming with the money in 5 days from Usk to Clare with 6 horses, and returning in 4 days with 4 horses, 32*s* 1¾*d*; for 7 salmon, price 14*d* each; for 72 lampreys, price 30*s*; for their carriage from Usk to Clare, and for expenses over 77 herons, 1 porpoise, and 10 sparrow-hawks, 63*s* 5½*d*; for the expenses of 3 destriers[19] of the lady kept at Usk, and the wages of the groom looking after them for 71 days, with their expenses from Usk to Clare, 63*s* 7*d*; for 84¼ ells of russet and blanket for the use of the lady, with 4*s* for carriage, 62*s* 5¼*d*, by 1 acquittance. £137 20¾*d* received from Sir Henry Motelot, receiver of Usk, namely, £62 9*s* 4*d* in cash; for the expenses of Alexander Charman, Sir Henry Motelot and others carrying this and doing other things, 41*s*

---

17 There were 2 loads in a *caretta* and 1 in a *chariotum*, but the account does not specify the difference between the two. The term 'litter' denotes bedding for animals.

18 These entries indicate that William de Manton was responsible for Elizabeth's finances, not just for the wardrobe. Previously these had been dealt with by the Chamber as Elizabeth's central financial office, but Wardrobe and Chamber were merged from this time. William also received the issues of the bailiwick of Cranborne.

19 The destrier was often used as a war-horse, but the lady used them for her carriage.

4*d*; money given to Sir Peter de Naylesworth and Eva de Lampaddok, 25*s* 4*d*; for 4 robes for divers servants in Wales and for the fee of the parkers of Caerleon and Trellech, £4 16*s*; for 93 oxen and 22 cows, with their expenses, £42 11*d*; for 55 pigs, with their expenses, £6 11*s* 4*d*; for the purchase of 542 conger eels, cod and ling, with their expenses, £11 11*s*;[20] for 171 1/4 yards of blue cloth, russet and blanket, with carriage to Clare, £6 6*s* 5 3/4*d*, by another acquittance.
Sum total: £230 18 1/4*d*.

Ireland. Sir William answers for £144 6*s* 8*d* received from Roger de Ewyas, the lady's attorney in Ireland, of which £133 6*s* 8*d* in cash; and for 3 horses bought from him, £11, by 1 acquittance of the lady made to him.
Sum total: £144 6*s* 8*d*.

Sale of wheat. Sir William answers for £23 received from William Edward, serjeant of Standon, for 63 quarters of wheat sold by him. £4 11*s* 1/2*d* received from Robert Mape, serjeant of Tonbridge Hall, for 14 quarters and 3 bushels of wheat sold by him. £10 3*d* received from Richard atte Pole, serjeant of Freckenham, for 35 quarters of wheat sold by him.
Sum total: £37 11*s* 3 1/2*d*.

Sale of hides and entrails of oxen. Sir William answers for £10 15*s* 6*d* received from Sir William de Berkwey for 135 hides of oxen and cows sold by him. 14*s* 5*d*, received from the same for the entrails of 13 oxen sold by him.
Sum total: £11 9*s* 11*d*.

Sale of sheepskins and entrails. Sir William answers for 44*s* 3 1/4*d* received from Sir William de Berkwey for 278 sheepskins sold by him. 22 1/2*d* received from the same for entrails of 28 sheep sold by him.
Sum total: 46*s* 1 3/4*d*.

Sale of rabbitskins. Sir William answers for 36*s* 11 1/4*d* received from Sir William de Berkwey for 676 rabbitskins sold by him.
Sum total: 36*s* 11 1/4*d*.

Sale of skimmings of fat. Sir William answers for 67*s* 10*d* received from Sir William de Berkwey for 148 gallons of skimmings of fat sold by him, price 5 1/2*d* a gallon.
Sum total: 67*s* 10*d*.

Sale of the issues of brewing. Sir William answers for 36*s* received from Sir William de Berkwey for malt dregs sold by him.
Sum total: 36*s*.

---

20 The reference to expenses in these three entries may well relate to costs of carriage.

Sale of old wheels. Sir William answers for 6s 8d received from one pair of old cart-wheels sold by Richard Charer. 14s received from John Reve of Chilton for 1 pair of old wheels sold to him.
Sum total: 20s 8d.

Small receipts. Sir William answers for 12$\frac{1}{2}$d received from the bailiff of Claret Hall for making 260 faggots of tithes there. 17$\frac{1}{2}$d received from the bailiff of Erbury for making 360 faggots of tithes from 'Alfidenheye' for the rector of Cavendish. 2s 11d received from the bailiff of Bardfield for 700 faggots of tithes for the vicar of Bardfield. 8s 11$\frac{1}{2}$d received from the reeve of Hundon for making 2,160 faggots of tithes in Hundon park. 20s 8d received from Robert Mareschal from payments of his horses, entered in the rolls and not paid.
Sum total: 35s $\frac{1}{2}$d.

Receipt of money by indenture. Sir William answers for £936 15s 4d received from Sir William de Oxwik by indenture.[21]
Sum total: £936 15s 4d.

Sold on account.[22] Sir William is charged with 29s 9d for divers items in the offices which are missing and are sold on account as appears elsewhere.
Sum total: 29s 9d.

Money due to the lady. Sir William answers for £17 13s 4d received from Sir William de Oxwik from the debt of Sir Ralph Ufford. £40 received from the same from the debt of Sir William de Ferrers.[23]
Sum total: £57 13s 4d.
Sum total of receipts: £2,248 3s 7$\frac{1}{2}$d.

Surplus on the last account. Sir William accounts for the surplus on the last account, 71s 8d.
Sum total: 71s 8d.

[Expenditure]

Payment of the lady's debts. Sir William accounts for the payment of the debts of divers creditors from the time of Sir William de Oxwik, the last clerk of the lady's chamber, as appears in 1 indenture sewn to the roll,[24] in part payment of £254 17s 9d, namely to Sir Andrew de

21 Until the Wardrobe and Chamber merged in 1351, the clerk of the Chamber handed money over to the Wardrobe for the household provisions. An indenture was drawn up to record what was delivered.

22 These were items in the account which were written off.

23 Sir Ralph Ufford married Elizabeth's daughter-in-law, Matilda of Lancaster. William de Ferrers was Elizabeth's grandson.

Bures, £20; to Anne de Lexedene, 110s; to the prior of Stoke, £20; to Robert Flemmyng, £42; to the lady for E' and K', £44; to Bartholomew Thomasin, £10 19s 6d; to William de Burton, £10 14d; to Walter Forest, £10; to Thomas Chemer, £14; to Henry de Norht', £9 12s 4d.

Sum total: £186 3s.

Payment made on the lady's order. Sir William accounts for a payment of £16 13s 4d to Sir Thomas de Cheddeworth due to him from the lady's debts.

Sum total: £16 13s 4d.

Purchase of wheat from the manors.[25] Sir William accounts for 63 quarters of wheat bought from William Edward, serjeant of Standon, on 29 August, £23. 80 quarters of wheat bought from Richard Segor, serjeant of Wood Hall, on 4 September, price 6s 8d a quarter, £26 13s 4d. 14 quarters and 3 bushels of wheat sold by Robert Mape, serjeant of Tonbridge Hall, on 28 September, £4 11s ½d. 35 quarters of wheat sold by Richard atte Pole, serjeant of Freckenham, on the same day, £10 3d. 90 quarters of wheat bought from the same man on the same day, price 6s a quarter, £27. 5 quarters of poor wheat bought from Andrew de Braundon, serjeant of Finchingfield, on the same day, price 5s a quarter, 25s. 26 quarters of wheat bought from Walter atte Mot, serjeant of Finchingfield, on the same day, price 6s a quarter, £7 16s. 155 quarters of wheat bought from Roger de Garbedons, reeve of Hundon, on the same day, price 6s a quarter, £46 10s. 74 quarters and 4 bushels of wheat bought from John Parker, serjeant of Erbury, on the same day, price 6s a quarter, £22 7s.

Sum total: £169 2s 7½d.

Purchase of wheat in the region. Sir William accounts for 38 quarters and 6 bushels of wheat bought from the rector of Glemsford in January, with 1d given to God, £11 14s 5½d. 3 quarters of wheat bought from Nigel Tebaud at Wickhambrook in April, 16s. 4 quarters

24 The indenture was dated 10 July 1351, and was stitched to the side of the roll. The debts were crossed out as they were paid. With some, a part payment was made, e.g. £20 to the prior of the monastery of Stoke by Clare out of a debt of £63 8s 11d. It is not clear what is meant by 'to the lady for E' and K''; here £44 was paid out of £60.

25 This section started with the purchase of grain and legumes, each of which was divided into purchases from the manors and from the region. Wheat, maslin, rye, peas and beans, barley, dredge, oats and malt were included. The sections on wheat and barley have been translated in full; for barley there is no entry for purchases from the region. The section on the purchase of oats from the manors has been given in full; typical entries have been selected for the purchases from the region.

of wheat bought at Cavendish in the same month, 26s 8d. 5 quarters of wheat bought from William Edward of Hundon in May, 33s 4d. 12 quarters of wheat, of which 4 bushels in profit, bought from Gilbert Wilde of Thurston, price 6s 4d a quarter, 72s 10d.[26] 2 quarters of wheat bought from John le Deye of Erbury in July, 12s. 14 quarters and 4 bushels of wheat bought in Clare market in August and September at divers prices, £4 8s 1d.

Sum total: £24 3s 4¹/₂d.

Purchase of barley from the manors. Sir William accounts for 5 quarters and 6 bushels of barley bought from John Alphei, serjeant of Claret Hall, on 26 April, price 6s 8d a quarter, 38s 4d. 23 quarters and 6 bushels of barley bought from Richard Segor, serjeant of Wood Hall, on 4 September, price 8s a quarter, £9 10s. 194 quarters of barley bought from Richard atte Pole, serjeant of Freckenham, on 28 September, price 6s 8d a quarter, £64 13s 4d. 1 quarter and 6 bushels of barley bought from Walter atte Mot, serjeant of Bardfield, on the same day, price 6s 8d a quarter, 11s 8d. 1 quarter and 2 bushels of barley bought from the same man as serjeant of Finchingfield on the same day, price 6s 8d a quarter, 8s 4d. 9 quarters and 7 bushels of barley bought from John Parker, serjeant of Erbury, on the same day, price 7s a quarter, 69s 1¹/₂d.

Sum total: £80 10s 9¹/₂d.

Purchase of oats from the manors. Sir William accounts for 1 quarter and 1 bushel of oats bought from Richard de Merston, reeve of Walsingham, on 26 December, price 2s 10d a quarter, 3s 2¹/₄d. 32 quarters and 1 bushel of oats bought from Thomas Spynk, serjeant of Brandon, on 10 July, price 3s 4d a quarter, 107s 1d. 25 quarters of oats bought from Walter de Caldecote, receiver of Brandon, on 4 August, price 3s 4d a quarter, £4 3s 4d. 3 quarters and 3¹/₂ bushels of oats bought from William Edward, serjeant of Standon, on 29 August, price 4s 4d a quarter, 14s 10³/₄d. 4 quarters of oats bought from Richard Segor, serjeant of Wood Hall, on 4 September, price 4s 6d a quarter, 18s. 10 quarters of oats bought from Robert Mape, serjeant of Tonbridge Hall, on 28 September, price 4s a quarter, 40s. 2 quarters and 1 bushel of oats bought from Richard atte Pole, serjeant of Freckenham, on the same day, price 3s 4d a quarter, 7s 1d. 2 quarters and 7 bushels of oats bought from Walter atte Mot, serjeant of Bardfield, on the same day, price 4s 6d a quarter, 12s 11¹/₄d. 1 quarter of oats bought from the same man as serjeant of Finchingfield on the same day, 4s 6d.

---

26 The term translated as profit, *avantagium*, represented the difference between a heaped and a razed measure.

5 quarters of oats bought from Richard atte Medwe, serjeant of Claret Hall, on the same day, price 3s 8d a quarter, 18s 4d. 164 quarters of oats bought from Roger Garbedons, reeve of Hundon, on the same day, of which 27 quarters was for making malt, price 4s a quarter, £32 16s. Sum total: £48 5s 4¹/₄d.

Purchase of oats in the region. Sir William accounts for 31 quarters of oats bought by John Gough in Wisbech at divers prices on 1 October, 62s 4d. For carriage of the oats from Wisbech to Anglesey by water, at 2¹/₂d a quarter, with 4d for porterage to the water, 6s 9¹/₂d. Paid to John Gough for 4¹/₂ days going there for the aforesaid purchase, 4s 6d. 100 quarters of oats bought at Wisbech by the same on 7 October, price 2s 2d a quarter, with 1d given to God, £10 16s 9d. Paid to the same for 5¹/₂ days going there for the aforesaid purchases, 5s 6d. For carriage of 73 quarters of the aforesaid oats from Wisbech to 'Wrydelington' and Anglesey, with 14d for porterage, 20s 11d ... 10 quarters of oats bought in Clare market at divers prices in December, 39s 4¹/₂d. 14 quarters and 2 bushels of oats bought in Clare market at divers prices in January, 60s 6¹/₂d ... 15 quarters and 5 bushels of oats bought at Wickhambrook at divers prices, 60s. 20 quarters of oats bought at Dullingham at divers prices, £4 2s ... 55 quarters of oats bought at Wisbech by John Gough on 29 June at 3s a quarter, £8 5s. For carriage of the same to Anglesey, with 11d for porterage to the water, 14s 8d. Paid to John Gough for 7 days going there for the purchase and to buy 20 quarters of beans, staying and returning, 7s ... 11 quarters and 5 bushels of oats bought in the neighbourhood of Clare at divers prices in August, 40s 2¹/₂d. 2 quarters and 1 bushel of oats bought at Clare in September, 7s 1d.
Sum total: £90 3s 10d.

Making of malt. Sir William accounts for the wages of John Hardi helping to make malt at Clare from 12 November to 15 January inclusive, namely for 10 weeks at 8d a week, 6s 8d. For the same John's wages, helping to make malt at Clare from 16 January to 5 March inclusive, namely for 7 weeks at 8d a week, 4s 8d. For wages of 1 woman cleaning out 15 malt-kilns there, at 3d each, 3s 9d. For the wages of John Hardi helping to make malt at Clare from 6 March to 4 June inclusive, namely for 12 weeks at 8d a week, 8s. Item, given to the same for his pay by agreement made with him for the whole of the aforesaid time, 2s. For wages of 1 woman cleaning out 25 malt-kilns in April, May and June, at 3d each, 6s 3d.
Sum total: 31s 4d.

Purchase of wines.[27] Sir William accounts for 2 pipes of Rhenish wine bought at Ipswich by John de Southam in October, containing 9 1/4 wine-jars, each jar containing 48 gallons, with 1d given to God, £14 9s 1d. For carriage of the same there, 12d. Paid to 1 groom coming from Ipswich with a letter to John concerning the arrival of the wines there, 6d. Paid to John for 3 1/2 days going from Clare to Ipswich and Harwich for the aforesaid purchase, with his passage by boat between Harwich and Ipswich on 2 occasions, 2s 1d. For 7 pots called 'cruskyns', 6d. For the expenses of 6 cart-horses for 2 days going from Clare to Ipswich to seek the wine, 2s 2d. 154 gallons of red wine bought from Matilda Mone at Clare to mix with vinegar, price 4d a gallon, 51s 4d. 2 tuns of red wine bought at Ipswich from Robert Tebaud in February, with 1d given to God, £18 1d. For boat hire to take the aforesaid tuns from the ship to the cart, 2d, and for their carriage there, 12d. Paid to John de Southam for 4 1/2 days going there for the purchase and carriage, 4s 6d. For the expenses of 2 cart-horses for 2 days going from Clare to Ipswich to seek the same, staying and returning, 3s 4d. 4 tuns of wine bought from John atte Forde of Colchester on 15 March, with 2d given to God, £30 13s 6d. For carriage of the same there, 16d. Paid to John de Southam for 5 1/2 days on 3 occasions going there for the aforesaid purchase, staying and returning, 5s 6d ... 1 pipe of Rhenish wine bought in London by Southam in May, with 1d given to God, £7 16s 1d, and containing 3 wine-jars, each jar containing 48 gallons. For carriage of the same there, 11d. Paid to John de Southam for 3 days going there for the said purchase, staying and returning, 3s. For the expenses of 6 cart-horses for 4 days going from Clare to London to seek the said pipe, staying and returning, 5s 1d. 6 pipes of red wine bought in London by John Southam in June, with 2d given to God, £16 13s 6d. For carriage of the same there, 2s 10d. Paid to John de Southam for 4 1/2 days going there for the purchase, staying and returning, 4s 6d.
Sum total: £133 5s 1 1/2d.

Purchase of oxen from the manors.[28] Sir William accounts for 1 bull, 5 oxen and 3 cows bought from William Edward, serjeant of Standon, on 29 August at 7s a head, 63s. 1 bullock bought from Richard Segor, serjeant of Wood Hall, on 4 September, 9s 6d. 18 oxen, cows and bullocks

27 Examples are given of purchases from each of the merchants patronised by the lady. Altogether, 14 tuns of red wine and 3 pipes of Rhenish wine were purchased. The tun contained 252 gallons and the pipe 126.

28 The purchases of meat comprised oxen, pigs, sheep, capons, rabbits and herons. The entries for oxen are given in full.

bought from Walter atte Mot, serjeant of Bardfield, on 28 September, at 6s a head, 108s. 5 oxen and 1 bull bought from Roger Garbedons, reeve of Hundon, on the same day at 8s a head, 48s. 4 cows bought from John Parker, serjeant of Erbury, on the same day at 8s a head, 32s.
Sum total: £13 6d.

Purchase of oxen from the region. Sir William accounts for 4 bullocks bought at Sudbury on 4 June at divers prices, 23s 9¼d. 93 oxen and 22 cows bought at Usk by Sir Henry Motelot, with their expenses from there to Lutterworth, £42 11d.
Sum total: £43 4s 8¼d.

Purchase of salt. Sir William accounts for 5 quarters of salt bought at Reach in May, price 4s a quarter, 20s. 6 quarters of salt of Poitou bought at Lynn in November, price 6s 4d a quarter, with 9d for its porterage and also of 6 barrels of white herrings there and at Anglesey, 38s 9d.[29] For the expenses of Cok Havering for 6 days going from Clare to see to the purchase and carriage, 2s. 6 quarters of salt of Poitou bought at Lynn in the same month, with 6d for porterage there, 39s 9d. For boat hire from there to Anglesey, 2s 4d. For Cok Havering's expenses going from Clare to Anglesey and from there to Lynn by water for the said purchase, with 9d for boat hire, 2s 3d. 5 quarters and 4 bushels of salt of Poitou bought at Colchester by Hugh Poulterer on 26 November, at 9s 4d a quarter, 51s 4d. For expenses for 2 days for 6 cart-horses to bring the salt to Bardfield, with 6d for Hugh's expenses for 1½ days, and 2d for porterage of the same to the cart, 4s 7d. 5 quarters and 6 bushels of salt bought at Wisbech by John Gough in the same month, price 5s a quarter, 28s 9d. For 1 barrel to put the salt in, with 5d for porterage of the salt, and 6d for cooperage and 3 hoops for the barrel, 2s 8¼d. 10 quarters of salt bought at Reach by Hugh Poulterer on 23 May, with 2d for his expenses, 40s 10d. 8 quarters of salt bought at Stourbridge [fair] on 12 September, price 5s 10d a quarter, with 2d for porterage, 46s 10d.[30]
Sum total: 14 1¼d.

Purchase of herrings.[31] Sir William accounts for 6 barrels of white

---

29 The salt of Poitou was a coarse salt.

30 Stourbridge fair was held at Cambridge.

31 The purchases of fish comprised herrings, stockfish (dried white fish), cod and conger eels, salmon, pike, lampreys, and one barrel of sturgeon. The entries for herrings, cod and conger eels, and salmon have been translated in full. A last comprised 12 barrels of white herring, or 20 cades of red (smoked) herring; the cade contained 500 or 720 fish.

herrings bought at Lynn, price 6s 8d a barrel, 40s. For carriage of the same and 6 quarters of salt of Poitou from Lynn to Anglesey, 6s. 5,000 white herrings bought at Cattiwade by Hugh Poulterer in the same month, with the salt for salting them and with porterage, 38s 7¹/₂d. For the expenses for 2 days of Hugh Poulterer going there to make the purchases, 6d. For the expenses for 1¹/₂ days of 6 cart-horses going from Clare to get them, 8d. 6 lasts of herrings bought at Yarmouth by Sir John de Lenne in November, of which 4 cost £4 6s 8d each, and 2 60s each, with 2d given to God, £23 6s 10d. For boat hire to take the herrings from one vill to the other, 4s 8d. For 1 building leased there to put the herrings in, with 2d for Cok Havering's ferry toll, and 12d for porterage, 18d. For the expenses for 5 days of Sir John de Lenne and Cok Havering going from Clare to Yarmouth to make the purchase and returning, 8s. For the expenses for 10 days of Cok Havering going there and staying, and carrying the herring from one vill to the other, with 1 hackney and 1 page for 9 days in the same month, 7s 1d. For Cok's expenses for 6 days going with 1 hackney and the cart on another occasion to Yarmouth to get the aforesaid herring, and returning, with 6d given to the page for shoes by Sir John de Lenne, 3s 2¹/₂d. 1 last and 9,000 red herrings bought from Robert Corby, bailiff of Southwold, on 28 September, the last costing £4 6s 8d, £8 4s 8d.
Sum total: £37 21d.

Purchase of cod and conger eels. Sir William accounts for 4 conger eels and 1 bream bought at Usk by Sir Henry Motelot in March, 3s 6d. 32 cod bought by Hugh Poulterer at Reach on 23 May, 25s. 33 cod bought by the same at Bury St Edmunds in the same month, 25s. For 2 baskets to put them in, with 6d for carrying them to Clare, 14d. 388 cod bought by the prior of Walsingham in July, £13 13s 8d. 34 cod bought at Colchester by Hugh Poulterer in September, 27s. 542 dried cod, conger eels and ling bought at Bristol by Sir H. Motelot, with their carriage from there to Tewkesbury, £11 11s.
Sum total: £29 6s 4d.

Purchase of salmon. Sir William accounts for 19 salmon bought for the lady's household by Sir Henry Motelot in March at divers prices, 68s 7d. 7 salmon bought by the same in April at 14d each, 8s 2d. 61 salmon bought at Stourbridge [fair] on 12 September, with 2d for porterage, £4 10s 2d.
Sum total: £8 6s 11d.

Purchase of spices.[32] Sir William accounts for 4 lb. currants bought

32 Entries have been selected to show the range of items purchased by the household.

from Bartholomew Thomasin on 28 October, price 6d a lb., 2s. 3 lb.
'sanders' bought from the same, price 20d a lb., 5s.[33] 33 lb. sugar
bought from the same on 15 November, price 18d a lb., 49s 6d. 6¹/₂
gallons of olive oil bought from the same, 8s 8d. 2 quires of paper
bought from the same, 8d. 62¹/₂ ells of canvas bought from John Not
in London on 15 November, 26s ... 44 lb. wax bought from the vicar
of Clare on 4 February, 20s. 10¹/₄ gallons of olive oil bought from
Bartholomew Thomasin on 23 February, price 14d a gallon, 11s 11¹/₂d.
For one barrel purchased to put the olive oil in, 11d. 3 quarters of
almonds bought from the same, 26s 3d. 1 peck of figs of Malaga bought
from Bartholomew Thomasin on 4 March, 18s ... 200 lb. rice, 20s. 10
lb. cinnamon, price 16d a lb., 13s 4d. 1 lb. saffron bought from
Bartholomew Thomasin, 13s ... 2 lb. liquorice, 5d ... 3 lb. pine-seeds,
18d ... 20 lb. ginger bought from Bartholomew Thomasin, 27s 4d. 20
lb. cinnamon, 23s 4d. 20 lb. pepper, 27s 4d. 20 lb. cumin, 5s ... 2 lb.
cloves, 13s 4d. 2 lb. cubebs, price 5s 6d a lb., with 8d for 1 barrel to put
them in, 11s 8d³⁴...
Sum total: £60 9s 6¹/₂d.

Purchase of confections.[35] Sir William accounts for 4¹/₂ lb. ginger and
4 lb. 'madrian' bought from Bartholomew Thomasin on 15 November,
12s 9d.[36] 4 lb. royal paste, 5s 4d. 2 boxes of royal paste weighing 7¹/₄ lb.
bought from the same on 18 December, 9s 8d. 3³/₄ lb. of 'pimonade', 2s
6d³⁷ ... 4¹/₂ lb. white anise confections, and 2 lb. vermilion anise
confections bought from the same on 29 March, 10s 1d. 2 lb. 'citronade'
bought from the same on 14 May, 5s 4d. 6 lb. plate-sugar, white and
red, bought from the same on the same day, 9s. 3 lb. confection of fistic
nuts, 7s. 6 lb. white and red comfits, 9s. For the expenses of 1 horse
carrying the confections from London to Clare, 12d ...
Sum total: £7 14s ¹/₂d.[38]

Purchase of horses. Sir William accounts for 1 sorrel horse bought
from Philip de Usk on 18 July for Robert Lucesone's cart, with 1d
given to God, 35s 1d. 1 grey horse bought from Sir William de Manton
for the same cart, 46s 8d. 1 white horse bought from Roger Ewyas in

33 These were for colouring food red.
34 Cubebs were small spicy berries of the pepper family.
35 Items have been selected to show the range of purchases.
36 'Madrian' was a kind of ginger.
37 This was a sort of electuary, a medicine combined with honey, syrup or a conserve.
38 After the purchase of confections, there follow short entries for the purchase of
   linen, parchment, wicks, tallow, vinegar and honey.

September, £4 13s 4d. 1 grey palfrey bought from the same in the same month, 66s 8d. 1 grey horse bought from the same in the same month, 60s.
Sum total: £15 21d.

Horses' expenses.[39] Sir William accounts for the expenses for 141/2 days in October of 12 cart-horses going from Clare to Tewkesbury to fetch 2 barrels of fish from there, and of 11 horses returning to Clare, 55s 5d. Paid to John de Rushton with 1 hackney going with the cart for the aforesaid time, 5s 3d ... For the expenses for 4 days in November of 10 destriers and foals going from Clare to Brandon to be kept there, 13s 5¹/₂d. Paid to Henry de Dene for 8 days going with them and returning, 8s. For the expenses for 5¹/₂ days in November of 7 cart-horses going from Clare to London to fetch the livery and returning, 8s 11d ... For the expenses for 4 days in April of 9 of the lady's destriers and foals coming from Brandon to Clare, with the wages of 3 grooms and 3 pages, 18s 5¹/₂d. Paid to Henry de Dene for 6 days going from Clare to fetch them and returning, 6s ... For the expenses for 2¹/₂ days of 5 cart-horses coming from London to Clare with spices in September, 3s 11d.
Sum total: £12 15s 6³/₄d.

Purchase of hay from the manors.[40] Sir William accounts for 756 botels of hay bought from Thomas Spynk, serjeant of Brandon for 756 horses kept there as if for 1 night, namely ¹/₂d a botel, 31s 6d.[41] 729 botels of hay bought from Walter de Caldecote, receiver of Brandon, for 729 horses kept there as if for 1 night, namely ¹/₂d a botel, 30s 4¹/₂d ... 738 botels of hay bought from Richard atte Pole, serjeant of Freckenham, on 28 September, price ¹/₂d a botel, 30s 9d. Hay from 30 acres of meadow purchased from Roger Garbedons, reeve of Hundon, on 28 September, price 4s an acre, £6. 3 cartloads of hay bought from the same on the same day, price 4s a load, 12s ...
Sum total: £21 3s.

Purchase of hay from the region.[42] Sir William accounts for the payment of 40s to Sir John Fermer at the lady's order for 18 stacks of hay bought from him in the preceding year and lost in the flood ... 10 cartloads of hay bought in the neighbourhood of Clare in May at divers prices, £4 9s

39 This section deals with the cost of carriage of provisions, and money spent in keeping certain horses on the demesne manors. Typical entries have been selected.
40 Selected entries are given.
41 The botel was a bundle of hay.
42 Entries haave been selected.

7*d* ... 79 cartloads of hay bought in the Bardfield neighbourhood in July and August, £12 15*s*. For expenses over the purchase and carriage of the same, as appears in the itemised account, 46*s* 2¹/₂*d*.[43]
Sum total: £46 5*s* 10¹/₂*d*.[44]

Purchase and making of charcoal and faggots.[45] Sir William accounts for the making of 35 quarters of charcoal in Hundon park in October, price for making a quarter 3¹/₂*d*, 10*s* 2¹/₂*d*. Making 51 quarters of charcoal there in the same month, at 3¹/₂*d* a quarter, 14*s* 10¹/₂*d*. Making 2,530 faggots at Claret Hall in February, at 5*d* per 100, 10*s* 6¹/₄*d*. Making 9,900 faggots in Hundon park in the same month, at 5*d* per 100, 41*s* 3*d* ... 5 quarters of sea coal bought on 20 April, 11*s* 3*d* ... Carriage of 11,300 faggots from Hundon to Clare, at 10*d* for carriage of 100, £4 14*s* 2*d* ... 5 quarters of sea coal bought at Stourbridge [fair] on 12 September, 10*s* ...
Sum total: £25 19*s* 8¹/₄*d*

Provision for the stable.[46] Sir William accounts for ... 1¹/₄ lbs. 'Popilion'[47] bought from Bartholomew Thomasin, 7*d*. 4³/₄ lb. turpentine bought from the same, 2*s* 9*d*. 60 cart-clouts bought for the carts by Richard Charer, 10*s* ... 1 iron band for the saddle of the Poultry, 6*d*.[48] 2 bridles purchased for 2 foals, 6*d*. 3 tanned bullock hides purchased for collars and mending harness, 5*s*. 1 gallon of oil for dressing these hides, 16*d*. 3 stones of skimmings of fat, 2*s* 3*d* ... 12 lb. salve, 18*d*. Thread to mend harness, 3*d*. Small nails and 'bordnail' for the carts, 2*d*. 8 ash trees bought by Richard Charer to repair the carriages and carts, 5*s* 6*d*. Timber bought from Thomas Carpenter by Richard Charer in February for the carriages and carts, 17*s* ...
Sum total: £19 2*s* 2¹/₂*d*.

Purchase of iron. Sir William accounts for 367 lb. Spanish iron bought at Barnwell on 20 June, 21*s* 4*d*. 1,000 lb. Spanish iron bought at Ipswich from Robert Tebaud in September, 53*s* 4*d*.
Sum total: 74*s* 8*d*.

---

43 Each department of the household kept its own accounts, and a summary was written in the wardrobe account.

44 This entry was followed by entries for the purchase of pasture and of litter (bedding for animals) from the manors and from the region.

45 Entries have been selected.

46 This entry consisted of small items of expenditure needed for the day-to-day running of the stables. A selection of entries has been included.

47 This was an unguent made from poplar buds.

48 Each department had horses and carts assigned to it.

Necessary expenses.[49] Sir William accounts for ... 8 lb. cotton thread bought from Bartholomew Thomasin on 15 November, 9s 4d. 1 pack-horse saddle bought in London by Sir W. de Oxwik in the same month, 12s 3d ... For the expenses for 4 days of 1 horse called piebald Charman sent from Brandon to Clare by the auditors, 17d ... Paid to William and Thomas Wayman going with the waggon and keeping the oxen of the household from 1 November to 8 January inclusive, namely for 10 weeks, each taking 8d a week, 13s 4d. Paid to 1 man helping to make candles of Paris for 3 days in February, 3d. Paid to John Bradefeld for 3 days in the same month going to divers manors to make an estimate of grain, 3s ... For carriage of one poor-quality porpoise from Newport to Usk and Clare, 14d. Paid to Walter the chamberlain being at Bardfield with 1 hackney for 2½ days before the lady's arrival, 12d. Paid to John Wardon, Robert Wolwy, and William, page of the wardrobe, there for the same time, 10d. Paid to 2 women collecting rushes there in prepara-tion for the lady's arrival, with 1d for candles bought there, 3d ... 7 pairs of shoes bought for Lady Athol by Margaret de Lalleford, 2s 11d ... 5 pairs of shoes bought for little Richard of the chamber, 20d. 9 pairs of shoes bought from Thomas de Cnaresbourgh, of which 3 for Cressoner, 2 for John of the buttery, and 4 for 2 little clerks of the chapel, 3s. 2 pairs of shoes bought for 2 little clerks of the chapel, 16d. Sum total: £11 14s 2½d.

Writs and legal expenses. Sir William accounts for 1 writ to William de Nessefeld for expediting the lady's business concerning her lands in Ulster, obtained by John Bataille in July, 18d. For John's expenses for 20 days in London and Chertsey suing out the writ, 40s. For sealing 2 writs to the escheator of Dorset for divers matters concerning the lands and business of Mautravers, obtained by Richard de Wodeham in July, 12d. Paid to Richard for 3 days going from Clare to London and back to acquire the same, 18d. 1 letter patent obtained in chancery by Sir John de Lenne to bear witness that Alexander Charman and John de Knaresburgh were the lady's attorneys in Ireland, with 2d spent on a box to put it in, 2s 2d.
Sum total: 46s 2d.

Purchase of cloths. Sir William accounts for 2 cloths of 'bruskyns' motley bought for the lady and the countess of Pembroke, £13 6s 8d.[50]

---

49 This is a miscellaneous entry, covering labouring jobs and journeys. Entries have been selected to show the range covered.

50 The term 'bruskyns' probably denotes that the cloth was of a bronze or tawny colour.

12 variegated cloths bought for the clerks and ladies at 51s 8d each, £31. 10 cloths of 'porre' motley and 10 striped cloths bought for the esquires at 51s 8d each, £51 13s 4d.[51] 8 striped cloths bought for the yeomen at 33s 4d each, £13 6s 8d. 5 cloths of brown motley and 5 striped cloths for the grooms at 30s each, £15. 2 cloths of tawny motley bought for the little clerks and maids, £4. For shearing the aforesaid cloths, 71s 6d. Paid to Sir William de Manton and Colynet de Morleye going from Clare to London to buy the cloths, with other expenses for packing them, 25s 8d. 2 green cloths bought for the pages, with 2s for shearing, 62s. 8 pieces of russet and 2 pieces of blanket containing 84$\frac{1}{4}$ ells bought by Sir H. Motelot, with their carriage from Usk to Clare in July, 62s 5$\frac{1}{4}$d. 106$\frac{3}{4}$ ells of russet and blanket bought at Usk by Sir H. Motelot, with their carriage from Usk to Clare in August, £4 10$\frac{1}{4}$d. 64$\frac{1}{2}$ ells of blue cloth, russet and blanket bought there by the said Sir H. with carriage from there to Clare in September, 45s 7$\frac{1}{2}$d.[52]
Sum total: £145 14s 9d.

Purchase of fur.[53] Sir William accounts for 2 furs of minever half-pured, each of 7 timbers, and 2 hoods, each of 50 bellies, £8 5s. 5 furs of gris each of 7 timbers, price 18s each, £4 10s. 16 hoods half-pured, each costing 6s 8d, 106s 8d. 20 furs of good popel and strandling, at 20s a couple, £10 … 3 furs of rabbitskins, 12s. 40 ermines bought for the lady in July, 40s.[54]
Sum total: £35 4d.

Purchase of budge.[55] Sir William accounts for 3 dozen furs of budge bought from Walter Forester of London at 48s a dozen, £7 4s. 4 dozen hoods of budge, price 30s a dozen, £6.
Sum total: £13 4s.

Purchase of lambs' furs. Sir William accounts for 7 dozen lambs' furs bought from Walter Forester of London, price 30s a dozen, £10 10s.
Sum total: £10 10s.

51 The word 'porre' meant leek, or vegetable pottage, possibly denoting that the cloth was pale green.

52 Russet was a medium- to low-quality woollen cloth, and blanket a cheap white woollen cloth.

53 Entries have been selected.

54 A fur denoted the fur lining of a robe. Minever, gris, popel and strandling were all terms to describe the fur of the Baltic squirrel. Minever half-pured was the white belly skin with some of the grey surrounding it; gris was the grey back of the winter skin; popel was the early summer skin; strandling the autumn skin. A timber was a bundle of 40 skins; Veale, *English Fur Trade*, pp. 215-29.

55 Budge was imported lambskins.

Foreign expenses.[56] Sir William accounts for the payment for 3 days for 7 greyhounds and 18 coursing hounds going from Clare to Tonbridge to take venison there in July, namely 1d a day for 2 greyhounds, and 1d a day for 3 coursing hounds, 2s 4$^1/_2$$d$. For their passage by ferry at Tilbury, with 6d for litter by the way, 12d. Paid to John the huntsman, 2 grooms and 1 page going with them, 18d. Paid to Robert Wolwy for 3$^1/_2$ days ending on 14 July going from Hundon to London with the lady's letters addressed to Sir John de Lenne, staying and returning, 7d ... Paid to Robert Wolwy for 11 days ending on 29 July going from Clare to Stanton Lacey to the earl and countess of Warwick with the lady's letters, staying and returning, with 1d for his ferry passage across the River Severn, 23d ... For the expenses of Alexander Charman, John Motelot, John Harpin and others carrying £80 from Usk to Clare, coming in 5 days with 6 horses, and returning in 4 days with 4 horses in July, 32s 1$^3/_4$$d$. Paid to Andrew de Waleden for 12 days in July going from Clare to Tonbridge to take deer, and from there to London to sue out divers writs and do other business for the lady, staying and returning, 18s ... Paid to Master Philip the cook for 2$^1/_2$ days ending on 17 August going from Clare to Lynn to investigate stockfish, staying and returning, 2s 6d. Paid to Sir John de Lenne going from Clare to Salisbury on the lady's business to the duke of Lancaster in August, 20s ... Paid to Robert Wolwy for 9 days ending on 1 September going from Bardfield to Cranborne with the lady's letters addressed to the receiver there, staying and returning, 18d ... For the expenses of Walter de Kirkeby for 9 days going from Clare to York to Lord Percy with the lady's letters, and for 13 days going from Clare to London on 2 occasions in September, 27s 3$^1/_2$$d$ ... Hiring 1 hackney for 9 days for John Whitheved going with Alice Benoit to Wormegay at the time Lady Bardolf gave birth, staying and returning, 18d.
Sum total: £10 19s 10$^1/_4$$d$.

Expenses of the household. Sir William accounts for the expenses of the household as appears in the diet roll in money, £434 17s 8$^1/_2$$d$.[57]
Sum total: £434 17s 8$^1/_2$$d$.

Delivery of money. Sir William accounts for the money delivered to Sir William de Oxwik, as appears in one indenture made to him, £16 2s.
Sum total: £16 2s.

56 These expenses were 'foreign' because they were normally concerned with the lady's business outside the household. Entries have been selected to show the types of item included, and the range of the lady's activities.

57 The diet roll gave totals in money for purchases, and also totals of stock used.

Delivery of money to the lady. Sir William accounts for money delivered to the lady, as appears in the itemised account, £55 6s 5¹/₂d. Sum total: £55 6s 5¹/₂d.

Fees at Michaelmas term. Sir William accounts for divers fees paid to divers of the lady's household for Michaelmas term last past, £32 3s 8d. Sum total: £32 3s 8d.

Sum total of all expenses and deliveries: £2,064 4s 2d. Thus Sir William owes £183 19s 5¹/₂d. Of which £40 was allowed to him by the lady, and the lady remitted the debts of Sir William de Oxwik with which he was charged. £12 6s 11d was allowed to him by the lady for divers things missing from the offices which were sold on account this year and in preceding years. Sum total: £52 6s 11d. So he owes £131 13s 6¹/₂d. The lady respited £17 13s 4d of the debts of Ralph de Ufford, as above. So Sir William owes £114 2¹/₂d net.

130. Extract from the account-book of Elizabeth Stonor, 1478 [From Public Record Office, London, C47/37/7, fo. 19v–20r; in English]

Item, paid on Friday after All Souls day for 7 oxen and 2 cows, price 11s an ox and 7s a cow, £4 11s.
Item, the Saturday following for pork, 3d.
Item, for 25 geese, 6s 3d.
Item, paid for 5 couple of cod and 4 couple of stockfish, 11s 10d.

Memorandum that my lady Dame Elizabeth Stonor and Christopher Holland have reckoned and accounted for the expenses of the household from 1 August to 9 November, in the eighteeenth year of Edward IV, and the aforesaid Christopher has been contented and paid for the same until 9 November.

[Signed] Elizabeth Stonor.

Expended in wheat from 1 August to 9 November next following, 20 quarters.
Expended in malt from 1 August to 9 November, 33 quarters.
Expended in beasts during the aforesaid time, 7 beasts.[58]
Expended in mutton for the same time, 14 [sheep].

---

58 The beasts presumably denote oxen.

131. Extract from the household roll of Joan de Valence, countess of Pembroke, 1296 [From Public Record Office, London, E101/505/25, m. 10; in Latin]

Sunday 3 June, at Sutton, the lady and Aymer and Sir R. de Inkepenne.[59] Poor, 24.
Pantry: 11*s*, from the stock at Brabourne.
Buttery: wine, ¹/₂ sester purchased, 22*d*; item, ¹/₂ sester from stock.[60]
Ale purchased, 12*s*.
Kitchen: for ¹/₂ ox, 1 sheep, ¹/₂ pig, 1 piece of bacon, 10*s* 8*d*; veal, 2*s* 6*d*; geese, 2*s*; poultry, 23*d*; eggs, 10*d*; milk, 7*d*; pottage and drinking water, 2*d*.
Sum total: 18*s* 8*d*.

Saucery: 1¹/₂*d*.
Porter's office: 5¹/₂*d*.
Stables: 76 horses; hay, 4*s* 9*d*; 4 quarters and 6 bushels of oats, 14*s* 3*d*; wages of 43 grooms, 5*s* 5¹/₂*d*; 2 lb. salve bought for the horses, 5*d*.
Sum total: 24*s* 10¹/₂*d*.
Sum total for the day: 57*s* 11¹/₂*d* [58*s* 11¹/₂*d*]

Offerings, 3*d*. To a groom bringing letters from Lady Isabella de Hastings, by gift of the lady, 6*d*. Item, for the wages of 1 groom for 6 days going to Bampton with the lady's letters, 9*d*.
Sum total: 18*d*.
Total sum for the day: 59*s* 5¹/2*d* [60*s* 5¹/₂*d*]

132. Elizabeth de Burgh's entertainment of the Black Prince and the bishop of Llandaff at Great Bardfield, 1358[61] [From Public Record Office, London, E101/93/20, m. 21; in Latin]

Tuesday 6 March. Number of messes: 81.[62] Pantry: 290 loaves from stock.
Buttery: 6 sesters of wine, and 100 gallons of ale from stock.
Kitchen: 568 herrings, 10 stockfish, 4 salt fish, 3 cod, 1¹/₂ salmon, 8 pike, 6 lampreys, 4 pieces of sturgeon, 5 crayfish and 50 whelks from stock. 42 codling, 9*s*; 1 conger eel, 4*s*; 12 mullet, 5*s*; 24 skate, 7*s* 6*d*; 50

---

59 Aymer was Joan's only surviving son and heir; he was styled earl of Pembroke from 1307.

60 The sester was used as a measure of wine.

61 The Black Prince and the bishop stayed for three days, 5–7 March. The entry for Tuesday 6 March has been translated. Fish was served because the visit occurred during Lent.

62 This information was put in the margin. The mess denoted the amount of food served to a group, usually consisting of two or four people.

whiting, 20*d*; 1 crayfish, 7*d*; 3 eels, 4*s*; 4 sticks of eels, 2*s* 4*d*; 3 sole, 5*d*; 400 oysters, 8*d*; 600 whelks, 2*s*; ¹/₄ porpoise, 11*s*; carriage of fish from Dunmow, 3*d*.

Stables: hay for 36 horses, 8 hackneys and 3 oxen from stock; provender for the same, 1 quarter and 3 bushels of oats, of which 1 bushel from increment; 168 loaves from stock; wages of 2 esquires, 4*d*; wages of 28 grooms and 6 pages, 4*s*.

Sum total for the kitchen: 48*s* 5*d*.

Sum total for the stables: 4*s* 4*d*.

Sum total of purchases: 52*s* 9*d*.

Sum total from stock: 114*s* 3*d*.

Sum total for the day: £8 7*s*.[63]

133. Three extracts from the daily household expenses of Alice de Brian, 1412–13 [From Public Record Office, London, C47/4/8B, fos 8r, 9v, 11r; in Latin]

Friday 16 December. The lady with her household. Visitors: Sir Richard Waldegrave with his son and servant at 1 meal; Richard Barbour, John Webbe with his son for the whole day.

Pantry: 40 white loaves and 4 black loaves; wine from what remained; ale from stock.[64]

Kitchen: ¹/₂ salt fish and 1 dried fish. Purchases: 100 oysters, 2*d*; 16 whiting and 9 plaice, 14*d*; 100 sprats, 4*d*.

Stables: hay from stock for 10 horses of the lady and visitors; 2 bushels of oats for provender for the same.

Sum total of purchases: 20*d*.

Number of messes:[65] breakfast, 3; dinner, 20; supper, 3. Total: 26.

Sunday 1 January. The lady with her household. Visitors: William Sampsom with his wife and servant, Edward Peyton with his servant, William Langham with his servant, the wife of Robert Dynham with her son, John Teyler with his son, Richard Scrivener, the bailiff of the manor with the harvest-reeve and 8 paid labourers, Margaret Brydbek, 1 harper, Agnes Whyte, for the whole day; Agnes Rokwode with her

---

63 The departmental totals only included purchases. The items from stock were given a money equivalent, and this was entered in the sum total for stock.

64 Alice did not have a separate buttery; the pantry dealt with both bread and drink.

65 The number of messes was entered in the margin of the book. Each mess normally numbered two or four people, and this group was served together at mealtimes; the mess denoted the amount of food served to each group. This information is found in a number of household accounts of the fourteenth and fifteenth centuries.

2 sons, daughter and maid, the vicar of Acton with his servant, Richard Appylton with his wife and servant, Thomas Malcher, with 300 tenants and other strangers, for 1 meal.

Pantry: 314 white loaves and 40 black loaves, of which 104 white and 14 black loaves were from the new baking; wine from what remained; ale from stock.

Kitchen: 2 pigs, 2 swans, 12 geese, 2 carcasses of mutton, 24 capons and 17 rabbits. Purchases: beef, 8s 2d; veal, 3s; 5 piglets, 2s 4d; 12 gallons of milk, 18d.

Stables: hay from stock for 18 horses of the lady and visitors; 2½ bushels of oats for provender for the same.

Sum total of purchases: 15s.

Number of messes: breakfast, 30; dinner, 160; supper, 30. Total: 200. [220]

Sunday 29 January. The lady with her household. Visitors: 2 friars from Sudbury, a man from Colchester, Colbrook, a paid labourer from Bures, at 1 meal.

Pantry: 46 white loaves and 6 black loaves; wine from what remained, ale from stock.

Kitchen: ¼ carcass of beef, 1 quarter of bacon, 1 carcass of mutton, 1 goose and 1 rabbit. Purchased: beef and pork, 2s 10d; 1 piglet, 5d.

Stables: hay from stock for 6 horses of the lady and visitors; 3 pecks of oats for provender for the same.[66]

Sum total of purchases: 3s 3d.

Number of messes: breakfast, 6; dinner, 20; supper, 18. Total: 44.

134. Details of the itinerary, residences and guests of Elizabeth de Burgh, 1349–50[67] [From Public Record Office, London, E101/93/4; in Latin]

22 November	Usk Prioress and convent of Usk
5 December	Usk Countess of Pembroke

66 There were four pecks in one bushel of grain.

67 These details are taken from a diet roll which gives full details of provisions consumed each day. The names of residences and guests were entered in the margin. In November 1349 Elizabeth was living in Usk. Of the visitors, the countess of Pembroke was Marie de St Pol, Elizabeth's closest friend; Ralph Lord Stafford married her niece, Margaret Audley; Lady Despenser was the widow of her nephew, Hugh le Despenser, who died in 1349; the Countess Warenne was Joan of Bar; the earl and countess of Northampton were William de Bohun and his wife Elizabeth; and the countess of Ulster was Elizabeth de Burgh, the namesake of her grandmother.

10 January	Usk Ralph Lord Stafford
26–7 January	Usk Ralph Lord Stafford, Lady Despenser
22 February	Usk Lady Talbot
10 April	Usk Countess of Pembroke
12 April	Usk and Troy[68]
13 April	Troy and Ross-on-Wye
14 April	Ross-on-Wye and Newent
15 April	Newent and Tewkesbury
16–18 April	Tewkesbury[69]
19 April	Tewkesbury and Stanway
20 April	Stanway and Chipping Norton
21 April	Chipping Norton and Bletchingdon
22 April	Bicester and Buckingham
23 April	Woburn
24–5 April	Chicksand
26 April	Chicksand and Litlington
27 April	Litlington and Radwinter
28 April	Radwinter and Clare
4 May	Clare Earl of Suffolk and Sir John Bardolf
8 May	Clare Countess Warenne
11 May	Clare Countess Warenne
11-13 May	Clare Countess of Northampton
14 May	Stoke by Clare
15 May	Clare
17-18, 21 May	Clare Earl of Northampton
20–1 May	Clare Isabella, Edward III's daughter
21 May–4 June	Clare Countess of Ulster
1 June	Clare Black Prince, John of Gaunt

135. Elizabeth de Burgh's private expenditure, 1351-52[70] [From Public Record Office, London, E101/93/12, m. 1, 2; in French]

68 When the household was on a journey, the places where it was in the morning and evening were noted. The removal of the whole household from Usk to Clare necessitated the use of 107 horses, 25 hackneys and 30 oxen. These numbers varied slightly during the journey.

69 The household did not move at weekends on this journey.

70 This expenditure was entered in a chamber-account. The chamber was Elizabeth de Burgh's principal financial office, but the chamber referred to here was her own chamber. Samples are given of two weeks' expenditure, and of her plans to build a house in London.

Item, given to the boy bishop on the eve of St Nicholas [5 December], with a pair of gloves price 2d, 6s 10d.[71]

Item, for the offering on the feast of St Nicholas [6 December] for the soul of Sir Gilbert de Clare, my lady's father, 3s.

Item, for the offering on the feast of the Conception of Our Lady by my lady and her household, 10d.

Item, for 2 lb. silk bought in London by Colynet, 40s.

Item, for 4 lb. thread of divers colours bought there, 12s.

Item, for 2 cressets of pewter bought for my lady on the same day, 3s. Delivered to my lady on 10 December, 40s.

Sum total for the week: 105s 8d.

Item, for the offering by my lady and her household on Christmas Day at 3 masses, 12s 8d.

Item, for the offering by my lady, Lady Bardolf and Lady Athol on the feast of St Stephen [26 December], 6d.

Item, delivered to Sir John FitzRalph on the same day by order of my lady, 100s.

Item, for the wages of Sir William Ailmer, chaplain at Bardfield, being there before my lady's arrival, from Michaelmas to 13 November, for 6 weeks, 6s.

Item, for 2½ ells of russet bought by Colynet for my lady, price 3s 4d an ell, 8s 4d.[72]

Item, paid to Colynet for ½ day going from Bardfield to Clare for a palm and other things, 6d.

Item, for 6 ells of canvas bought by Walter the chamberlain for the little clerks, 4s.

Item, for 3 ells of russet bought by the aforesaid Walter for Hywel ap Thomas, 3s 7d.

Item, given to Simon, the groom of Sir Robert Cokerel, by the said Walter, 2s.

Item, for the offering by my lady and Lady Bardolf and Lady Athol on the feast of St Thomas [29 December], 3d.

Item, given to Sir Richard de Kelleshulle, justice, on the same day, 40s.

Item, given to a clerk of Sir Richard on the same day, 3s 4d.

Item, delivered to my lady for sending to the countess of Ulster on 30 December, 100s.

Sum total for the week: £14 14d.

Item, paid to Sir John de Lenne for houses leased in Aldgate by order

---

71 It was usual for this to be a time of celebration and licence.
72 The ell measured 45 inches (1¼ yards); i.e. 1.143 metres.

of my lady, with 1*d* given to God, 66*s* 9*d*.

Item, for parchment bought by Master Richard the carpenter for the design, 4*d*.

Item, given to Master Richard by Sir John de Lenne, 10*s*.[73]

136. Extract from the account for Elizabeth de Burgh's falcons, 1338– 39 [From Public Record Office, London, E101/92/9, m. 10; in Latin]

John de Lenne [clerk of the wardrobe] accounts for the costs of 1 [peregrine] falcon and 2 lanner falcons in the custody of John Falconer from 30 September to 31 October inclusive, namely for 32 days, the falcon costing $^1/_2d$ a day and the lanner $^1/_4d$, 2*s* 8*d*. For the cost of 1 falcon in his custody from 30 September to 20 October inclusive, namely for 21 days, 10$^1/_2d$. Paid to the same John, 1 groom and 1 page staying behind at Clare with the said falcons for 3 days ending on 6 October, at 4$^1/_2d$ a day, 13$^1/_2d$. Paid to the same John Falconer searching in divers places for 1 lost falcon, staying and returning, for 6 days ending on 28 October, at 4$^1/_2d$ a day, 2*s* 3*d* ... Paid to John Revesale for 11 days ending on 6 December going from Bardfield to Woodham Ferrers and back to take partridges, taking 3$^1/_2d$ a day for himself, his page and dogs, 3*s* 2$^1/_2d$ ... For the costs of 1 goshawk in the custody of John de Clakton from 11 January to 13 February inclusive, namely for 34 days, at $^1/_2d$ a day, 17*d* ... For pigeons and meat bought by John de Revesale for the lady's sparrowhawks in July, 2*s*. Paid to John Falconer keeping the falcons at Bardfield from 2 June to 19 July inclusive, namely for 48 days, at 2*d* a day, 8*s*. Paid to Nicholas Falconer keeping the lady's falcons at Bardfield from 14 April to 1 June inclusive, and from 19 July to 27 July inclusive, namely for 58 days, taking 1$^1/_2d$ a day, 7*s* 3*d* ... Sum total: £6 4*s* 9$^1/_2d$.

137. Grant by Henry V to his grandmother, Joan de Bohun countess of Hereford, of hunting rights in Hatfield Forest, 1414 [From Public Record Office, London, C66/393, m. 29; in Latin]

The king greets all those to whom these letters come. You should

---

73 These three entries in January 1352 refer to the house which Elizabeth had built in the outer precinct of the convent of the Minoresses outside Aldgate by Richard de Felstede. For Elizabeth's connections with London, see J. C. Ward, 'Elizabeth de Burgh, Lady of Clare (d. 1360)', in C. M. Barron and A. F. Sutton, eds, *Medieval London Widows 1300-1500*, London, 1994, pp. 29-45.

know that, on account of the sincere love and deep affection which we have towards our very dear grandmother Joan countess of Hereford, we have granted her for life all the game within our forest of Hatfield, to have as our gift. The countess or her servants may hunt in the forest in summer and winter as often as she pleases, and carry away the beasts of the chase taken there, and dispose of them as she wishes, without any interference or hindrance from us or any of our foresters or officials whatsoever. In testimony of this, we have had drawn up these our letters patent. Witnessed by the king at Westminster on 9 January.

138. Examples of plate, furnishings and jewellery bequeathed by Philippa countess of March, 1378[74] [From Nichols, *Collection of All the Wills of the Kings and Queens of England*, pp. 99–101; in French]

Item, I bequeath to the church of Bisham all my chapel complete with all its appurtenances, namely vestments, books, chalices, cruets, silver candlesticks, painted and embroidered tablets, to serve at the altar of St Anne, before which altar my body will be buried in the second arch opposite my most honoured lord, my father, on whose soul may God have mercy; with the exception of my best vestments with three copes to match which I bequeath to the abbey of Wigmore, and my white vestments which I bequeath to the house of Limebrook. I bequeath to the same altar of St Anne the best tablet of gold that I bought from John Paulyn. I bequeath to serve at the same altar of St Anne two silver basins with the arms of Mortimer and Montagu in enamel on the base. Item, I bequeath to Edmund my son a bed of blue taffeta embroidered with asses marked on the shoulder with a rose, namely a complete canopy, three curtains of taffeta, a quilt embroidered to match, four tapestry hangings, six hangings of worsted, one canvas, one mattress, two pieces of fustian, a white counterpane, a pair of linen sheets, a coverlet of worsted for the same bed, a blue coverlet lined with trimmed minever, a kerchief of minever and blue camaka, one cup and an ewer of crystal garnished with gold. Item, [to Edmund] one gold ring with a ruby enamelled with russet. Item, to Edmund my son one gold ring with a piece of the true Cross and the inscription, 'In the name of the Father, Son and Holy Spirit, amen'. Item, to Edmund a

---

74 For other examples of furnishings, see nos. 68, 69. Philippa was the daughter of William Montagu earl of Salisbury, and this explains her burial in the priory founded by her father at Bisham. Wigmore and Limebrook were both Mortimer foundations.

blue clasp with two hands holding a diamond. Item, a pair of rosaries with the beads of red crosses enamelled; to keep the aforesaid ring with the true Cross, the clasp and rosaries with my blessing. Item, to Edmund one silver goblet with cover with the escutcheon of the arms of Mortimer. Item, to the same Edmund one gilt goblet with cover decorated with a rose.

139. Examples of plate and furnishings bequeathed by Matilda Lady St John, 1452. [From Lambeth Palace Library, London, Register of John Kemp, fo. 314r; in Latin]

Item, I bequeath to Thomas St John, my son, two silver basins engraved with the arms of my lord, his father. Item, I bequeath to the same Thomas twelve dishes, four salt-cellars and three chargers of silver ... Item, I bequeath to the same Thomas one bed of red worsted embroidered with parrots, with the tester and everything for it. Item, I bequeath to the same Thomas one whole bed of silk with the tester of black worsted and everything for it. Item, I bequeath to the same six livery beds. Item, I bequeath to the same Thomas one missal with one chalice and two cruets of silver. Item, I bequeath to the same Thomas one vestment of blue and red velvet, with the whole apparatus for the altar. Item, I bequeath to the same Thomas all my great bed of arras with all its equipment. Item, I bequeath to the same Thomas all my green tapestry hanging in the chamber with the bankers for the same.[75] Item, I bequeath to the same Thomas one great mattress with two pieces of fustian and six pairs of linen sheets.[76] Item, I bequeath to the said Thomas all my bed of black and white worsted with all its equipment. Item, I bequeath to John Halsham my son one little bed of tapestry with little green hangings, one mattress, one pair of blankets and two pairs of linen sheets. Item, I bequeath to the said John one basin with one ewer of silver, with the borders engraved with holly leaves ...

140. Examples of the lady's dress from the accounts of Mary de Bohun, countess of Derby, 1387-88[77] [From Public Record Office, London, DL28/1/2, fos 19-25; in Latin]

---

75 Bankers were the tapestry coverings for benches.

76 Fustian was a strong cloth, made of cotton, or a mixture of cotton and flax.

77 These accounts are arranged under the types of cloth or fur. The purchase of each type of cloth is given, followed by the way in which it was used for the lady, her children, retainers and servants. Select examples have been translated.

Delivered to William Thornby, the lady's tailor, 6 yards of scarlet for 2 furred robes for the lady against Christmas. 6 yards of scarlet delivered to him for 2 robes lined with tartarin in the summer.[78]
Delivered to William Thornby 1¼ yards of blue shortcloth for stockings for the lady.
Delivered to William Thornby 2¼ yards of black longcloth for a cloak and hood for the lady embroidered with harebells, as below.
Delivered to William Thornby 6 yards of green longcloth for 2 robes lined with tartarin for the lady for hunting.
Delivered to William Thornby 3 gold brocades 'de cypre', 1 white, 1 black and the other blue, for 3 robes for the lady.[79]
Delivered to William Thornby 1 white and blue brocade for 1 robe for the lady. And delivered to him for 1 gown for the duchess of Gloucester 1½ black and red silk brocades.
Delivered to Peter Swan 1½ yards of white and blue satin to embroider 1 cloak for the lady with harebells.
Delivered to William Thornby to trim 1 embroidered cloak of black cloth for the lady, 12 ermines.
Delivered to William Thornby to fur-line one of the lady's robes of scarlet, 15 timbers of pured minever. Delivered to the same to fur-line 1 of the lady's robes of white and blue silk brocade, 15 timbers of pured minever. Delivered to the same to fur-line 1 embroidered cloak of black cloth for the lady, 10½ timbers and 5 bellies of pured minever. Paid to Peter Swan for embroidering 1 short cloak of black cloth for the lady, embroidered and powdered with harebells, 40s.

141. The employment of a goldsmith and an illuminator by Elizabeth de Burgh, 1339 [From Public Record Office, London, E101/92/9, m. 10; in Latin]

John de Lenne [clerk of the wardrobe] accounts for payment to Robert the illuminator and Thomas the goldsmith staying behind at Bardfield, the lady being at Clare and going on pilgrimage to Walsingham, from 21 August to 3 October inclusive, namely for 42 days, each taking 2d a day, 14s 8d.[80]

78 Scarlet was an expensive woollen cloth, dyed in grain with kermes. Tartarin was a type of silk.
79 The patterns were partly woven with gold thread.
80 This entry was put among the foreign expenses on the wardrobe account.

142. The servants of Elizabeth countess of Salisbury, according to her will of 1414 (the servants were remembered in hierarchical order)[81]
[From Lambeth Palace Library, London, Register of Henry Chichele, Part 1, fo. 268b; in Latin]

I bequeath to Sir Hugh my chaplain a gold vestment, a missal and a breviary, price £10, to pray for my soul; item, to Sir William Cressy chaplain for the same reason 100s; item, to Sir John Boklond chaplain for the same reason 5 marks; item, to Sir John Wythy chaplain for the same reason 40s; item, to Sir John Axbrigge chaplain for the same reason 40s; item, to Sir Robert Loveringe chaplain for that reason 20s ... Item, I bequeath and leave to Agnes Grene my chief damsel 100 marks for her long service; item, [to her] two best robes furred with trimmed minever; to Katherine Pule my other damsel for that reason £10 and two robes furred with trimmed minever; item, [to] Alice Auncelle my other damsel for that reason £10 and two robes furred with minever; item, to William Grene esquire for his long service 100 marks; item, to Raulyn Bush esquire for the same reason 100 marks; item, to Patrick Mohon for that reason 20 marks; item, to Thomas Huntele esquire for that reason 100 shillings; item, to Thomas Bolour esquire for that reason 40s; item, to fitz Bussh esquire for that reason 5 marks; item, to William Short my auditor for the same reason 50 marks; item, to Anastasia my chamber-maid for the same reason 6 marks and a robe of russet furred with gris;[82] item, to Walter de Warderobe for that reason 100s; item, to Haukyn Greynard usher of my chamber 5 marks; item, to John Holeway yeoman of my chamber 40s; item, to Edward Legh my butler 100s; item, to Richard Pykenot usher of my hall 5 marks; item, to Jankyn my blacksmith 4 marks; item, to John Wyght cook 40s; item, to William Pomeray buyer 40s; item, to Hugh Short clerk 5 marks; item, to Walter Gardyner 26s 8d; item, to Roger atte Ford doorkeeper 40s; item, to John Newbury yeoman 5 marks; item, to Robert Parker yeoman 40s; item, to Joan Holeway laundress 20s and a robe lined with black buckram.[83] Item, I bequeath and leave for the maintenance and sustenance of Master John Fole at the discretion of my executors £10; item, to Adam Blaunchard groom of my chamber 40s; item, to John Goldhurst another groom of my chamber 13s 4d; item, to William Dosse groom of my buttery 26s 8d; item, to William groom of my hall 20s; item, to William Somere

81 See also no. 108 for the household servants of Isabella Lady Morley.
82 Gris was the grey back of the winter skin of the Baltic squirrel.
83 Buckram was a fine cotton or linen material.

groom of my kitchen 26s 8d; item, to William Fouler groom of my stable 20s; item, to Walter Bouke groom of my stable 20s; item, to John Scolard another groom of my stable 20s; item, to John Weylond another groom of my bakehouse;[84] item, to William Stathe groom of my said bakehouse 13s 4d; item, to Richard Parker[85] of my said kitchen 20s; item, to Robert Thresshe groom of my poultry 13s 4d; item, to Raulyn another poor groom 20s; item, [to] John Broun poor man of my house 13s 4d. Item, I bequeath to Jonet Newbury a robe of blue cloth furred with minever. Item, I bequeath to Edward Legh for his wife a green robe lined with buckram. Item, I bequeath to Sir William Yllemynstre friar to pray for my soul 40s; item, to John Hibard my servant 20s.

84 The amount of the legacy was not entered in the register.
85 Judging by the context the word groom has been omitted at this point.

VI: Religion

Men and women of the nobility and gentry living in the world were encouraged to practise their religion through attendance at Mass, private prayer on behalf of themselves and the dead, works of charity, pilgrimage, and material support of the Church. Alternatively, they could enter a monastery or nunnery to take up a life of religion. These two forms of life have parallels with each other; the noble household had its round of services in the chapel, and a noblewoman, if she chose, could live a religious life and remain in the world, while secular concerns inevitably impinged on life in the nunnery. There is copious evidence for women's involvement in religion, notably in charters and wills, but also in didactic treatises, devotional literature, household accounts and episcopal visitations. However, all this evidence leaves the important questions of motivation and piety unanswered; the historian has to look at the outward actions and has little means of assessing the degree of inner piety.

Much of the information on religious activity comes from charters and wills, and caution has to be exercised in the use of both. Charters are particularly important for the late eleventh and twelfth centuries and survive in abundance for many of the monastic houses founded at that time; some pose problems of authenticity and they were rarely dated. Both men and women were involved in issuing and consenting to charters. Grants to a religious house were a matter for family concern; grants made by a woman were confirmed by her husband and son, and occasionally the lord, while her husband's grants were witnessed and agreed to by his wife.[1] Although the grants usually state that they were intended to help towards the salvation of the souls of the grantor and his family, it is rare to obtain an insight into the circumstances of the grant, still less the influences behind it. Later charters can give more details, but it is only when supplementary information survives that it is possible to see the factors underlying a foundation; this is apparent in the case of the hospital at Heytesbury.[2] After the Statute

1 See nos. 72-5.

2 M. A. Hicks, 'Piety and lineage in the Wars of the Roses: the Hungerford experience', in R. A. Griffiths and J. Sherborne, eds, *Kings and Nobles in the Later Middle Ages: A Tribute to Charles Ross*, Gloucester, 1986, p. 100.

of Mortmain of 1279, a considerable amount of additional information can be gathered from the mortmain licences, as for Heytesbury and for Marie de St Pol's foundations.[3]

The problems posed by the interpretation of wills have been widely voiced.[4] Although they throw much light on the family, household, furnishings and religious practice from the late thirteenth century onwards, it is essential to be aware of their limitations. Wills were usually made on the testator's death-bed; hence the statement at the beginning of the will that the testator was whole in mind even though sick in body. After the committal of the soul to God and the saints, it was usual to make provision for burial and requiem masses, and then for bequests to be made to the Church and works of charity, and to the family and household. Obviously, testators were selective in the items they chose to bequeath, and it must not be assumed that they were disposing of all their possessions. The will by no means detailed all their wealth, and a statement was generally included that the residue of the possessions was to be used by the executors at their discretion for the benefit of the testator's soul. The testator was not concerned with estates which were passed on according to the laws of inheritance or family arrangements. The will was not concerned with earlier gifts and benefactions; the testator might well have already made provision for requiem masses by founding a chantry.[5] The appointment of the executors was crucial for the carrying out of the will, and they bore a heavy responsibility.[6] It is rare to know to what extent the provisions of the will were actually carried out.

Because of their land and wealth, noble and gentry women were expected to be generous in their support of the Church, and this generosity was a means by which they could gain salvation.[7] These religious endowments, however, have to be put in their ecclesiastical, family and social context. All people were influenced by contemporary fashions in endowment; there is a strong contrast between the 'boom'

---

3 S. Raban, *Mortmain Legislation and the English Church, 1279-1500*, Cambridge, 1982, pp. 132-4, 140-1.

4 R. N. Swanson, *Church and Society in Late Medieval England*, Oxford, 1989, pp. 265-8; C. Burgess, 'Late medieval wills and pious convention: testamentary evidence reconsidered', in M. Hicks, ed., *Profit, Piety and the Professions in Later Medieval England*, Gloucester, 1990, p. 14. The word 'will' is widely used as a generic term; in fact, the testament dealt with personal property, and the will with real property; see above, no. 42.

5 Elizabeth de Burgh founded a chantry at Anglesey priory in 1335; L. C. Loyd and D. M. Stenton, eds, *Sir Christopher Hatton's Book of Seals*, no. 74.

6 Archer and Ferme, 'Testamentary procedure', pp. 13-15.

in monastic foundations of the twelfth century, and the much fewer grants, often to ascetic orders, later; the later period saw frequent bequests to the friars and a concern for requiem masses, whether in the parish church or in a religious house. Walsingham epitomises a twelfth-century foundation while Hinton, Clare and Denny point to the later medieval trend.

Family considerations were almost always taken into account. The foundations at Walsingham, Hinton and Clare show that these were a family concern in which both men and women were involved. The connections between many families and churches were long-lasting, and continued to be maintained when a new family took over an estate on marriage to the heiress. Women maintained links with the religious houses connected with their own natal families as well as those of their husbands; thus Anne countess of Stafford chose to be buried at Lanthony Secunda priory and continued to support her father's college at Pleshey. In many cases this emphasis on family can be linked with strong feeling towards one's neighbourhood, as expresssed in gifts to both parish churches and local monasteries and hospitals.[8]

All these grants benefited the Church, but also brought tangible advantages to the woman and her family. In a few cases, such as Anglesey priory, founded by Richard de Clare earl of Hertford for Augustinian canons, rights of patronage were inherited by a woman. More widespread benefits came from the masses celebrated for the souls of members of the family. Even when the foundation took the form of a college or hospital, it was regarded as a chantry endowed to help the soul through Purgatory. Chantries are first found in the twelfth century but their number increased rapidly after c.1250. Whether they were permanent, like a college or hospital, or founded for a term of years, they aimed to provide daily or weekly services, usually masses, for the benefit of particular individuals in this life and of their souls after death. Their popularity is partly to be explained by the increasing emphasis placed by the Church on the Mass as the means by which God exercised his grace towards mankind, and this

---

7 Anselm's letter to Richard son of Count Gilbert and his wife Rohaise concerning the founding of St Neots priory stressed the importance of grants to the Church made by lay people. It is significant that Richard and Rohaise made a joint approach to Anselm as abbot of Bec to send monks to St Neots; F. S. Schmitt, *Sancti Anselmi Cantuariensis Archiepiscopi Opera Omnia*, Edinburgh, 1946, III, pp. 220-1.

8 A transition is sometimes found with the family's loyalty switching from a local monastery to the parish church. For the case of Etchingham, see N. Saul, *Scenes from Provincial Life: Knightly Families in Sussex 1280-1400*, Oxford, 1986, pp. 140-6.

was further heightened by the institution of the feast of Corpus Christi in 1264. The widespread belief in Purgatory as the place which the soul had to pass through after death, and and the consideration that the time the soul spent in Purgatory could be shortened by means of the prayers of the living and requiem masses explain why chantries and other forms of commemoration figure largely in late medieval wills.[9]

Foundations expressing the woman's own individual wishes, independent of family, could usually only be made by widows who had already met their family obligations. Thus Ela countess of Salisbury moved her husband's Carthusian foundation from Hatherop to Hinton before making her own foundation at Lacock, a nunnery which she subsequently entered and of which she became abbess; even so, she ensured that she had her eldest son's consent for what she was doing. Marie de St Pol's foundation of a house of Minoresses (Franciscan nuns) at Denny was again her own choice, and illustrates the ruthlessness needed by many patrons in pushing their plans to a successful conclusion.[10] Women, like Marie de St Pol, were important founders of colleges at Oxford and Cambridge in the later Middle Ages, and in Marie's case was a matter of individual choice.[11]

As far as the noblewoman's own religious life was concerned, religious teaching in childhood was regarded as vital, and this was especially important in the later Middle Ages as lay people came increasingly to participate in religious practice. For the knight of La Tour Landry, women's education consisted primarily of learning about the Scriptures. With greater importance attached to Mass, men and women needed to know how to prepare devoutly for the service, and follow it prayerfully; works such as *The Lay Folk's Mass Book* helped them to do

9 J. Le Goff, *The Birth of Purgatory*, Aldershot, 1984, pp. 289-95; E. Duffy, *The Stripping of the Altars: Traditional Religion in England 1400-1580*, New Haven, 1992, pp.338-76.

10 Women were responsible for the foundation of three out of the four houses of Minoresses in England in the late thirteenth and fourteenth centuries. These nuns followed the Isabella Rule, approved by Urban IV in 1263, and followed at Longchamp, the house founded in 1255 by Isabella, sister of Louis IX of France. The English foundations are discussed by A. F. C. Bourdillon, *The Order of Minoresses in England*, Manchester, 1926.

11 Marie's work can be compared with Elizabeth de Burgh, and especially with Margaret Beaufort; Ward, *English Noblewomen*, pp. 156-60; Jones and Underwood, *The King's Mother*, pp. 202-31. In the case of Balliol College Oxford, Devorguilla de Balliol was developing a foundation initiated by her husband. Education was regarded as important for the household clerks; Elizabeth de Burgh was sending clerks to Oxford and London (to study law) in the early 1330s.

this. Sermons were an important teaching aid on religious, pastoral and moral matters. Devotional literature in the vernacular was available to women, and is recorded in some wills.[12] Growing literacy among noblewomen by the fifteenth century meant that they could make use of their own books of hours as well as other religious works. It is likely that the wills only record a small sample of the books in use, but they indicate their significance in late medieval religion.[13] Use of these books could give a measure of individuality to the woman's religious observance, as does the evidence for ownership of rosaries and relics, and devotion to particular saints.[14]

A few noblewomen became recluses, usually when they were widowed. It was for a group of three ladies, possibly of the Mortimer family, living as recluses in the vicinity of a great house, that the *Ancrene Riwle* was written as a guide in the thirteenth century. This lay stress on a life of contemplation, and emphasised the need for penance and confession.[15] More women lived out their lives as nuns, while others took the veil after they were widowed. There is no means of knowing for how many this was the result of a genuine vocation, and how many adopted this form of life as a result of parental or financial pressure. Entry into a nunnery required a money payment, but this may have been lower than some parents would have to pay for a dowry on marriage.[16] Information about the nun's life is largely derived from

12 Excerpts from instructional and devotional texts are included in R. N. Swanson, ed., *Catholic England: Faith, Religion and Observance before the Reformation*, Manchester, 1993, pp. 78-147.

13 S. G. Bell, 'Medieval women book owners: arbiters of lay piety and ambassadors of culture', in M. Erler and M. Kowaleski, eds, *Women and Power in the Middle Ages*, Athens, 1988, pp. 149-87; J. Boffey, 'Women authors and women's literacy in fourteenth- and fifteenth-century England', in C. M. Meale, ed., *Women and Literature in Britain, 1150-1500*, Cambridge, 1993, pp. 159-82; C. M. Meale, '"... alle the bokes that I haue of latyn, englisch and frensch": laywomen and their books in late medieval England', *ibid.* pp. 128-58.

14 J. Catto, 'Religion and the English nobility in the later fourteenth century', in H. Lloyd-Jones, V. Pearl and B. Worden, eds, *History and Imagination: Essays in honour of H. R. Trevor-Roper*, London, 1981, pp. 48-50.

15 M. B. Salu, trans., *The Ancrene Riwle*, Exeter, 1990; B. Millett, 'Women in No Man's Land: English recluses and the development of vernacular literature in the twelfth and thirteenth centuries', in C. M. Meale, ed., *Women and Literature*, pp. 86-103. Examples of noblewomen recluses are given in M. W. Labarge, *Women in Medieval Life*, London, 1986, pp. 122-8.

16 See above, the will of William Berland, 1383, no. 16. This may be compared with evidence at Shaftesbury from the late eleventh century; K. Cooke, 'Donors and daughters: Shaftesbury abbey's benefactors, endowments and nuns, c. 1086-1130', *Anglo-Norman Studies, XII. Proceedings of the Battle Conference of 1989*, ed. M. Chibnall, Woodbridge, 1990, pp. 29-30, 37-42.

visitations, but since these aimed at searching out deficiencies and failures, they cannot be accepted as a complete picture. An insight of a different kind is provided by the description of the office of cellaress at Barking abbey. The position of the abbess had parallels with that of the widow, in that she had responsibilty for lands and services. Her election needed royal assent, and in times of political disturbance she might find herself called on to keep a noblewoman confined.[17] Nuns also had their connections with the world outside. As many were from noble and gentry families, they maintained contact with the world through their families. Nunneries were used for the education of young children,[18] and nuns were entertained by noblewomen at their residences.[19] Even the stricter orders, like the Minoresses, were not cut off from the rest of noble society.

For the woman living in the world, the intensity of religous observance and piety would clearly vary from one individual to another. Some widows chose to become vowesses, taking a vow of chastity in the presence of the bishop;[20] Margaret Beaufort was unusual in taking the vow during the lifetime of her third husband.[21] The daily life of Cecily duchess of York towards the end of her life implies a constant round of prayer, public and private, in the midst of a noble household. Although this should not be taken as typical, the stress in the later Middle Ages on the importance of the private chapel shows that the lady and her household had a religious life in addition to their secular concerns.[22] Elizabeth de Burgh's private expenditure points to a yearly cycle of masses for the living and the dead, including relatives, officials and servants. This was combined with the use of the local parish church from time to time. Other aspects of household life conformed to religious tenets. Fast days were marked by abstinence from meat; in Lent dairy products were also banned. Friday and Saturday were

17 See above, no. 102; Elizabeth de Burgh at Barking abbey.

18 See above, no. 63; the children of the de la Pole family at Bungay and Bruisyard.

19 See above, no. 134.

20 For examples of the ceremony when the vowess took her vow, see R. N. Swanson, ed., *Catholic England*, pp. 173-4; M. C. Erler, 'Three fifteenth-century vowesses', C. M. Barron and A. F. Sutton, eds, *Medieval London Widows*, pp. 165-7.

21 Jones and Underwood, *The King's Mother*, pp. 187-8.

22 This is brought out in the securing of indulgences from the papacy to have private altars, confessors and other religious privileges; e.g. *Calendar of Entries in Papal Registers relating to Great Britain and Ireland: Papal Letters*, IV, p. 47: in 1365, an indulgence was granted to Maurice de Berkeley and his wife to have a portable altar, to have Mass celebrated before daybreak, and Mass and other divine offices celebrated privately in places under interdict.

always fast days, as were the vigils of certain feasts, and sometimes Wednesdays. The Church's feast days were times for celebration, although households varied as to which feasts were especially honoured.

Pilgrimage played an important part in the religious lives of many noblewomen, with Canterbury and Walsingham as popular destinations.[23] Some noblewomen travelled abroad, as did Elizabeth Luttrell to Santiago de Compostella. Few women followed Eleanor of Castile's example in going on crusade, but some made financial contributions, and others, like Eleanor de Bohun, transmitted family crusading traditions to their own children.[24]

Good works were regarded as an integral part of these women's religious activity, and charity was viewed as securing remission of time in Purgatory. Depictions of the seven works of mercy often show them being performed by women, and the relief of poverty was regarded as the responsibility of the lady and her household.[25] This took a variety of forms. Household accounts point to the presence of poor people in some households and the feeding of the poor.[26] Both casual and regular almsgiving were recorded. The washing of the feet of the poor on Maundy Thursday was carried out by Mary de Bohun. Some women, like Margaret Lady Hungerford, devoted resources to the foundation of hospitals and almshouses.[27] Many wills provided for the presence of the poor round the coffin at the lady's funeral, clothes and money being given in return for the prayers which were regarded as especially beneficial to the deceased.

The importance of death, Purgatory and salvation in the later medieval world has often been emphasised. Religious observance during life and at and after death was designed to help the woman towards salvation. About 1400, opinion and practice were polarised, some feeling that as unworthy sinners they were completely dependent on God for salvation; this view was held among the Lollards and

23 See above, no. 57, for Matilda of St Hilary's pilgrimage to Thomas Becket's shrine at Canterbury.

24 See above, no. 34; S. Lloyd, *English Society and the Crusade, 1216-1307*, Oxford, 1988, pp. 102-6; C. Tyerman, *England and the Crusades, 1095-1588*, Chicago, 1988, p. 180.

25 P. H. Cullum, '"And hir name was charite": charitable giving by and for women in late medieval Yorkshire', in P. J. P. Goldberg, ed., *Woman is a Worthy Wight*, chapter 7.

26 See above, nos. 131, 133, for the households of Joan de Valence and Alice de Brian.

27 Hospitals in the Middle Ages were essentially devoted to the care of the old and poor.

also much more widely, and is typified by the will of Anne Latimer in 1403.[28] Many, however, felt that they needed requiem masses, and most wills specified particular numbers or types or periods of masses for the benefit of the testator and others named by her. The desire for a splendid funeral was expressed in many of these wills, some making provision for their tomb, though rarely in as much detail as Isabella Despenser, countess of Warwick. The funeral and tomb were not simply for the individual woman concerned. Many chose to be buried beside their husbands or in association with parents and ancestors. As so often in their religious activities, they were thinking in terms of family, status, and their place in society and the locality. They wanted a permanent memorial.

143. The foundation of the priory at Walsingham for Augustinian canons, 1153 [From British Library, London, Cotton MS. Nero E vii, fo. 8r; in Latin]

Geoffrey de Favarches greets all the faithful people of holy Church which is in Christ. Be it known to you that I have given and granted in perpetual alms to God and St Mary and to Edwy my clerk the chapel which my mother founded in Walsingham in honour of Mary, ever Virgin, in order to establish the religious order which he will provide, for the salvation of my soul and those of my parents and friends.[29] I have also given him possession of the church of All Saints of the same vill and all its appurtenances, both in lands and tithes and rents and homages and everything which Edwy possessed on the day when I undertook the journey to Jerusalem; and specifically 20s a year from my demesne for two-thirds of the demesne tithes; and also the land of Snoring which Hawise gave to God and the aforesaid chapel, namely ½ an acre in the vill of Snoring which lies next to the land and house of Thovy, and eight acres in the arable fields of the same vill, together with the shares in the meadow which belong to the same land. In order that the aforesaid Edwy and his successors, professed to the regular life, may hold this by perpetual right in ecclesiastical possession without disturbance, I corroborate and confirm this my gift

---

28 K. B. McFarlane, *Lancastrian Kings and Lollard Knights*, Oxford, 1972, p. 214; M. G. A. Vale, *Piety, Charity and Literacy among the Yorkshire Gentry, 1370-1480*, Borthwick Papers no. 50, York, 1976, pp. 12-13; J. A. F. Thomson, 'Orthodox religion and the origins of Lollardy', *History*, LXXIV, 1989, pp. 39-55; M. Aston, '"Caim's castles": poverty, politics and disendowment', in *Faith and Fire: Popular and Unpopular Religion 1350-1600*, London, 1993, p. 128.

29 The chapel was said to be built on the model of the holy house at Nazareth.

and grant by testimony of my charter and my seal to the honour of God and blessed Mary, ever Virgin. The witnesses of this gift and grant are Alan the priest of 'Turlfordia' etc.

144. Grant by Matilda de Clare countess of Gloucester and Hertford to the priory of Augustinian friars at Clare, 1276–89[30] [From British Library, London, Harley MS. 4835, fo. 4r; in Latin]

Men present and future should know that I Matilda de Clare countess of Gloucester and Hertford in my pure and liege widowhood have given, granted and by this my present charter confirmed to God and the friars of St Augustine of Clare and their successors, for the salvation of my soul and the soul of Sir Richard de Clare, late earl of Gloucester and Hertford, and for the salvation of the souls of our ancestors and successors, two acres of meadow with their appurtenances which I have of the gift and feoffment of Susanna, formerly the wife of Walter Swayn of Clare. They lie in the meadow called 'Eldemelnemede' next to the site of the friars of the order of St Augustine on one side, and of Walter Lambert of Belchamp on the other, one end abutting on the pasture once held by Hugh Dolefen, and the other on the meadow which I had of the gift and feoffment of William Thurstan of Clare and Matilda his wife. To have and to hold all the aforesaid meadow with its appurtenances to God and the friars and their successors of me and my heirs or assigns well and in peace, freely and quietly for ever by rendering yearly to the lords of the fee due and accustomed service for all services, aids, suits, customs and demands belonging to me or to my heirs or my assigns. I Matilda and my heirs and assigns will warrant, acquit and defend for ever all the aforesaid meadow with appurtenances to God and the aforesaid friars and their successors against all men. So that this my gift, grant and confirmation may have the validity of perpetual authority, I have affixed my seal to the present charter. Witnessed by Sir Walter son of Humphrey, Sir Hugh son of Adam, Richard de Goseford, William de Goseford, Peter Hubert, Walter le Palmer, Geoffrey Sellar, John Pye, John de Clare, Robert Mainard, William Thurstan and others.

30 This house had been founded by her husband, Richard de Clare earl of Gloucester and Hertford in 1248.

145. Charter of Ela countess of Salisbury, founding the Charterhouse at Hinton, 1227 [From Dugdale, *Monasticon Anglicanum*, VI, p. 5; in Latin]

Ela countess of Salisbury gives eternal greeting in the Lord to all sons of holy mother Church to whom the present writing comes. Be it known to you all that my lord and late husband, William Longespee earl of Salisbury, wished to build a house of the Carthusian order. With my assent and good will he gave to the order the manor of Hatherop [Gloucestershire] and his wood of 'Bradene' in its entirety, and the land of Chelworth which he had of the gift of Henry Basset so that the monks and brothers might remain there to serve God for ever according to the Carthusian custom and order.[31] However, because the monks and brothers destined for that place could not find in those lands a place suitable for their order, although they stayed there for several years, I, wishing for God's sake to complete what my husband had begun well, in my liege power and widowhood after his death have given and granted and by this my charter confirmed to the Carthusian order all my manor of Hinton, with the advowson of the church and the park and all its other appurtenances without anything reserved to me or my heirs, in exchange for the aforesaid lands. I have done this for my husband's soul, and the soul of Earl William my father, and for my salvation and that of my children, and for the souls of all my ancestors and heirs. Similarly I have granted all my manor of Midsummer Norton with the advowson of the church and all its other appurtenances, without any reservation to me or my heirs. However, I have reserved to me and my heirs the military services of all those who hold of me in the aforesaid manors by military service, except the service of Richard the parker and his heirs from one virgate of land which he holds in Hinton; this service will belong to the monks and brothers for ever, or Richard is to hold that virgate of land by keeping the park or by military service; saving also to me and my heirs droveways which are outside the bounds of the aforesaid manors. These possessions are for the foundation, building and maintenance for ever of a house of the Carthusian order in honour of God and blessed Mary and St John the Baptist and All Saints in Hinton park in the place which is called Place of God. To have and to hold to the monks and brothers serving God there in pure and perpetual alms according to the custom and order of the church of La Chartreuse. I and my heirs will warrant the aforesaid lands with appurtenances to the monks and

31 William Longespee was the bastard brother of Richard I, and his title and all his lands came to him by right of his wife.

brothers against all people, and will defend them from all services, customs and secular demands. In order that this my gift, grant and confirmation may remain valid and firm for ever, I have strengthened it with the testimony of the present writing and the impression of my seal. Witnessed by Lord Jocelin [of Wells] bishop of Bath, Lord Richard [Poore] bishop of Salisbury, Master Edmund de Abendon treasurer of Salisbury, Master Elias de Derham canon of Salisbury, Reginald de [Caune] then sheriff of Wiltshire, Bartholomew de Turbervill, William Gereberd, Walter de Pavily, John Gereberd, Baldwin son of William then steward of the earl of Salisbury, Michael de Cheldrinton, William de Burneford, Nicholas de Hedinton clerk, Roger Lond ...

146. Grant by Ela countess of Salisbury to the nunnery she founded at Lacock, *c.* 1236[32] [From Dugdale, *Monasticon Anglicanum*, VI, pp. 502-3; in Latin]

Men present and future should know that I Ela countess of Salisbury, for God and for the soul of Earl William Longespee my husband, and of all his and my ancestors, and for the salvation of myself and of William Longespee, my eldest son, and of all my other children and my heirs, in my widowhood and liege power have given, granted and by my present charter confirmed to God and blessed Mary and St Bernard, and to the nuns serving God at Lacock, my manor of Lacock, with the advowson of the church of the same manor and with all its appurtenances; and the manor of Hatherop with all its appurtenances; and the manor of Bishopstrow with all its appurtenances; and half the manor of Heddington with all its appurtenances, which belong to me as a result of the final concord concerning the honour of Trowbridge made between Humphrey de Bohun and me in the lord king's court;[33] and the advowson of the church of Shrewton; with all liberties and free

32 Ela founded Lacock priory for Augustinian canonesses in 1229-30; it was upgraded to an abbey when she became abbess there in 1240, having taken the veil in 1238. Her grants were made with the close co-operation of her eldest son William, with whom two agreements were concluded in 1236. In these, Ela promised to hand over all her inheritance to William on 1 November; the only reservation in the second agreement was the wardship of her son Nicholas which she held of William's grant. Summaries of these agreements are given in *Lacock Abbey Charters*, ed. K. H. Rogers, Wiltshire Record Society, XXXIV, 1979, pp. 11-13; they are printed in the original in W. G. Clark-Maxwell, 'The earliest charters of the abbey of Lacock', *Wiltshire Archaeological and Natural History Magazine*, XXXV, 1907-08, pp. 203-5.

33 According to this final concord, made in 1229, Bishopstrow and half of Heddington were to pass to Ela.

customs, in all places and in all things, without any reservation.
Wherefore I wish the nuns, who are going to serve God at Lacock for
ever, to have and hold all the aforesaid manors in free, pure and
perpetual alms, completely free and quit of all secular service due to
the lord king and his bailiffs, and to me and my heirs, and of all kind
of service and exaction for whatever reason it may be demanded. I Ela
and my heirs will warrant, defend and acquit to the nuns against all
men and women for ever all the aforesaid manors, with the advowsons
of the churches of Shrewton and Lacock, and with all their other
appurtenances, as free and quit as any alms which can be given.
Witnessed by Sir Walter de Godarvile, Thomas de Ebelesbourn,
Nicholas Malemains, Adam rector of Gaddesden, Richard Longespee,
John de Moul, Master Roger de Stokes, Sir Roger de Baskervile, Peter
de Salceto, Sir Peter parson of Trowbridge, Philip de Depeford clerk,
Thomas Makerel clerk, Robert de Holte clerk and others.

147. Licence by Edward III to Marie de St Pol countess of Pembroke to transfer the convent of the Minoresses from Waterbeach to Denny and to grant the nuns the manor of Denny, 1339[34] [From Dugdale, *Monasticon Anglicanum*, VI, p. 1551; in Latin]

Edward by the grace of God king of England, lord of Ireland and duke
of Aquitaine greets all those to whom the present letters come. You
should know that, in return for the remission and quitclaim of all the
right and claim which she had in the castles and vills of Hertford and
Haverford, and in the manors of Higham Ferrers, Monmouth and
Hadnock, we formerly granted to our beloved Marie, who was the wife
of Aymer de Valence late earl of Pembroke, the manor of Denny with
its appurtenances in Cambridgeshire, among other lands and tenements,[35] to have for her whole life and afterwards, in return for the
good service which she has given us, and also in return for £250
which we have received from her by the hands of the venerable father
Henry bishop of Lincoln, then our treasurer. We have granted for us
and our heirs that Marie should have and hold the manor of Denny
with appurtenances to her and her heirs, together with knights' fees,

---

34 This is one of a series of documents concerned with the transfer which was not
effected until 1351 by which time most of the nuns had moved from Waterbeach to
Denny; Bourdillon, *Order of Minoresses*, pp. 19-22. For a full account of Marie de St
Pol, see H. Jenkinson, 'Mary de Sancto Paulo, foundress of Pembroke College,
Cambridge', *Archaeologia*, LXXXVI, 1915, pp. 401-46. Marie's will provided for her
burial in the choir of Denny church in the habit of a Minoress; she died in 1377.

35 The quitclaim and exchange were made in March 1327.

liberties and everything else belonging to that manor, of us and our heirs and of the other capital lords of that fee by the due and accustomed services for ever. On behalf of ourselves and our heirs, we remit all right and claim which we had or could have in the manor to Marie and her heirs, as is more fully set out in divers of our letters patent. Marie has now petitioned us that the house of the abbess and sisters of the Minoresses of Waterbeach, our beloved in Christ, is on a restricted, low and bad site, and is otherwise unsuitable for their life, and that we should grant her permission to transfer the abbess and sisters from Waterbeach to the manor of Denny, and give and assign that manor to the abbess and sisters so as to construct houses and buildings there for their habitation, and to have and hold to them and their successors for ever. Considering the zeal of the countess for the increase of divine worship and works of piety, and also taking her views into account, we have granted by our special grace, for us and our heirs, to the abbess and sisters that they may move from Waterbeach to the manor of Denny whenever they and the countess please, there to live according to the rule of their order for ever, without hindrance or impediment from us or our heirs or any of our officials. We have also granted to the countess of our more copious grace that she can give and assign the manor of Denny, with knights' fees, liberties and all its other appurtenances, to the abbess and sisters, to have and hold to them and their successors for ever, to be used for their habitation, and for making and maintaining chantries and other alms and pious works, according to the ordinance of the countess. Similarly we have given special licence to the same abbess and sisters that they can receive the manor with its appurtenances from Marie, and construct and erect houses and buildings for their habitation there, and hold the manor, thus built up, with all its appurtenances to them and their successors for ever, according to the tenor of the present letters, and notwithstanding the published statute about not putting lands and tenements in mortmain. We do not wish Marie or her heirs, or the abbess and sisters or their successors to be hindered, molested in any way, or oppressed because of the matters mentioned or because of the statute by us or our heirs, our justices, escheators, sheriffs or other of our bailiffs or officials whatsoever. Yet saving to us and our heirs and other chief lords of that fee the services due and accustomed. In testimony of this, we have had these our letters patent drawn up. Witnessed by Edward duke of Cornwall and earl of Chester, our dearest son, keeper of England. Given at Berkhamsted on 14 April.

148. Licence granted by Edward III to Marie de St Pol countess of Pembroke to found Pembroke College at Cambridge, 1347[36] [From Public Record Office, London, C66/222, m. 9; in Latin]

The king greets all those to whom these letters come. You should know that of our special grace, on behalf of ourselves and our heirs as far as in us lies, we have granted and given licence to our beloved kinswoman, Marie de St Pol countess of Pembroke that she can found a house of scholars in the town of Cambridge for a warden and thirty scholars or more according to the will of the countess. They are to live there for ever, observing certain rules, and studying there in divers faculties in the university, according to the ordinance to be made by the countess. She can give and assign to the warden and scholars one, two or three suitable messuages and sites with appurtenances in the same town for the habitation of the warden and scholars, whether these be held of us in chief or of others; she can also grant advowsons of churches to the value of £100 a year, according to their valuation for taxation,[37] which are not held of us in chief, to have and hold to the warden and scholars and their successors for ever. Similarly we have given special licence to the same warden and scholars that they can receive the aforesaid messuages and sites, with appurtenances, and the advowsons from the countess, and appropriate the churches, and hold them once appropriated to them and their successors for their own uses together with the aforesaid messuages and sites for their habitation and support for ever, as has been stated in this letter, notwithstanding the published statute about not putting lands and tenements in mortmain. We have previously taken inquisitions which used to be done in this case. Saving to us and the chief lords of those fees the services due and accustomed. In testimony of this, we have had these our letters patent drawn up. Witnessed by the king at Guildford on 24 December.

149. Extracts from Edward IV's licence for the foundation of an almshouse at Heytesbury by Margaret Lady Hungerford, 1472[38] [From Dugdale, *Monasticon Anglicanum*, VI, pp. 725-6; in Latin]

36 The foundation is discussed by D. R. Leader, *A History of the University of Cambridge*, I, *The University to 1546*, Cambridge, 1988, pp. 83-4.

37 This valuation was probably based on the Valuation of Pope Nicholas IV, 1291.

38 For the background to this foundation, see Hicks, 'Piety and lineage', p. 100. Robert Lord Hungerford died in 1459, and Walter ten years earlier.

The king greets all to whom these letters come. You should know that as a perpetual memorial and at the pious desires of the devout, especially those who are mindful of the salvation of souls, it is fitting for us to give gracious consent. Because it is holy and beneficial to pray for the dead, we at the humble petition of Margaret, who was the wife of Robert late Lord Hungerford, knight, have granted of our special grace and given licence on behalf of ourselves and our heirs to the same Margaret, to John Cheyne of Penn esquire, and to John Mervyn esquire, acting on their own or together, that they or two or one of them may make, found, create, erect and establish an almshouse. The house is to be for one chaplain, twelve poor men and one woman for ever. The chaplain is to be warden of the same house at Heytesbury in Wiltshire. There is to be divine service and other prayers every day in the parish church of Heytesbury for ever, for our good estate, for our best beloved consort Elizabeth queen of England, for the reverend father in Christ Richard Beauchamp bishop of Salisbury, while we are all alive, and for our souls after we have died; and also for the good estate of the aforesaid Margaret, John and John, and of Master James Goldwell, apostolic protonotary, dean of the cathedral church of St Mary at Salisbury, while they live; and for the souls of Robert Hungerford and of Margaret when she has died; and also for the souls of Robert's parents, Walter Hungerford, late Lord Hungerford, and Katherine his deceased wife, and of Margaret's parents, William Lord Botreaux and Elizabeth his deceased wife; and for the soul of George Westby esquire; and also for the souls of the aforesaid John Cheyne, John Mervyn and James Goldwell, after their deaths, and for the souls of all the faithful departed. Certain other things are to be done and prayed for for ever according to the ordinance of Margaret, John and John, or any others involved in this ... Moreover of our more copious grace we have granted and given licence on behalf of us and our heirs to Margaret, John and John that they or two or one of them can give and grant to the aforesaid warden, poor men and woman the manors of Little and Great Cheverell, with appurtenances, in the aforesaid county, for their support when the almshouse is made, founded, created, built and established. They can also grant them two messuages with appurtenances in Heytesbury which Walter Hungerford, late Lord Hungerford, recently acquired from John de Borgh esquire, whether they be held of us or of others, for the habitation of the warden, poor men and woman and their successors; and twenty cartloads of wood for their fuel from the wood of South Leigh in Wiltshire, with the advowson of the church of Great

Cheverell only excepted. To have and hold in free, pure and perpetual alms for ever the aforesaid manor and messuages, with appurtenances, with the one exception, to the warden, poor men and woman and their successors, and for them to have and receive yearly the aforesaid twenty cartloads of wood from the aforesaid wood by the supervision of its keeper at the time, or without his supervision if he cannot or will not attend to this when asked, without impediment. In testimony of this, we have had these our letters patent drawn up. Witnessed by the king at Westminster, 20 February.

150. The exercise of patronage by Elizabeth de Burgh over Anglesey priory, 1333[39] [From British Library, London, Harley Charter 47 E38; in Latin]

Be it known to all by means of the present letters that we Elizabeth de Burgh, lady of Clare and sister and one of the heirs of Sir Gilbert de Clare, late earl of Gloucester and Hertford, of famous memory, have clarified the right of patronage which we have over Anglesey priory when a vacancy [in the office of prior] occurs. On behalf of ourselves and our heirs, in written form, we have granted and confirm to the canons of the monastery and their successors the following concessions which are to be observed for ever. Whenever the monastery shall happen to be vacant through the death or resignation [of the prior], the canons ought to send one of their number to us if we are in the kingdom of England, or to our steward of Clare then in office if we are outside the kingdom, to announce the vacancy and seek licence to elect a prior from his own church or elsewhere. When the licence has been procured, the canons may freely proceed to the election. Once the election has been made, they are to present the elected man to us and our heirs as patron and seek our consent. We have however granted to the canons and their successors that neither we nor any of our heirs or successors nor anyone in our name by reason of our patronage over the monastery may commit any waste there during the vacancy by selling, bestowing and disposing of their goods, or by making any change which could be proved to be to the loss of the monastery. So that there should be no occasion for removal or destruction, we wish and have granted to the canons on behalf of ourselves and our heirs that in time of vacancy, for as long as the vacancy lasts, we and our successors may only have one man who, on account of the acknowl-

39 Anglesey priory was founded _c._ 1212 for Augustinian canons by Richard de Clare earl of Hertford.

edgement of our right of patronage, may take simple seisin and who may make no destruction, as said above. When he takes seisin in this form, he is to hand over and commit all their goods to the sub-prior or to his deputy and to other more discreet officers of the aforesaid house to preserve and keep them to the use of the monastery, appointing also a groom to keep the gate of the priory in place of the janitor, eating and drinking in the canons' refectory at the table of the lay brothers during the vacancy, until they are provided with a prior and pastor. We have granted this liberty to the aforesaid canons and their church, and we do not wish ourselves or any of our heirs or successors or anyone acting in our name to attempt or do anything contrary to it to the prejudice of the monastery. In order that this our grant and confirmation may have full validity and effect for ever, our seal has been attached to the present letter. Witnessed by Sir John de Cantebrig, Sir Alexander de Walsham, Sir John de Wauton, Sir Walter Trayly, knights, Sir Thomas de Cheddeworth, Master William de Brampton, John de Engayn of Teversham, William Muchet of Fen Ditton and others. Given at Anglesey on Wednesday after the feast of St Matthew, apostle and evangelist [22 September], 1333, in the seventh year of the reign of King Edward III.

151. Extracts from the will of Anne countess Stafford, 1438, showing connections maintained with the religious foundations of her own parents and ancestors[40] [From Lambeth Palace Library, London, Register of Henry Chichele, Part 1, fo. 479r; in English]

In the name of God, amen. I Anne countess of Stafford, Buckingham, Hereford and Northampton and lady of Brecon, of whole and advised mind, ordain and make my will in the English tongue in this form for my greatest profit, reading and understanding. First I bequeath my soul to Almighty God, and my body to be buried in the church of Lanthony near Gloucester in the place that I have earlier ordained and have made my tomb. I bequeath to the same church 100 marks in money or in the value of such of my movable goods as will seem best according to the discretion of my executors ... After my debts, wrongs and extortions, and rewards of my servants have been paid and satisfied, I bequeath £20 a year to be paid by my executors for twenty years from certain lands and tenements which are in the hands of my

40 See above, no. 33, for the connection of the Bohun family with the priory of Lanthony Secunda; Anne's mother was Eleanor de Bohun. Lanthony Secunda was synonymous with Lanthony by Gloucester.

feoffees to the priests to perform divine service daily for me during the aforesaid term in the college of Pleshey, according to the form of the will which I made before and which is written and sealed with my seal[41] ...

152. Excerpts from *The Book of the Knight of La Tour Landry* concerning prayer and piety [From *The Book of the Knight of La Tour Landry*, ed. T. Wright, Early English Text Society, original series XXXIII, revised edition 1906, chapters, 2, 20, 101;[42] in English]

The first work or labour that a man or woman should start with is to serve God. Every time he wakes, he ought to acknowledge God in thought and prayer that He is His Lord, Creator and Maker. When he rises, he should say his matins or orisons, if he is a clerk, giving thanks and praise, so as to say, 'All people, praise the Lord', and 'Let us bless the Father and the Son', and to say prayers which praise and thank God. For it is a higher and worthier thing to praise and thank God than to make requests to Him and ask for gifts and rewards. Praise and thanksgiving make up the service of the angels which praise and worship God for ever. It is better to thank God than to make requests, for he knows better what man or woman needs than they do themselves. Afterwards, every day before you go to sleep, you ought to praise God for the souls which have died; if you do this, the dead pray for you. Do not forget to pray to the blessed Virgin Mary who prays for us day and night, and do not forget to recommend yourself to the saints. When this has been done, you may sleep the better. Also you ought to pray every time you wake, and you ought not to forget.

The pleasure of all good women ought to be to visit and feed the poor and fatherless children and to nourish and clothe young little children, as did a holy woman who was countess of Mans, who always fed thirty fatherless children and said it was her recreation. Therefore she was loved by God and had a good life and death; at her death was seen a great light which shone clearly and was full of small children, Innocents, around her.

Yet I say to you that obedience to God and the fear of God comes before marriage, since we ought first to obey our Creator who made us in his semblance and image. The law's first command is to obey God;

41 This will has not survived.

42 This work was translated into English in the fifteenth century, and printed by Caxton in 1484.

for no woman ought to put service to her husband before service to God, from whose service comes profit to the soul which is everlasting. For, as Scripture says, all the good service done by the body makes for salvation for the soul, since the wealth of the soul has no equal. Therefore the wife is bound first to obey and serve God, and afterwards her husband, by the pledge of marriage, and to pray for him, and counsel him kindly and patiently for the good of his soul, and so turn him away from every evil deed, inasmuch as lies in her power. Every good woman is bound to do this.

153. Two letters of King John relating to the election of an abbess of Barking, 1215 [From T. D. Hardy, ed., *Rotuli Litterarum Clausarum, 1204-24*, pp. 181, 202; in Latin]

The king greets the prioress and convent of Barking. We ask you more attentively to place in authority as your abbess Lady Sarah de Walebr', nun and your sister, hearing our prayers as effectively as you wish us to hear yours in expediting your business and defending and maintaining your liberties everywhere. Witnessed by the king at Southampton, 30 January.

Lord P[eter des Roches] bishop of Winchester is ordered to apply all care and solicitude so that the aunt of Robert de Ros, nun at Barking, be promoted as abbess there, and, if this cannot be done, that the sister of John de Bassingeburn, prioress of 'Elleschirch' be promoted as abbess, and, if neither of them can be promoted, that the prioress of Barking be promoted as abbess, and that you in no way allow the sister of Robert FitzWalter to be promoted as abbess there.[43]

154. The injunctions of Archbishop John Peckham for the abbey of Barking, 1279 [From C. T. Martin, ed., *Registrum Epistolarum Johannis Peckham, Archiepiscopi Cantuariensis*, Rolls Series, 3 vols, 1882-86, I, pp. 81-6; in Latin]

Friar John, by divine permission humble minister of the church of Canterbury, primate of all England, greets with the grace and benediction of the Lord Jesus Christ the beloved daughters in Christ

---

43 'Elleschirch' was probably the nunnery of Elstow in Bedfordshire; Robert FitzWalter was the leader of the baronial party in 1215. Sibyl the prioress was elected but only held office for about two months. On 31 August Mabel de Boseham received the house's temporalities as abbess.

... the abbess and convent of Barking.[44] You are converted to serve laudably, as we believe, in the castles of the Lord, as we rejoice to have found by diligent investigation in the recent visitation. However, in the many dangers of the fragile present the virgin's delight is easily harmed by fact or rumour, unless, encircled with the arms of discipline and the arguments of chastity, it sweeps away the opportunities for disparagement by the perverse people with whom it is surrounded. Wherefore the venerable brother in Christ Lord John [Chishull], by grace of God bishop of London, handed over to you articles to be inviolably observed as a guide for your reputation, and we are adding certain points which, if obeyed, will keep you commended to God and men. First therefore we ordain that the divine office be celebrated by you devoutly and wholly, as laudable custom used to see to in the past; we forbid you to admit the mutilation of the office which certain monks, hopefully not with the spirit of demons, are said to have rashly suggested to you. For the praise of the Most High constitutes angelic life rather than earthly. Therefore the abbreviation of Lauds is seen to be contrary to custom and opposed to the celestial citizens. In celebrating Lauds, the hour of midnight is to be observed as most acceptable to God and the angels for the office of Matins.[45] Compline should be said at the proper time every day, so that with the chatterers excluded an opportunity should be prepared for prayer and quiet. At these and at the rest of the hours[46] all should assemble, unless prevented by illness or an occupation of salutary obedience. Moreover the place appointed for the celebration of the mass of the glorious Virgin should be so provided that the company of the nuns singing there are separated by a space from others who are present. We do not approve of the celebration of the Feast of Innocents being done by children, but regard this with displeasure; it should by no means be begun by the children nor should they intermingle with the nuns in any way until after vespers of the blessed John the Evangelist is finished.[47] Consequently however the nuns may not be absent from the same office, but all men and women and adolescents should be excluded from the choir at that time, and the nuns make good the

44 The name of the abbess is missing.

45 Matins and Lauds constituted the night office; Compline was the last office for the day. The daily round of services is discussed in D. Knowles, *The Monastic Order in England*, Cambridge, 1950, pp. 448-53.

46 This term is used to denote the offices or services in the church each day.

47 The feast of the Innocents on 28 December commemorated the massacre of the Innocents by King Herod. The feast of St John the Evangelist was on 27 December.

defects of the children, so that divine praise be not turned into a
mockery, which is wrong. They may receive the holy sacrament of the
eucharist on all the principal feasts and on each day of their
professions, unless they are absent for an unavoidable reason, or with
the permission of the abbess. Because we have learned that after the
office of the dead the priests in the notable company of clerks cross
from the church through the cloister to the parlour where they stay,
attending to drinking up the chalices and many other matters, we
condemn this custom for ever as corrupt, wishing in such a case that
those who need the refreshment of drink should receive it in the house
of the principal priest by dispensation of the cellaress. When the
requisite lights are prepared for the feast of the Purification [of the
Virgin Mary], we forbid the sacrist to invite any outsiders to the feast,
but only those labouring with her in the workshop of the lights, and
she should refund what she saves in superfluous costs in candles well
enough produced for the office of matins; and she should not provide
sour wine for the ministry of the altar. Moreover we have learned that
the priests keep the Host in their bed-chambers,[48] because they cannot
come into the nuns' enclosure to get it in cases of sudden illness among
parishioners. Because it is audacious, irreverent and mad to put the
King of glory in a common and contemptible place, we order by virtue
of obedience that henceforth the same most divine body be kept with
due precaution in a sacred place or oratory, accessible always to the
priests. We have also decreed that silence be regularly observed at
appointed places and times, since, as St James says, religion is vain
which does not stop the tongue from uttering undue things.[49] By grace
of this we ordain that no lay person, man or woman, no religious man
even, should come to the parlour after sunset, or remain to talk, unless
by chance for clear necessity, with the whole company [of nuns], and
with the permission of the abbess. At that time, moreover, all other
approaches to the cloister are to be shut, so that no entry or exit be
then open. Two trustworthy and blameless nuns are to be assigned to
check this carefully, and are bound by obedience to do this every day,
in remission of all their sins. Furthermore, the abbess should not dare
to remain in her chamber about that time, except for an essential
reason, and she should do this very seldom for honouring her guests,
or for business which cannot be dealt with at another time. She should
hasten to return thence, joined always by the more mature or more

48 Peckham in referring to the Host used the term 'the body of Our Lord Jesus Christ'.
49 Epistle of St James, chapter 1, verse 26.

prudent of the convent, on whose counsels she should rely. As often as she can, especially on solemn days, she should eat in the convent. Because the aforesaid bishop forbade the nuns to presume to spend time, eat, drink or sleep in chambers, by enjoining this on pain of anathema, we make an additional decree that no man, lay or religious, should enter the same chambers, and we decree this on pain of excommunication which we now pronounce. We make an exception if, by chance, and would that it does not happen, the infirmary was so greatly burdened with other sick nuns, or if anyone's illness was so wretched that it was necessary to put her in a chamber. In this case we allow only the confessor and doctor, and also father or brother, to have access to her, so that all suspicion is excluded and all other evasion denied, and he who has entered is to leave quickly. However, in the offices which cannot be done by women, the entry of workmen is to be allowed with the same precautions. In all other cases outsiders are to be excluded from the cloister and the inner offices as far as strict necessity permits. Moreover the confessions of the healthy nuns are to be heard in a place public and open to all. However, except in the case of confession, let a nun, the bride of Christ and the companion of angels, be ashamed to admit or even prolong solitary talk with any man, but rather no one called to have talk with any stranger should approach the caller alone, but have with her one companion at least who can give testimony of the innocence of all she has heard and seen. Moreover no servant of the house who is removed for scandal or infamy is ever to be reinstated to that or another office in the monastery. We forbid on pain of excommunication which we pronounce against all people that no one of this kind should enter the enclosures of the house without our or the bishop's permission, except in case of calamity. If at the instigation of the devil it should happen that any son of perdition should himself or through a procuress as intermediary suggest anything forbidden to any of you, she should quickly disclose this by obedience to the abbess, notwithstanding a promise to conceal this by a given pledge that was circumvented or by an oath. For we decree that such obligations are invalid, because a pledge owes nothing to perfidy nor an oath to the injury of the Creator. What we believe of religious persons, especially those women who make a vow without permission of their superior or God, is that they bind themselves much more to the perplexities of the devil. In sending out nuns to visit mortals, we order these four rules to be observed. First, that they should be sent out only for an essential and inevitable reason, such as especially the imminent death of parents, beyond which reason we know of scarcely any other sufficient to consider. Second, they should always be sent to a place not far distant and remote from all suspicion, taking care that they do not lodge with monks or canons or in other religious houses, because the malice of lay people frequently disgraces the reputation of such more easily. Third, that no one should leave except with a trustworthy and blameless company of nuns and servants. Fourth, that speed of return be insisted on with a short period of time being set, and she who is found to have sinned by delaying should by no means be sent out for a long time afterwards. We entreat you, dearest daughters, to be mindful that the foundation of the monastic profession is the denial of one's own will and the humility of obedience, which is the foundation of all virtues. On the other hand, we have truly learned that some of you, would that it were not very many, are tardy in obedience and do not easily accept laborious occupations which are imposed on you by way of obedience. To eradicate this danger, you, abbess, should take pains to obey the decrees of us and of your bishop just as you wish to be obeyed by those subject to you. If you find that any nun dislikes difficult obediences, you should take away the consolable obediences, especially leaving the house, until she consents to obey you. And if she is found disobedient for a third time, it is to be announced to the bishop at once. However, may the peace of God which passes all understanding keep your hearts, so that if any nun taunts another she may humbly ask pardon, and if the matter is notorious she should kiss her foot in chapter.[50] Farewell in Christ and the glorious Virgin. Recite these our ordinances four times a year along with the letters of the bishop or on the day after. Given at Orsett, 19 November 1279, in the first year of our consecration.

155. Extracts from the Office of the Cellaress of the Monastery of Barking, fifteenth century[51] [From British Library, London, Cotton MS. Julius D viii, fos 40r–47v; in English]

This is the charge belonging to the cellaress of the monastery of Barking, as follows.

---

50 This is a reference to the daily meeting in the chapter-house.

51 This document should be compared with lay household management, above, nos. 127, 129-33. It opens with the Office's receipts which are given in full. The provision of supplies is arranged according to the type of foodstuff and according to the needs of the Church's year, and details are also given of anniversaries and pittances; examples of all these topics are included.

The arrears. When she comes into office, she must look first at what is owed to the office by divers servants and rent-gatherers, and see that it is paid as soon as possible.

Great Warley. And then she must receive yearly from the collector of Great Warley 50s at Michaelmas, and 50s at Easter.

Bulphan. And also from the collector of Bulphan yearly 50s at Michaelmas and 50s at Easter.

Mucking. And also from the collector of Mucking yearly £4 at the aforesaid terms. And also 60s from the farms there at the said two terms.

Hockley. And also from the collector of Hockley at the feasts of Michaelmas and Easter £10 in equal portions.

Tollesbury. And also from the collector of Tollesbury at the said two feasts in equal portions …[52]

Wigborough. Also from the collector of Wigborough at the said two feasts in equal portions, £10.

Ingatestone. And also from the collector of Ingatestone at the aforesaid two feasts in equal portions, 48s.

Slapton. And also from the collector of Slapton at the said two feasts in equal portions, £8.

Lidlington. And also from the farmer of Lidlington at the said two feasts in equal portions, £16.

Uphall. And also from the farmer of Uphall, £6 13s 4d a year.

Downshall. And also from the farmer of Downshall, 56s 8d a year.

Wangeyhall. And from the farmer of Wangeyhall, 66s 8d a year.[53]

Barking. And also from the collector of the rents and services of Barking and Dagenham belonging to the aforesaid office, £12 18s a year.

London. And also from the canons of St Paul's in London for a yearly rent, 22s a year. From the prior and convent of St Bartholomew's in London, 17s a year. From John Goldyngton for a yearly rent from divers tenements at St Mary 'Schorehogge' in London, 22d a year. And she should receive yearly 33s 4d from a tenement in Friday Street in London, but it is not known where it stands, and she should receive yearly 30s of the rent of the Tyburn, but it is not paid.

The issues of the larder. And also she must be charged with all the ox hides that she sells, and all the entrails of the oxen, and all the tallow coming from the oxen that she sells, and also for any mess of beef that she sells, and all these are called the issues of the larder.

52 The manuscript is defective at this point.

53 This sum was crossed out and £4 10s substituted in another hand.

The foreign receipt. And also if she sells any hay belonging to her office she must charge herself with it, and it is called a foreign receipt. Sum total of all the aforesaid charge ...[54]

Grain. With part of the aforesaid sum she must purvey yearly 3 quarters of malt for the tuns of St Ethelburga and Christmas, for each occasion 12 bushels.[55] Then she must pay to the brewer of each tun, 20d. Then she must purvey 1 quarter and 7 bushels of wheat for the pittance of William Dune, Lady Matilda Loveland, Lady Alice Merton, and Lady Matilda the king's daughter.[56] And for rissoles in Lent and to bake with eels on Shrive Thursday.[57] And then she must pay the baker for baking each pittance, 6d. And also she must purvey 2 bushels of green peas for the convent in Lent every year. And then she must purvey 1 bushel of green beans for the convent against the summer.

Stock. She must purvey 22 good oxen a year for the convent.

Provisions for Advent and Lent. Also she must purvey 2 cades of red herring for the convent in Advent. And 7 cades of red herring for the convent in Lent. And also 3 barrels of white herring for the convent in Lent. And also she must purvey 112 lb. almonds for the convent in Lent, and 18 salt fish for the convent in Lent.[58] And 14 or 15 salt salmon for the convent in Lent. And 3 pecks and 24 lb. figs. And 1 peck raisins for the convent in Lent, and also 28 lb. rice for the convent in Lent, and 8 gallons of mustard for the convent.

Rissole silver. And also she must pay to every lady of the convent and also to the prioress, two cellaresses and the kitchener for their double allowance for the rissole silver, payable sixteen times a year to each lady and double ¹/₂d each time, but it is now only paid twice, namely at Easter and Michaelmas. Also she must pay to each lady of the convent and to the aforesaid four doubles 2d for their 'cripsis' and 'crumkakes' always paid at Shrovetide.

Anniversaries. And also she must pay for five anniversaries, namely Sir William vicar, Dame Alice Merton, Dame Matilda the king's daughter,

---

54 The manuscript is defective at this point.

55 St Ethelburga was the first abbess of Barking, c. 666-95.

56 Lady Matilda the king's daughter was the daughter of King John, and was abbess between 1247 and 1252. Matilda Loveland was abbess between 1258 and 1275, and Alice Merton between 1276 and 1291.

57 Shrive Thursday was Maundy Thursday.

58 The almonds were pounded and mixed with water as a substitute for milk in Lent, as dairy products were forbidden.

Dame Matilda Loveland, and William Dune, and also purvey twelve gallons of good ale for William's pittance on the day of his anniversary.

Offerings, wages and gifts of the cellaress. And also she must pay as an offering to two cellaresses 12d a year, and then she shall pay the steward of the household 20d each time he brings home the money from the courts. And then she shall give to the steward of the household at Christmas 20d. To my lady's gentlewoman, 20d;[59] and to each gentleman, 16d; and to each woman as it pleases her to do. Similarly to the grooms. And then she must buy a sugar loaf for my lady at Christmas. And also she must pay her clerk 13s 4d for his wages; to her yeoman cook, 26s 8d; and she shall pay for a gown for her groom cook; and 2s a year to her pudding-wife.

Hiring of pasture. Then she must be sure of pasture for her oxen, as her servants may inform her.

Mowing and making of hay. And also to see that her hay be mown and made as required.

Costs of repairs. Then she must see that all kinds of buildings within her office are kept in repair, both at her farms and manors, and in the monastery.

Livery of herring. To each lady of the convent for every day of the week in Lent four herrings red and white, that is for each lady twenty-eight herrings a week, and to the priory for five days in the week four herrings each day, the five days being Monday, Tuesday, Wednesday, Thursday and Saturday, and on Sunday they receive fish, and on the Friday figs and raisins.[60]

Livery of salt fish. To each lady of the convent every other week one mess of salt fish, and to the prioress, two cellaresses and kitchener for the double allowances every other week in Lent one mess of salt fish for each double. And to the priory every other week in Lent two messes of salt fish. Each salt fish contains seven messes.

Livery of salt salmon. To each lady of the convent in Lent every other week one mess of salt salmon, and similarly to each of the four doubles one mess of salmon, and similarly every other week to the priory two messes of salt salmon. Each salmon gives nine messes.

---

59 'My lady' denoted the abbess.

60 The reference to the priory probably denotes the priests serving the abbey.

156. The daily life of Cecily duchess of York, *c.* 1485-95[61] [From *A Collection of Ordinances and Regulations for the Government of the Royal Household*, London, Society of Antiquaries, 1790, pp. 37-9; in English]

Orders and rules of the princess Cecily.

A concise account of the order, rules and organisation of the household of the most excellent princess Cecily, late mother of the most noble prince, King Edward IV.

It seems to me necessary to understand her own routine concerning God and the world.

She is accustomed to rise at seven o'clock and her chaplain is ready to say with her matins of the day and matins of Our Lady. When she is fully ready, she hears a Low Mass in her chamber and after Mass she takes some breakfast. She goes to the chapel to hear the divine service and two Low Masses, and from there to dinner. During dinner, she hears a reading on a holy subject, either Hilton on the contemplative and active life, Bonaventure on the infancy of the Saviour, the Golden Legend, St Matilda, St Katherine of Siena, or the Revelations of St Bridget.[62] After dinner she gives audience for an hour to all who have any business with her. She then sleeps for a quarter of an hour. After sleeping she continues in prayer until the first bell rings for Evensong. Then she enjoys a drink of wine or ale. Without delay her chaplain is ready to say both evensongs with her, and, after the last bell has rung, she goes to the chapel and hears Evensong sung. From there she goes to supper where she repeats the reading which was heard at dinner to those who are in her presence. After supper she spends time with her gentlewomen in the enjoyment of honest mirth. One hour before going to bed she takes a cup of wine, and then goes to her private closet where she takes her leave of God for the night, bringing to an end her

61 The duchess's daily routine forms the first part of these household ordinances and this is followed by the rules for the household, showing that even when the lady was living a devout life the household still needed to be organised on a considerable scale. The first part of the document is discussed and set in context by C. A. J. Armstrong, 'The piety of Cicely, duchess of York: a study in late medieval culture', in *England, France and Burgundy in the Fifteenth Century*, London, 1983, pp. 135-56.

62 The Life of Christ attributed to Bonaventure was not actually by him. In her will Cecily bequeathd The Golden Legend, the Life of St Katherine of Siena and a book of St Matilda of Hackeborn to her granddaughter Bridget, who became a Dominican nun at Dartford priory. Her granddaughter Anne, who was prioress of Syon abbey, was bequeathd a book containing works by Bonaventure and Hilton, and a book of the Revelations of St Bridget; J. G. Nichols and J. Bruce, *Wills from Doctors' Commons*, Camden Society, old series, LXXXIII, 1863, pp. 2-3. The books of St Matilda, St Katherine and St Bridget were all mystical works. Syon was a double monastery following the Augustinian Rule as reformed by St Bridget.

prayers of the day. By eight o'clock she is in bed. I trust to Our Lord's mercy that this noble princess divides up the hours to his great pleasure.

The rules of the house.

On eating days at dinner there is a first dinner by eleven o'clock during the time of High Mass for carvers, cupbearers, sewers and officers.[63]

On fasting days by twelve o'clock, a later dinner for carvers and waiters.

On eating days, supper for carvers and officers at four o'clock, and for my lady and the household at five o'clock.

When my lady is served with the second course at dinner and supper, the chamber and the hall are rewarded with bread and ale according to the discretion of the usher. There are no rewards from the kitchen, except to ladies and gentlewomen, the head officers if they are present, the dean of the chapel, the almoner, the gentlemen ushers, the carvers, cupbearers and sewers, the cofferer, the clerk of the kitchen and the marshal.

No one dines in their offices, except only the cooks, the scullery, the saucery, the porters, and the bakers if they are occupied with baking.

On Sunday, Tuesday and Thursday, the household at dinner is served with boiled beef and mutton and one roast; at supper 'leyched' beef and roast mutton.[64]

On Monday and Wednesday at dinner, one boiled beef and mutton; supper, as above.

On fasting days, salt fish, one fresh fish and butter; at supper, salt fish and eggs.

Wine daily for the head officers when they are present, the ladies and gentlewomen, the dean of the chapel, the almoner, the gentlemen ushers, the cofferer, the clerk of the kitchen and the marshal.

On Friday payment is made for all kinds of fresh food. At the end of every month payment is made for all kinds of other things. The wages for the chapel are paid at the end of each quarter.

Every half year the wages are paid to the household, and livery cloth once a year. Payment of fees outside the household is made once a year.

Proclamation is made four times a year in the market towns round Berkhamsted to find out whether the purveyors, caterers and others make true payment of my lady's money or not, and whether my lady's servants pay their own debts or not; if any fault is found, a remedy is to be provided immediately in recompense.

---

63 The rules distinguish between eating days when meat was served, and fasting days when fish was eaten. The sewer, like the carver and cupbeareer, served at table.

64 A leche could be either sweet or savoury, and was sliced, like brawn or gingerbread.

There are no breakfasts, except only for the head officers when they are present, the ladies and gentlewomen, the dean and the chapel, the almoner, the gentlemen ushers, the cofferer, the clerk of the kitchen and the marshal.

All other officers who have to meet to write up their records have their breakfast together in the Counting-house, after the writing has been done. The remains of every office are to be taken at the end of each month, to see whether the officers are in arrears or not.

Livery of bread, ale, fire and candle is assigned to the head officers if they are present, the married ladies and gentlewomen, the dean and chapel, the almoner, chaplains, gentlemen ushers, cofferers, clerk of the kitchen, the marshal, and all the gentlemen within the house if they do not sleep in the town, namely, full livery of all the above things from the feast of All Saints [1 November] to the feast of the Purification of Our Lady [2 February]; and after the Purification half livery of fire and candles until Good Friday, when the time for fire and candle ceases. To all sick men is given a privilege of having all such things as may ease them. If he is a gentleman and prefers his own diet, he has 16d for his weekly board and 9d for his servant, and nothing out of the house. If any man becomes unfit to work, he still has during my lady's life the same wages that he had when he might do best service, and 16d for his weekly board and 9d for his servant. If he is a yeoman, 12d; a groom or a page, 10d.

157. The projected pilgrimage of Sir Andrew Luttrell and his wife Elizabeth to Santiago de Compostella, 1361 [From Public Record Office, London, C54/199, m. 22; in Latin]

The king greets the mayor and bailiffs of Dartmouth or Plymouth. Because our beloved and faithful Andrew Luttrell and Elizabeth his wife and some others in their company are about to set out to [the shrine of] St James with our permission, we order you without delay to have delivered to Andrew one ship out of the ships not arrested for the passage of our beloved and faithful Richard de Stafford, seneschal of Gascony, in either of the ports of Dartmouth or Plymouth where Andrew shall choose to embark. The ship should be suitable for the passage of Andrew and Elizabeth, and twenty-four persons, men and women, and twenty-four horses in their company. Only the ships ordained for the seneschal's passage are excepted, notwithstanding certain mandates or commissions to the contrary. Witnessed by the king at Easthampstead, on 25 July.

158. Elizabeth de Burgh's private expenditure on religious purposes, 1351-52[65] [From Public Record Office, London, E101/93/12; in French]

Item, delivered to Sir Piers de Ereswelle on 5 February to give to divers religious men in Cambridge to sing masses for Sir Thomas de Cheddeworth, 25s.[66]

Item, given to the friars of Clare, Sudbury and Babwell for the same reason, 20s.

Item, given to the friars of Chelmsford for the same reason, 10s.

Item, for the offering of my lady and her household on 13 February for the soul of Sir Thomas de Cheddeworth, 3s 1d.

Item, for the offering on the same day in Finchingfield church for Sir Thomas, 2s.

Item, for the offering on the same day in Bardfield church for Sir Thomas, 2s.

Item, paid to Geoffrey le Chapemaker of Clare on 5 March for making two clasps and four ornaments of silver for a book for my lady, 20d.

Item, paid to a Franciscan friar of Cambridge on 12 March for illuminating a book of my lady's, 15s 4d.

Given to a Carmelite friar who preached at Bardfield in the lady's chapel on 25 March, 6s 8d.

Item, for the offering of my lady and the damsels on the day of the Annunciation of Our Lady [25 March], 10d.

Item, given to an Augustinian friar who preached at Bardfield church on Palm Sunday, 6s 8d.

Item, for the offering of my lady and her household on the same day for the soul of Lady Margaret countess of Gloucester, 2s 4d.[67]

Item, given to 50 poor people on Maundy Thursday, 9d to each of them, 37s 6d.

Item, delivered to Sir Piers on the same day to give to the poor, 24s 6d.

Item, for the offering of my lady and Lady Athol on Good Friday at the Cross, 6d.[68]

65 These payments are taken from Elizabeth de Burgh's chamber account in which her private expenditure was recorded, and should be compared with the earlier excerpts, above, no. 135. The entries selected illustrate commemoration of her family and officials, offerings at services in the household chapel, use of parish churches, relief of the poor, and ownership of books.

66 Sir Thomas de Cheddeworth was a close adviser of Elizabeth from the early 1320s; see above, no. 102. Sir Piers de Ereswelle was Elizabeth's almoner.

67 Margaret was Elizabeth's sister.

68 Elizabeth countess of Athol was the lady's granddaughter.

Item, for the offering of my lady and her household on Easter Day, 7s 5d.

Item, given on 21 April to seven men of Tregrug going to the Holy Land, 6s 8d.[69]

Item, given to a child baptised in the presence of the lady in Clare church on 28 May, 3s 4d.

Item, for the offering of my lady and her household in Clare church on the feast of the Assumption of Our Lady [15 August], 4s 11d.

Item, given to two children who were baptised in the lady's presence on the same day, 5s.

Item, given to a Dominican friar who preached before my lady on the same day, 10s.

159. Mary de Bohun countess of Derby's almsgiving on Maundy Thursday, 1388 [From Public Record Office, London, DL28/1/2, fos 20v, 26r; in Latin]

Delivered for 18 gowns and hoods given in the lady's almsgiving on Maundy Thursday to 18 poor women, 35¼ yards of russet shortcloth.[70]

Money distributed on Maundy Thursday to 18 poor women, 9s.

160. The celebration of the feast of Corpus Christi by Elizabeth de Burgh at her house in the outer precinct of the convent of the Minoresses outside Aldgate, London, 1358[71] [From Public Record Office, London, E101/93/20, m. 19d; in Latin]

Thursday 31 May. Feast of Corpus Christi.

Pantry: 6 quarters of wheat supplied which gave 1,150 loaves and 3 pecks of flour. 510 loaves from stock used. Fruit purchased, 4d.

Buttery: 24 sesters of wine from stock. 150 gallons of ale bought in London, 25s.

Kitchen: ½ a quarter of beef, 2 bacons, 1½ quarters of dishes of boar, and 6 deer from stock. 1½ carcasses of beef, 29s; 6½ pigs, 30s 6d; 2½ carcasses of mutton, 6s 3d; 12 calves, 27s 8½d; 3 heads and 2 dishes of boar, 9s 4d.

69 Tregrug was one of Elizabeth's manors in Wales.

70 Mary was probably eighteen years old.

71 The scale of the celebration can be seen by comparing it with other expenditure for that week; the sum total of purchases for the week came to £28 11s ½d, and total expenditure on the day before and the day after came to £5 16s 11½d, and £2 19s 6d respectively.

Poultry: 3 swans, 7 herons, 5 squirrels, 24 rabbits, and 3 geese from stock. 12 piglets, 13s; 2 swans, 10s; 60 capons, 30s; 4 hens, 10d; 47 geese, 13s 5¹/₂d; 16 lambs, 14s 8d; 10 egrets, 25s;[72] 130 chickens, 16s 3d; 8 rabbits, 16d; 1,300 eggs, 9s 9d; 17 gallons of milk, 17d; 4 gallons of cream, 16d; 3 cheeses, 12d; onions, 7d.

Hall and chamber: rushes purchased, 9s 3d.

Stables: hay for 26 horses, and 10 hackneys from stock. For their provender, 7 bushels and 1 peck of oats, and 124 loaves from stock; wages of 6 grooms and 1 page, 10d.

Sum total for the pantry: 4d

Sum total for the buttery: 25s

Sum total for the kitchen: 102s 9¹/₂d

Sum total for the poultry: £6 18s 7¹/₂d

Sum total for the hall and chamber: 9s 3d

Sum total for the stables: 10d

Sum total of purchases: £13 16s 10d

Sum total from stock: £4 19s 6d

Sum total for the day: £18 16s 4d

No. of messes: 136

161. The will of Margaret de Thorp, 1347, which refers to her psalter [From Borthwick Institute of Historical Research, York, Archiepiscopal Register, 10, fo. 330r; in Latin]

In the name of God, amen. I Margaret de Thorp, wife of Sir William de Thorp knight, make my testament in this form. First I bequeath my soul to Almighty God, and my body to be buried in the church of Thorpe near Newark and the necessities for my burial. Item, I bequeath half a mark to the painted image of St Lawrence. Item, I bequeath one silver cup to make a chalice to serve the altar of the chapel of the Holy Trinity of Thorpe. Item, I bequeath my psalter to the aforesaid chapel to serve there for as long as it may last, passing from heir to heir without any alienation. If there is any remainder of my goods not bequeathed, I give and leave it to Sir William my husband. To fulfil and do all this I appoint as my executors Sir William my husband, whom I wish to be chief executor, and Sir Philip Spenser, and Sir Adam de Everingham of Rockley. Given at Thorpe on Saturday after the feast of St Martin [17 November] 1347.

---

72 An egret is a small white heron.

162. Extract from the will of Elizabeth countess of Northampton, 1356, giving details of ownership of a relic[73] [From Lambeth Palace Library, London, Register of Simon Islip, fo. 122; in Latin]

Item, the cross which I used to carry made of the wood of the Lord's true cross and in which there is a thorn of the Lord's crown.

163. Extract from the will of Mary Lady Roos, 1394, giving details of her burial, tomb, requiem masses and family bequests, including peronal religious possessions[74] [From Borthwick Institute of Historical Research, York, Archiepiscopal Register 14, fo. 47v–48r; in Latin]

In the name of God, amen. I Mary Lady Roos of Orby, being sound of mind, make my testament in this form. First I leave my soul to God and blessed Mary and all the saints, and my body to be buried in the monastery of the blessed Mary at Rievaulx in the choir near the body of Sir John Roos lord of Helmsley my husband. Item, I leave my best beast to offer on the day of my burial for my mortuary. Item, I bequeath 100s to make a marble stone for my tomb like the one that lies over Lady Margaret de Orby my grandmother in the church of St Botolph [Boston]. Item, I bequeath £5 for the cost of the coffin, wax and other expenses round my body on the day of my burial. Item, I bequeath 100s to be distributed to the poor on the same day. Item, I bequeath £24 for the support of certain priests celebrating masses in the monastery of Rievaulx or in other places at the choice of my executors for my soul, and the souls of my husband and father and mother for one year after the day of my burial. Item, I bequeath to my dearest brother the lord earl of Northumberland one gilt cup. Item, I bequeath to Lady Roos my mother two gilt spoons, and one ring with a diamond. Item, I bequeath to Sir Henry Percy my dearest kinsman one tablet of gold. Item, I bequeath to Lady Percy one pair of rosaries of gold. Item, I bequeath to Sir Ralph Percy my kinsman my best pair of rosaries of gold and one gold ornament. Item, to my sister of Clifford one gilt goblet.[75] Item, to Isabella Percy twenty marks, with

---

73 Elizabeth died in her husband's lifetime and her will stated that it was made with his permission. This bequest was one of several to the Dominican friars of London; Elizabeth specified that she was to be buried in the choir of their church.

74 Mary was the daughter-in-law of Beatrice Lady Roos (no. 167), and the half-sister of Henry Percy earl of Northumberland. Her mother was the daughter and heiress of Sir John de Orreby.

75 Elizabeth Lady Clifford was the sister of Mary's husband, John Lord Roos.

my mantle and gown of scarlet and fur-lined, and with the French book of the duke of Lancaster, and my green primer which once belonged to my lord and father, to pray for my soul.[76]

164. Extract from the will of Isabella Despenser, countess of Warwick, 1439, giving details of her tomb [From *The Fifty Earliest English Wills*, ed. F. J. Furnivall, Early English Text Society, original series, LXXVIII, 1882, pp. 116-17; in English]

In the name of God, amen. This is the testament and last will of Lady Isabella countess of Warwick, made in London on 1 December 1439. First I bequeath my soul to Almighty God, and my body to be buried in the abbey of Tewkesbury in the place that I have assigned. My great 'templys'[77] with the pale rubies are to be sold for the highest price, and the money delivered to the abbot and house of Tewkesbury so that they do not grumble about my burial or about anything that I will have done about my body. My image is to be made completely naked, with nothing on my head and the hair cast back, and is to be of the size and design that Thomas Porchalyn has made. At my head, there is to be Mary Magdalene laying my hands across [my breast]. On the right hand side of my head there is to be St John the Evangelist, and on the left St Anthony, and at my feet a scutcheon of my arms impaled with my lord's and supported by two griffins. All round my tomb poor men and women are to be depicted in their poor array with their beads in their hands[78]...

165. The will of Katherine Peverel, 1375[79] [From Lambeth Palace Library, London, Register of Simon Sudbury, fo. 90r–v; in Latin]

In the name of God, amen. On Sunday after the feast of St Luke the evangelist [21 October], 1375, I Katherine, widow of Sir Andrew

---

76 This book was written by Henry duke of Lancaster and entitled *Livre de Seyntz Medicines*.

77 These were jewels worn on the forehead.

78 The naked image reflects the contemporary view that wealth was transient and that the body would decay. This description can be compared with the tomb at Ewelme of Alice duchess of Suffolk where her naked body was depicted at the base of the tomb with her clothed figure on top. Devotion to particular saints was widespread in the late Middle Ages.

79 This will, and those of Anne Latimer and Beatrice Lady Roos, have been given in full, in order to show how religious bequests, and those to family and servants, could vary from will to will. This was partly the result of differing religious beliefs and attitudes, but was also an individual matter. Katherine Peverel's will shows the great importance attached by many to their own locality.

Peverel knight, make my testament in this form. First I bequeath my soul to God and blessed Mary and all his saints, and my body to be buried in the monastery of Lewes according to the disposition of the prior there. Item, I bequeath twenty marks to the prior and monks there to pray for my soul. Item, I bequeath to the shrine of St Richard of Chichester, 40s. Item, I bequeath to the friars of Shoreham, 20s. Item, I bequeath to the friars of Lewes 20s. Item, I bequeath to the friars of Arundel, 20s. Item, I bequeath to the Dominican friars of Chichester, 20s. Item, to the Franciscan friars of Chichester, 20s. Item, I bequeath to the prior and convent of Hardham, 66s 8d. Item, to the prior and convent of Pynham, 20s. Item, I bequeath to the prioress and nuns of Rusper, 66s 8d. Item, I bequeath to the prioress and nuns of Easebourne, 20s. Item, I bequeath to the abbot and convent of Dureford, 100s. Item, I bequeath to the hospital of St James of Chichester, ¹/₂ mark. Item, I bequeath to the hospital of St Katherine of Shoreham, ¹/₂ mark. Item, I bequeath to the hospital of St Mary Magdalene of Bidlington, 20s. Item, I bequeath to the hospital of [St Nicholas in] Westout in Lewes, ¹/₂ mark. Item, I bequeath to the hospital of St James [of Sutton] by Seaford, ¹/₂ mark. Item, I bequeath to Sir Robert vicar of Cowfold, 100s. Item, I bequeath to the same Robert my best horse called piebald. Item, I bequeath to Nicholas Wilcombe, 40s. Item, I bequeath to John Bysshopeston, 100s. Item, I bequeath to Andrew Peverel, a kinsman of my lord, 40s. Item, I bequeath to Sir Robert Rett of Slindon, 40s. Item, I bequeath to Katherine Depham my maid for her marriage, 100 marks, and also half of the cloth and bed-hangings of my chamber. Item, I bequeath to William Boteller, 40s. Item, I bequeath to Walter atte Brok 40s. Item, to William the baker, one mark. Item, I bequeath to Roger Helewes 20s. Item, I bequeath to John Deubonee 20s. Item, to John the logger, 20s. Item, I bequeath to John Bayoun 13s 4d. Item, to the lord earl of Arundel my brother, [blank]. Item, to Sir Richard, son of the aforesaid earl, my second best horse. Item, I bequeath to the church of Shermanbury 20s. Item, I bequeath to Sir John Denarkes, formerly my chaplain, 13s 4d. Item, I bequeath to Sir Richard Cosyn, formerly my chaplain, ¹/₂ mark. Item, to Sarah my maid, 13s 4d. Item, I bequeath to Sibyl my servant, 20s. Item, I bequeath to Richard my chamberlain, 20s. Item, I bequeath to the laundress, ¹/₂ mark. Item, I bequeath to Robert Seman, 100 sheep. Item, I bequeath to Katherine Depham my maid one of my horses called sorrel, or the lady's palfrey. Item, I bequeath 100s to be divided among my faithful servants in my household according to the disposition of my executors. To ordain, dispose and carry out this will faithfully in the aforesaid form I make and appoint as my executors Sir Richard Arundel my nephew, the prior of Lewes Nicholas Wylcombe, Sir Robert vicar of Cowfold, John Bysshopeston, Robert Seman. I bequeath to each of them 100s if they undertake the task of executing the will, and otherwise not. The remainder of all my goods I wish to be distributed by the disposition of my executors in the celebration of masses and in almsgiving for the souls of Sir Andrew Peverel and Sir Henry Husee, formerly my husbands, and for my soul, our debts being paid first. In witness of this, I have affixed my seal to this will. Given at Ewhurst on the day and year aforesaid.

166. The will of Anne Latimer, 1402[80] [From Public Record Office, London, Prob. 11/3 Marche, fo. 18v; in English]

In the name of God, amen. On 13 July 1402, I Anne Latimer, thanking God in his mercy for having such mind as he vouchsafes, and desiring that God's will be fulfilled in me and in the use of all the goods that I have been given to keep, make my testament with that in mind in this form. First I place my soul in the hands of God, praying to him humbly that by his grace he will take as poor a present as my wretched soul to his mercy. I will that my body be buried at Braybrooke beside my lord and husband Thomas Latimer, if God wills. I bequeath to the repair of the chancel and the parsonage of the church at Braybrooke 40s. 40s also to make the bridge which my lord began. I also bequeath £20 to be doled out to needy poor men known by the discretion of the overseers and executors of my will. To Roger my brother, 40s. To Alison Bretoun, five marks. To Kalyn Okham, 20s. To Anneys, 20s. To Magote Deye, 20s. To Thomas Fetplace, 26s 8d. To William, my brother's man, 3s 4d. To William Leycestrechyre, 10s. I also bequeath 40s to be divided among the rest of my servants by the discretion of the executors and overseers of this testament. The rest of my goods I wish to be sold and doled out to needy poor men according to the law of God, by the advice and discretion of the overseers and executors of this will. To execute, ordain and accomplish this will truly, I principally desire and pray Master Philip, abbot of Leicester, and Sir Lewis Clifford, and Robert parson of Braybrooke to be overseers, so that all these things may be fulfilled according to the law of God. For my executors of this will I ask Sir Robert Lethelade parson of

---

80 This will, with no provision for masses, and a stress on works of charity, has been associated with the Lollards, but was typical of a wider group of people c. 1400.

'Kynmerton', Thomas Wakeleyn, Sir Henry Slayer parson of Warden, and John Pulton. May these things be done in the name and worship of God, amen. In witness of this will I affix my seal. Witnessed by: Sir Robert priest of Braybrooke, Thomas Fetplace and Alison Bretoun. Written on the year and day aforesaid.

167. Will of Beatrice Lady Roos, 1414[81] [From Borthwick Institute of Historical Research, York, archiepiscopal register 18, fos. 357v–358v; in Latin]

In the name of God, amen. On 26 June 1414, I Beatrice Lady Roos, being sound of mind and whole of memory, make my testament in this form. First I leave my soul to Almighty God and the blessed Virgin Mary and all the saints, and my body to be buried in the choir of the priory church of Warter. Item, I bequeath my best beast for my mortuary. Item, I bequeath forty marks sterling to be distributed to the poor on the day my funeral ceremonies are celebrated. Item, I wish for twenty-four torches of pure wax and five tapers to be lit and burnt at the time of the said ceremonies, and for each taper to weigh ten pounds of wax. Item, I bequeath 100 marks for as many masses as can profitably be celebrated after my death for my soul and the souls of my husbands, ancestors and parents, and all the faithful departed, at York and in divers monasteries, abbeys, priories, convents of mendicant friars, hospitals, parish churches and chapels in Yorkshire. Item, I bequeath £50 sterling to two chaplains celebrating mass daily for my soul and the soul of Thomas de Roos my husband and the souls of all the faithful departed in the parish church of Helmsley for five years after my death. Item, I bequeath £20 to one chaplain to celebrate mass daily in the aforesaid form in the chapel of Storthwaite for four years after my death. Item, I bequeath £6 for celebrating four masses of the Trinity and the Annunciation of the Blessed Virgin Mary and four requiem masses for my soul and the souls of all the faithful departed with all possible haste after my death. Item, I bequeath £10 for thirty trentals of St Gregory to be celebrated within a year of my death.[82] Item, I bequeath to the prior of Warter 40s, to the subprior 20s, to each canon there who is a priest 6s 8d, and to each canon who is not a priest 3s 4d. Item, I bequeath to Beatrice Chetwyn, canoness of Aconbury,

---

81 Beatrice was the daughter of Ralph earl of Stafford and Margaret Audley; Thomas Lord Roos was her second husband and died in 1384. Her eldest son John, husband of Mary Percy, died in 1393, and her son William died later in 1414.

82 A trental was a set of thirty requiem masses.

53s 4d. Item, I bequeath fifteen marks to the convents of Franciscan, Dominican and Carmelite friars within the city of York, namely five marks to each convent. Item, I bequeath 100*s* to the convent of Augustinian friars of York. Item, I bequeath 6*s* 8*d* to each lazar-house in the suburbs of York. Item, I bequeath 40*s* to the anchoress of Leake. Item, I bequeath 40*s* to the anchoress of Nun Appleton. Item, I bequeath ten marks to be distributed among my tenants, especially the needy of Roos and 'Munkwyk'. Item, I bequeath £10 to my needy tenants in Melbourne, Seaton Ross, and Storthwaite. Item, I bequeath 6*s* 8*d* each to seven poor old men of my household and to two pages of the kitchen. Item, I bequeath ten marks to Master John Birkwod, Augustinian friar. Item, I bequeath £4 to Master John Murscugh of the Franciscan order. Item, I bequeath five marks to Robert Flete my chaplain. Item, I bequeath five marks to John Kyngeston my chaplain. Item, I bequeath five marks to Agnes Taillour living in my household. Item, I wish that each servant or inmate of my household who is not remunerated by me in my lifetime should be recompensed by my executors according to what will seem reasonable to them and according to length of service. Item, to William Lord Roos, my son, two basins of silver-gilt, one silver goblet with a cover called 'Fawconberge', one complete blue bed with its hangings embroidered with white roses and the arms of Roos and Stafford, and one of the best horses from my stable, except my mortuaries. Item, I bequeath to Margaret Lady Roos, William's wife, one pair of linen sheets called 'Rysyngshetes', and one silver-gilt goblet with a cover which I was given by William Lord Roos my son. Item, I bequeath to Elizabeth Lady Clifford, my daughter, one great vessel with seven vessels inside it, called the great bowl. Item, I bequeath to Matilda Clifford, Elizabeth's daughter, one silver-gilt vessel with a cover which John Lord Roos, my son, bequeathed to me in his will, and one smaller silver basin from my chamber with the silver ewers belonging to it. Item, I bequeath to William Mapilton my servant one silver vessel with a cover called the little bowl. Item, I bequeath to Thomas de Rolleston rector of Kirby Misperton one silver goblet with a cover marked on the knob with two 'b's. Item, to William de Rolleston vicar of Helmsley one silver goblet with a cover marked on the knob with the number 157. Item, I bequeath to John Cheston one silver goblet with a cover which the same John recently bought for me, decorated on the cover and the base of the goblet with birds and forked branches. Item, I bequeath to John de Chaumbre, formerly my servant, one silver goblet with a cover chased like a chalice. Item, I bequeath to Robert de

Hoton my servant one silver goblet with a cover decorated on the cover and the base of the goblet with branches and leaves of yew, and which I recently acquired from John Cheston's purchase. Item, I wish that all the palls and covers for my body be distributed and divided among the damsels of my chamber according to the disposition and discretion of my executors. Item, I wish that all common and poor-quality beds in my wardrobe be divided and distributed among especially needy poor people by the disposition of my executors as will seem to them best for the salvation of my soul. Item, I wish that all lands and tenements, rents and services, with all their appurtenances, which I recently acquired from John Arnald in the vill and territory of Seaton Ross in Spalding moor be sold by my executors and the feoffees for the same, at the highest price they can advantageously get, and the money received by my executors be distributed in works of charity in the best way that they know, saving the annuities granted to Richard Coke, Robert Messag', John Biron and Alice his wife, and Robert Ogle for the term of their lives. Item, I give and bequeath to the high altar of the priory of Warter one whole vestment of blue cloth of gold, namely three albs, with two tunicles, one chasuble, one cope, one altar-frontal, and one reredos, with appurtenances, two tall silver candle-sticks, one better chalice of silver-gilt, two cruets, and one pax-board of silver, one pair of censers, and one silver bell. Item, I bequeath to the parish church of Helmsley one whole vestment of chequered white and red velvet. Item, I bequeath to the parish church of Hemingbrough one whole vestment, price ten marks. The rest of all the essential vestments and books and other ornaments belonging to my chapel I wish to be distributed and divided for ecclesiastical use in divers needy places, according to the discretion and disposition of my executors as will seem best for the salvation of my soul. Item, I bequeath to each of my executors administering my goods in the lawful way 100s, to be received for their labour over and above due expenses. The remainder of all my goods not bequeathd or given above I give and bequeath to John de Aske esquire, Sir John Levesham rector of the church of Brompton, Richard Gascoygne, William Mapilton, John Cheston, Robert Hoton, Sir Thomas Rolleston rector of the church of Kirby Misperton, and William Rolleston vicar of Helmsley whom I ordain, make and appoint as my executors, so that they ordain and dispose of the aforesaid remainder as will seem best and most beneficial for the salvation of my soul. Item, I request and pray William Lord Roos my most dear and well beloved son, Thomas [Langley] bishop of Durham, and John Prophet dean of the cathedral church of York to be supervisors of this my written will for reverence to God and for the sake of charity. Witnessed by William Chetwyn, Bartholomew Bygod and Ralph Bygod esquires. In testimony of all this I have affixed my seal to this present will on the day and in the year of the lord aforesaid.

Glossary

Advowson   The right of patronage over parish churches and certain monasteries.

Affinity   The group of retainers who received fees and liveries from a lord.

Amercement   A financial penalty levied by a court; its equivalent at the present day is the term 'fine'.

Bailiwick   A grouping of estates, often on a geographical basis, for purposes of administration and exploitation.

Demesne manor   A manor in the lord's hands and exploited by him, as opposed to the manors held as knights' fees by his vassals The term 'demesne' is also used to describe the lord's land on the manor, as distinct from the land farmed by the peasants.

Distraint   The taking of goods in order to enforce a judicial decision.

Dower   The land held by a noblewoman after the death of her husband, originally assigned by the husband at the time of the marriage. From *c.* 1200 one-third of the husband's land came to be allocated to the widow.

Dowry   The money payment made by the bride's father at the time of the marriage.

Enfeoffment to use   Grant of lands to a group of people, known as feoffees, who held the lands to the use of a named beneficiary.

Entail   Grant of land laying down a specific line of inheritance.

Escheator   A royal official responsible for land which came into the king's hands; he held inquisitions *post mortem* and proofs of age, and allocated dower. His area of responsibility varied, but from the fourteenth century it was usual to appoint members of the county gentry to this office.

Farm, farmer   A manor which was farmed was leased out to a farmer or leaseholder.

Fine   Agreement with the king or lord, for which a sum of money was paid.

Honour   A lordship comprising the lord's demesne manors and the knights' fees held by his vassals, and centred on the chief castle of the lord of the honour. The most important vassals in the twelfth century are described as honorial barons. The lord of the honour held the honour court which vassals were obliged to attend, and had the right to levy feudal incidents from his vassals: relief when a vassal's heir succeeded to a holding, and wardship and marriage when a vassal had died leaving an heir who was a minor.

Jointure   Land held jointly by husband and wife, and held by the wife for life in the event of the death of her husband.

Liberty   An area where a lord had special judicial privileges. A specific privilege is described as a liberty or a franchise.

Linear measures   The yard measures 0.9144 m. and the foot 0.3048 m. The ell measures 1.143 m. The perch measured 5¹/₂ yards, but there could be local variations.

Liquid measures   The tun contained 252 gallons and the pipe 126 gallons. The sester often contained 4 gallons, but a sester of sweet wine contained 2 gallons and a sester of ale could contain 12–14 gallons.

Maritagium   Gift of land by the bride's father or close relation designed to provide the married couple with the means of livelihood for themselves and their children.

Mess   The amount of food served to a group of people, normally numbering two or four, who were served together at mealtimes. It can also be used to denote a dish of food.

Octave   A week (eight days) after a specified date.

Pannage   Payment for pasturing pigs in the lord's woods.

Primer   Book of Hours, containing a shortened version of the Divine Office, particularly the Office of Our Lady, the Office for the Dead, penitential psalms, the litany, and prayers. The owner often added to the prayers.

Quarter   Measure of grain, normally containing eight bushels, although there were local variations. The bushel contained four pecks.

Quindene   A fortnight (fifteen days) after a specified date.

Receiver   The central financial official on the honour.

Reeve   A villein who was responsible for the running of a demesne manor. Demesne manors are also found in the charge of a bedel or serjeant.

Sac and soc, toll and team, and infangenetheof   Judicial privileges included in late eleventh- and twelfth-century charters, denoting the lord's right to hold a court, deal with pleas concerning cattle, and do justice on a thief caught in possession of stolen property on the demesne.

Seisin   Possession of land.

Steward   Chief official on the honour, and from the thirteenth century mainly responsible for the holding of courts.

Tally   Receipt for payment. The term 'acquittance' was also used to denote a receipt.

Tenant-in-chief   A person who held directly from the Crown by knight service.

Vassal   A person who held land from a lord in return for performing homage and swearing fealty to the lord. The vassal's holding was termed a fief, and he owed the service of a specific number or specific fraction of knights to the lord; he was therefore said to hold, for instance, $1/2$ or 20 knights' fees. If summoned, he owed knight service in his lord's contingent in the feudal host, the royal army, and also castleguard at his lord's or a royal castle. The services could be discharged by a money payment. He owed feudal incidents to his lord.

View of frankpledge Many lords had the right to hold the view of frankpledge on their manors so as to check on the tithings, in which men were grouped for policing purposes, and to deal with minor law and order offences. A lord who had this franchise is said to have exercised leet jurisdiction.

Warranty Guarantee of tenure.

Bibliography of printed works

Acheson, E., *A Gentry Community: Leicestershire in the Fifteenth Century, c. 1422-c. 1485*, Cambridge, 1992.

Adams, N. and C. Donahue, Jun., eds, *Select Cases from the Ecclesiastical Courts of the Province of Canterbury, c. 1200-1301*, Selden Society, CXV, 1978-79.

Alexander, J. and P. Binski, eds, *Age of Chivalry: Art in Plantagenet England, 1200-1400*, London, 1987.

Altschul, M., *A Baronial Family in Medieval England: the Clares, 1217-1314*, Baltimore, 1965.

Amt, E., ed., *Women's Lives in Medieval Europe: A Sourcebook*, London, 1993.

Archer, R. E., 'Rich old ladies: the problem of late medieval dowagers', in A. Pollard, ed., *Property and Politics: Essays in Later Medieval English History*, Gloucester, 1984, pp. 15-35.

Archer, R. E., 'The estates and finances of Margaret of Brotherton, c. 1320-1399', *Historical Research*, LX, 1987, pp. 264-80.

Archer, R. E., '"How ladies ... who live on their manors ought to manage their households and estates": women as landholders and administrators in the later Middle Ages', in P. J. P. Goldberg, ed., *Woman is a Worthy Wight: Women in English Society c. 1200-1500*, Gloucester, 1992, chapter 6.

Archer, R. E. and B. E. Ferme, 'Testamentary procedure with special reference to the executrix', in *Medieval Women in Southern England*, Reading Medieval Studies, XV, 1989, pp. 3-34.

Armstrong, C. A. J., 'The piety of Cicely, duchess of York: a study in late medieval culture', in *England, France and Burgundy in the Fifteenth Century*, London, 1983, pp. 135-56.

Aston, M., '"Caim's castles": poverty, politics and disendowment', in *Faith and Fire: Popular and Unpopular Religion 1350-1600*, London, 1993, pp. 95-131.

Backhouse, J., *Books of Hours*, British Library, London, 1985.

Backhouse, J., *The Luttrell Psalter*, British Library, London, 1989.

Barber, R. and J. Barker, *Tournaments: Jousts, Chivalry and Pageants in the Middle Ages*, Woodbridge, 1989.

Bell, S. G., 'Medieval women book owners: arbiters of lay piety and ambassadors of culture', in M. Erler and M. Kowaleski, eds, *Women and Power in the Middle Ages*, Athens, 1988, pp. 149-87.

Blamires, A., ed., with K. Pratt and C. W. Marx, *Woman Defamed and Woman Defended: An Anthology of Medieval Texts*, Oxford, 1992.

Boffey, J., 'Women authors and women's literacy in fourteenth- and fifteenth-century England', in C. M. Meale, ed., *Women and Literature in Britain, 1150-1500*, Cambridge, 1993, pp. 159-82.

Bourdillon, A. F. C., *The Order of Minoresses in England*, Manchester, 1926.

Brewer, J. S. and R. Howlett, eds, *Monumenta Franciscana*, 2 vols, Rolls Series, London, 1858-82.

Britnell, R. H., 'Minor landlords in England and medieval agrarian capitalism', *Past and Present*, no. 89, 1980, pp. 3-22.

Brooke, C. N. L., *The Medieval Idea of Marriage*, Oxford, 1989.

Brundage, J. A., *Law, Sex and Christian Society in Medieval Europe*, Chicago, 1987.

Burgess, C., 'Late medieval wills and pious convention: testamentary evidence reconsidered', in M. Hicks, ed., *Profit, Piety and the Professions in Later Medieval England*, Gloucester, 1990, pp. 14-33.

Carpenter, C., *Locality and Polity: A Study of Warwickshire Landed Society, 1401-1499*, Cambridge, 1992.

Carpenter, D. A., 'Was there a crisis of the knightly class in the thirteenth century? The Oxfordshire evidence', *English Historical Review*, XCV, 1980, pp. 721-52.

Catto, J., 'Religion and the English nobility in the later fourteenth century', in H. Lloyd-Jones, V. Pearl and B. Worden, eds, *History and Imagination: Essays in honour of H. R. Trevor-Roper*, London, 1981, pp. 43-55.

Chibnall, M., 'Women in Orderic Vitalis', *Haskins Society Journal*, II, 1990, pp. 105-21.

Clanchy, M. T., *From Memory to Written Record: England 1066-1307*, London, 1979.

Clarke, A., J. Caley, J. Bayley, F. Holbrooke and J. W. Clarke, eds, *Rymer's Foedera, 1066-1383*, 4 vols, Record Commission, London, 1816-69.

Cooke, K., 'Donors and daughters: Shaftesbury abbey's benefactors, endowments and nuns *c.* 1086-1130', in M. Chibnall, ed., *Anglo-Norman Studies XII: Proceedings of the Battle Conference 1989*, Woodbridge, 1990, pp. 29-45.

Coss, P. R., *Lordship, Knighthood and Locality: A Study in English Society, c. 1180-1280*, Past and Present Publications, Cambridge, 1991.

Coss, P. R., 'Sir Geoffrey de Langley and the crisis of the knightly class in thirteenth-century England', *Past and Present*, no. 68, 1975, pp. 3-37.

Coss, P. R., 'Bastard feudalism revised', *Past and Present*, no. 125, 1989, pp. 27-64.

Crawford, A., 'Victims of attainder: the Howard and de Vere women in the late fifteenth century', in *Medieval Women in Southern England*, Reading Medieval Studies, XV, 1989, pp. 59-74.

Crouch, D., *William Marshal: Court, Career and Chivalry in the Angevin Empire 1147-1219*, London, 1990.

Crouch, D., *The Image of Aristocracy in Britain, 1000-1300*, London, 1992.

Cullum, P. H., '"And hir name was Charite": charitable giving by and for women in late medieval Yorkshire', in P. J. P. Goldberg, ed., *Woman is a Worthy Wight: Women in English Society c. 1200-1500*, Gloucester, 1992, chapter 7.

Davies, R. R., 'Baronial accounts, incomes and arrears in the later Middle Ages', *Economic History Review*, second series, XXI, 1968, pp. 211-29.

Davis, N., ed., *Paston Letters and Papers of the Fifteenth Century*, 2 vols, Oxford, 1971-76.

Denholm-Young, N., *Seignorial Administration in England*, Oxford, 1937.

Denholm-Young, N., 'The Yorkshire estates of Isabella de Fortibus', *Yorkshire Archaeological Journal*, XXXI, 1934, pp. 388-420.

Douglas, D. C., *William the Conqueror*, London, 1964.

Douglas, D. C. and G. W. Greenaway, eds, *English Historical Documents 1042-1189*, London, 1953.

Duby, G., trans. B. Bray, *The Knight, the Lady and the Priest: The making of Modern Marriage in Medieval France*, Harmondsworth, 1983.

Duffy, E., *The Stripping of the Altars: Traditional Religion in England 1400-1580*, New Haven, 1992.

Dugdale, W., *Monasticon Anglicanum*, J. Caley, H. Ellis and B. Bandinel, eds, 6 vols, London, 1817-30.

Dyer, C., *Standards of Living in the Later Middle Ages: Social Change in England c. 1200-1520*, Cambridge, 1989.

Erler, M. C., 'Three fifteenth-century vowesses', in C. M. Barron and A. F. Sutton, eds, *Medieval London Widows 1300-1500*, London, 1994, pp. 165-83.

Fairbank, F. R., 'The last earl of Warenne and Surrey and the distribution of his possessions', *Yorkshire Archaeological Journal*, XIX, 1907, pp. 193-264.

Farley, A. and H. Ellis, eds, *Liber Censualis vocatus Domesday Book*, 4 vols, Record Commission, London, 1783-1816.

Furnivall, F. J., ed., *The Fifty Earliest English Wills*, Early English Text Society, original series, LXXVIII, 1882.

Gairdner, J., ed., *The Paston Letters, 1422-1509*, 4 vols, reprint of edition of 1872-75, Edinburgh, 1910.

Given-Wilson, C., *The English Nobility in the Late Middle Ages: the Fourteenth-Century Political Community*, London, 1987.

Goldberg, P. J. P., *Women, Work and Life Cycle in a Medieval Economy: Women in York and Yorkshire, c. 1300-1520*, Oxford, 1992.

Goodman, A., 'The countess and the rebels: Essex and a crisis in English society (1400)', *Transactions of the Essex Archaeological Society*, third series, II, 1970, pp. 267-79.

Gray, H. L., 'Incomes from land in England in 1436', *English Historical Review*, XLIX, 1934, pp. 607-39.

Greenway, D. E., ed., *Charters of the Honour of Mowbray, 1107-91*, British Academy, Records of Social and Economic History, new series, I, 1972.

Harding, A., *England in the Thirteenth Century*, Cambridge, 1993.

Hardy, T. D., ed., *Rotuli Litterarum Clausarum in Turri Londinensi Asservati, 1204-27*, 2 vols, Record Commission, London, 1833-44.

Hardy, T. D., ed., *Rotuli de Oblatis et Finibus in Turri Londinensi Asservati, Tempore Regis Johannis*, Record Commission, London, 1835.

Hardy, T. D., ed., *Rotuli Litterarum Patentium in Turri Londinensi Asservati, 1201-16*, Record Commission, London, 1835.

Hardy, T. D., ed., *Rotuli Chartarum in Turri Londinensi Asservati, 1199-1216*, Record Commission, London, 1837.

Harper-Bill, C., ed., *The Cartulary of the Augustinian Friars of Clare*, Suffolk Records Society, Suffolk Charters, XI, 1991.

Harper-Bill, C. and R. Mortimer, eds, *Stoke by Clare Cartulary*, 3 vols, Suffolk Records Society, Suffolk Charters, IV-VI, 1982-84.

Harvey, S., 'The knight and the knight's fee in England', *Past and Present*, no. 49, 1970, pp. 3-43, and reprinted in R. H. Hilton, ed., *Peasants, Knights and Heretics*, Cambridge, 1976, pp. 133-73.

Haskell, A. S., 'The Paston women on marriage in fifteenth-century England', *Viator*, IV, 1973, pp. 459-71.

Helmholz, R. H., *Marriage Litigation in Medieval England*, Cambridge, 1974.

Hicks, M., 'Piety and lineage in the Wars of the Roses: the Hungerford experience', in R. A. Griffiths and J. Sherborne, eds, *Kings and Nobles in the Later Middle Ages: A Tribute to Charles Ross*, Gloucester, 1986, pp. 90-108.

Hicks, M., 'The piety of Margaret, Lady Hungerford (d. 1478)', *Journal of Ecclesiastical History*, XXXVIII, 1987, pp. 19-38.

Hicks, M., 'The last days of Elizabeth countess of Oxford', *English Historical Review*, CIII, 1988, pp. 76-95.

Holmes, G. A., *The Estates of the Higher Nobility in Fourteenth-Century England*, Cambridge, 1957.

Holmes, G. A., 'A Protest against the Despensers, 1326', *Speculum*, XXX, 1955, pp. 207-12.

Holt, J. C., *Magna Carta*, second edition, Cambridge, 1992.

Holt, J. C., 'Politics and property in early medieval England', *Past and Present*, no. 57, 1972, pp. 3-52.

Holt, J. C., 'Feudal society and the family in early medieval England: I. The revolution of 1066', *Transactions of the Royal Historical Society*, fifth series, XXXII, 1982, pp. 193-212.

Holt, J. C., 'Feudal society and the family in early medieval England: II. Notions of patrimony', *Transactions of the Royal Historical Society*, fifth series, XXXIII, 1983, pp. 193-220.

Holt, J. C., 'Feudal Society and the family in early medieval England: III. Patronage and politics', *Transactions of the Royal Historical Society*, fifth series, XXXIV, 1984, pp. 1-25.

Holt, J. C., 'Feudal society and the family in early medieval England: IV. The heiress and the alien', *Transactions of the Royal Historical Society*, fifth series, XXXV, 1985, pp. 1-28.

Hudson, J., *Land, Law and Lordship in Anglo-Norman England*, Oxford, 1994.

Hudson, J., 'Life-grants of land and the development of inheritance in Anglo-Norman England', in M. Chibnall, ed., *Anglo-Norman Studies, XII: Proceedings of the Battle Conference, 1989*, Woodbridge, 1990, pp. 67-80.

Illingworth, W. and J. Caley, eds, *Placita de Quo Warranto*, Record Commission, London, 1818.

Jenkinson, H., 'Mary de Sancto Paulo, foundress of Pembroke College, Cambridge', *Archaeologia*, LXXXVI, 1915, pp. 401-46.

Jones, M. K. and M. G. Underwood, *The King's Mother: Lady Margaret Beaufort, Countess of Richmond and Derby*, Cambridge, 1992.

Kingsford, C. L., ed., *The Stonor Letters and Papers, 1290-1483*, 2 vols, Camden Society, third series, XXIX, XXX, 1919.

Knowles, C. H., 'Provision for the families of the Montfortians disinherited after the battle of Evesham', in P. R. Coss and S. D. Lloyd, eds, *Thirteenth Century England I: Proceedings of the Newcastle upon Tyne Conference, 1985*, Woodbridge, 1986, pp. 124-7.

Knowles, D., *The Monastic Order in England*, Cambridge, 1950.

Knowles, D. and R. N. Hadcock, *Medieval Religious Houses, England and Wales*, London, 1971.

Labarge, M. W., *A Baronial Household of the Thirteenth Century*, London, 1965.

Labarge, M. W., *Women in Medieval Life*, London, 1986.

Lamond, E., ed., *Walter of Henley's Husbandry*, Royal Historical Society, London, 1890.

Lander, J. R., 'Attainder and forfeiture, 1453-1509', *Historical Journal*, IV, 1961, pp. 119-51.

Lander, J. R., 'Marriage and politics in the fifteenth century: the Nevilles and the Wydevilles', *Bulletin of the Institute of Historical Research*, XXXVI, 1963, pp. 119-52.

Le Goff, J., *The Birth of Purgatory*, Aldershot, 1984.

Lloyd, S., *English Society and the Crusade, 1216-1307*, Oxford, 1988.

Loengard, J. S., '"Of the gift of her husband": English dower and its consequences in the year 1200', in J. Kirshner and S. F. Wemple, eds, *Women of the Medieval World*, Oxford, 1985, pp. 215-55.

Loyd, L. C. and D. M. Stenton, eds, *Sir Christopher Hatton's Book of Seals*, Oxford, 1950.

Luard, H. R., ed., *Annales Monastici*, 5 vols, Rolls Series, London, 1864-69.

Lucas, A. M., *Women in the Middle Ages: Religion, Marriage and Letters*, Brighton, 1983.

Lyte, H. C. M., *A History of Dunster*, 2 vols, London, 1909.

McFarlane, K. B., *Lancastrian Kings and Lollard Knights*, Oxford, 1972.

McFarlane, K. B., *The Nobility of Later Medieval England*, Oxford, 1973.

Macray, W. D., ed., *Chronicon Abbatiae Rameseiensis*, Rolls Series, London, 1886.

Maddicott, J. R., *Law and Lordship: Royal Justices as Retainers in Thirteenth- and Fourteenth-Century England*, Past and Present supplement, no. 4, 1978.

Maitland, F. W., ed., *Bracton's Note Book*, 3 vols, London, 1887.

Malory, Sir Thomas, edited by J. Cowen, *Le Morte D'Arthur*, 2 vols, Harmondsworth, 1986.

Martin, C. T., ed., *Registrum Epistolarum Johannis Peckham, Archiepiscopi Cantuariensis*, 3 vols, Rolls Series, London, 1882-86.

Mason, E., ed., *The Beauchamp Cartulary: Charters 1100-1268*, Pipe Roll Society, new series, XLIII, 1980.

Mate, M., 'Profit and productivity on the estates of Isabella de Forz, 1260-92', *Economic History Review*, second series, XXXIII, 1980, pp. 326-34.

Meale, C. M., '"... alle the bokes that I haue of latyn, englisch and frensch": laywomen and their books in late medieval England', in C. M. Meale, ed., *Women and Literature in Britain, 1150-1500*, Cambridge, 1993, pp. 128-58.

Mertes, K., *The English Noble Household, 1250-1600: Good Governance and Politic Rule*, Oxford, 1988.

Miller, E. and J. Hatcher, *Medieval England - Rural Society and Economic Change 1086-1348*, London, 1978.

Millett, B., 'Women in No Man's Land: English recluses and the development of vernacular literature in the twelfth and thirteenth centuries', in C. M. Meale, ed., *Women and Literature in Britain, 1150-1500*, Cambridge, 1993, pp. 86-103.

Milsom, S. F. C., 'Inheritance by women in the twelfth and early thirteenth centuries', in M. S. Arnold, T. A. Green, S. A. Scully and S. D. White, *On the Laws and Customs of England: Essays in honor of Samuel E. Thorne*, Chapel Hill, 1981, pp. 60-89.

Morgan, D. A. L., 'The individual style of the English gentleman', in M. Jones, ed., *Gentry and Lesser Nobility in Late Medieval Europe*, Gloucester, 1986, pp. 15-35.

Newton, S. M., *Fashion in the Age of the Black Prince: A Study of the Years 1340-1365*, Woodbridge, 1980.

Nichols, J., *A Collection of All the Wills of the Kings and Queens of England*, London, 1780.

Nichols, J. G. and J. Bruce, eds, *Wills from Doctors' Commons: A Selection from the Wills of Eminent Persons proved in the Prerogative Court of Canterbury, 1495-1695*, Camden Society, old series, LXXXIII, 1863.

Orme, N., *From Childhood to Chivalry: The Education of the English Kings and Aristocracy 1066-1530*, London, 1984.

Palgrave, F., ed., *Rotuli Curiae Regis, 6 Richard I - 1 John*, 2 vols, Record Commission, London, 1835.

Palmer, R. C., 'Contexts of marriage in medieval England: evidence from the king's court *circa* 1300', *Speculum*, LIX, 1984, pp. 42-67.

Patterson, R. B., ed., *Earldom of Gloucester Charters: The Charters and Scribes of the Earls and Countesses of Gloucester to ad 1217*, Oxford, 1973.

Payling, S., *Political Society in Lancastrian England: The Greater Gentry of Nottinghamshire*, Oxford, 1991.

Pisan, Christine de, trans. S. Lawson, *The Treasure of the City of Ladies or The Book of the Three Virtues*, Harmondsworth, 1985.

Plucknett, T. F. T., *A Concise History of the Common Law*, fourth edition, London, 1948.

Plucknett, T. F. T., *Legislation of Edward I*, Oxford, 1949.

Pollard, A., 'Estate management in the later Middle Ages: the Talbots and Whitchurch, 1383-1525', *Economic History Review*, second series, XXV, 1972, pp. 553-66.

Pollock, F. and F. W. Maitland, *The History of English Law before the time of Edward I*, 2 vols, second edition, Cambridge, 1898.

Power, E., *Medieval English Nunneries c. 1275-1535*, Cambridge, 1922.

Powicke, F. M., *King Henry III and the Lord Edward*, 2 vols, Oxford, 1947.

Pugh, T. B. and C. D. Ross, 'The English baronage and the income tax of 1436', *Bulletin of the Institute of Historical Research*, XXVI, 1953, pp. 1-28.

Raban, S., *Mortmain Legislation and the English Church, 1279-1500*, Cambridge, 1982.

Rawcliffe, C., *The Staffords, earls of Stafford and dukes of Buckingham, 1394-1521*, Cambridge, 1978.

Richmond, C., *The Paston Family in the Fifteenth Century: The First Phase*, Cambridge, 1990.

Richmond, C., 'Religion and the fifteenth-century gentleman', in R. B. Dobson, ed., *The Church, Politics and Patronage in the Fifteenth Century*, Gloucester, 1984, pp. 193-208.

Richmond, C., 'The Pastons revisited: marriage and the family in fifteenth-century England', *Bulletin of the Institute of Historical Research*, LVIII, 1985, pp. 25-36.

Richmond, C., 'Thomas Lord Morley (d. 1416) and the Morleys of Hingham', *Norfolk Archaeology*, XXXIX, 1984-86, pp. 1-12.

Riley, H. T., ed., *Thomae Walsingham Historia Anglicana*, 2 vols, Rolls Series, London, 1863-64.

Riley, H. T,. ed., *Johannis de Trokelowe et Henrici de Blaneford Chronica et Annales*, Rolls Series, London, 1865.

Roberts, C., ed., *Excerpta e Rotulis Finium in Turri Londinensi Asservatis, Henry III, 1216-72*, 2 vols, Record Commission, London, 1835-36.

Rogers, K. H., ed., *Lacock Abbey Charters*, Wiltshire Record Society, XXXIV, 1979.

Rose, G. and W. Illingworth, eds, *Placitorum in Domo Capitulari Westmonasteriensi Asservatorum Abbreviatio*, Record Commission, London, 1811.

Rosenthal, J. T., *The Purchase of Paradise: Gift Giving and the Aristocracy, 1307-1485*, London, 1972.

Rosenthal, J. T., 'Aristocratic marriage and the English peerage, 1350-1500: social institution and personal bond', *Journal of Medieval History*, X, 1984, pp. 181-94.

Ross, C. D., 'The household accounts of Elizabeth Berkeley, countess of Warwick, 1420-1', *Transactions of the Bristol and Gloucestershire Archaeological Society*, LXX, 1951, pp. 81-105.

Ross, C. D., 'Forfeiture for treason in the reign of Richard II', *English Historical Review*, LXXI, 1956, pp. 560-75.

Ross, C. D. and T. B. Pugh, 'Materials for the study of baronial incomes in fifteenth-century England', *Economic History Review*, second series, VI, 1953-54, pp. 185-94.

Rothwell, H., ed., *English Historical Documents 1189-1327*, London, 1975.

Round, J. H., ed., *Rotuli de Dominabus et Pueris et Puellis de XII Comitatibus (1185)*, Pipe Roll Society, XXXV, 1913.

Rubin, M., *Corpus Christi: The Eucharist in Late Medieval Culture*, Cambridge, 1991.

Salu, M. B., trans., *The Ancrene Riwle*, Exeter Medieval English Texts and Studies, Exeter, 1990.

Sanders, I. J., *English baronies: A Study of their Origin and Descent, 1086-1327*, Oxford, 1960.

Saul, N., *Knights and Esquires: the Gloucestershire Gentry in the Fourteenth Century*, Oxford, 1981.

Saul, N., *Scenes from Provincial Life: Knightly Families in Sussex, 1280-1400*, Oxford, 1986.

Scattergood, V. J. and J. W. Sherborne, eds, *English Court Culture in the Later Middle Ages*, London, 1983.

Shahar, S., *The Fourth Estate: A History of Women in the Middle Ages*, London, 1983.

Shahar, S., *Childhood in the Middle Ages*, London, 1990.

Sheehan, M. M., 'The influence of canon law on the property rights of married women in England', *Mediaeval Studies*, XXV, 1963, pp. 109-24.

Sheehan, M. M., 'Choice of marriage partner in the Middle Ages: development and mode of application of a theory of marriage', *Studies in Medieval and Renaissance History*, new series, I, 1978, pp. 1-33.

Sheehan, M. M., 'Marriage theory and practice in the conciliar legislation and diocesan statutes of medieval England', *Mediaeval Studies*, XL, 1978, pp. 408-60.

Simpson, A. W. B., *An Introduction to the History of the Land Law*, Oxford, 1961.

Sir Gawain and the Green Knight, trans. B. Stone, second edition, Harmondsworth, 1974.

Stafford, P., 'Women in Domesday', in *Medieval Women in Southern England*, Reading Medieval Studies, XV, 1989, pp. 75-94.

Stapleton, T., ed., *Plumpton Correspondence*, Camden Society, old series, IV, 1839.

Stenton, F. M., *The First Century of English Feudalism*, second edition, Oxford, 1961.

Stenton, F. M., ed., *Facsimiles of Early Charters from Northamptonshire Collections*, Northamptonshire Record Society, IV, 1927.

Stubbs, W., ed., *Gesta Regis Henrici Secundi Benedicti Abbatis*, 2 vols, Rolls Series, London, 1867.

Swanson, J., 'Childhood and childrearing in *ad status* sermons by later thirteenth-century friars', *Journal of Medieval History*, XVI, 1990, pp. 309-31.

Swanson, R. N., *Church and Society in Late Medieval England*, Oxford, 1989.

Swanson, R. N., ed., *Catholic England: Faith, Religion and Observance before the Reformation*, Manchester, 1993.

Thompson, S., *Women Religious: The Founding of English Nunneries after the Norman Conquest*, Oxford, 1991.

Turner, R. V., 'The Mandeville inheritance, 1189-1236: its legal, political and social context', *Haskins Society Journal*, I, 1989, pp. 147-72.

Tyerman, C., *England and the Crusades, 1095-1588*, Chicago, 1988.

Vale, M. G. A., *Piety, Charity and Literacy among the Yorkshire Gentry, 1370-1480*, Borthwick Papers, no. 50, York, 1976.

Veale, E. M., *The English Fur Trade in the Later Middle Ages*, Oxford, 1966.

Walker, D., 'Miles of Gloucester, earl of Hereford', *Transactions of the Bristol and Gloucestershire Archaeological Society*, LXXVII, 1958, pp. 66-84.

Walker, S. S., 'Proof of age of feudal heirs in medieval England', *Mediaeval Studies*, XXXV, 1973, pp. 306-23.

Ward, J. C., *English Noblewomen in the Later Middle Ages*, London, 1992.

Ward, J. C., 'Fashions in monastic endowment: the foundations of the Clare family, 1066-1314', *Journal of Ecclesiastical History*, XXXII, 1981, pp. 427-51.

Ward, J. C., 'The place of the honour in twelfth-century society: the honour of Clare 1066-1217', *Proceedings of the Suffolk Institute of Archaeology and History*, XXXV, 1983, pp. 191-202.

Ward, J. C., 'Royal service and reward: the Clare family and the Crown, 1066-1154', in R. A. Brown, ed., *Anglo-Norman Studies XI: Proceedings of the Battle Conference 1988*, Woodbridge, 1989, pp.261-78.

Ward, J. C., 'Sir John de Coggeshale: an Essex knight of the fourteenth century', *Essex Archaeology and History*, XXII, 1991, pp. 61-6.

Ward, J. C., 'Elizabeth de Burgh, Lady of Clare (d. 1360)', in C. M. Barron and A. F. Sutton, eds, *Medieval London Widows 1300-1500*, London, 1994, pp. 29-45.

Waugh, S. L., 'Marriage, class and royal lordship in England under Henry III', *Viator*, XVI, 1985, pp. 181-207.

Waugh, S. L., 'Tenure to contract: lordship and clientage in thirteenth-century England', *English Historical Review*, CI, 1986, pp. 811-39.

Wentersdorf, K. P., 'The clandestine marriages of the Fair Maid of Kent', *Journal of Medieval History*, V, 1979, pp. 203-31.

Wood-Legh, K. L., *Perpetual Chantries in Britain*, Cambridge, 1965.

Woolgar, C. M., ed., *Household Accounts from Medieval England,* 2 vols, British Academy, Records of Social and Economic History, new series, XVII, XVIII, Oxford, 1992-93.

Wright, S. M., *The Derbyshire Gentry of the Fifteenth Century,* Derbyshire Record Society, VIII, 1983.

Index